How to Raise Your Child
to Be a Winner

How to Raise Your Child to Be a Winner

A Proven Program that Shows How to Guide Your Child—from Infancy on—to Ultimate Self-Fulfillment

BY

GENE R. HAWES, HELEN GINANDES WEISS,

AND MARTIN S. WEISS

RAWSON, WADE PUBLISHERS, INC.
New York

Library of Congress Cataloging in Publication Data

Hawes, Gene R
    How to raise your child to be a winner.

    Includes bibliographical references and index.
    1. Children—Management.   I. Weiss, Helen
Ginandes, joint author.   II. Weiss, Martin S.,
joint author.   III. Title.
HQ772.H377   1980   649′.1   79-91331
ISBN 0-89256-132-7
LC. 79-91331

Published simultaneously in Canada by McClelland and Stewart, Ltd.
Manufactured in the United States of America by Fairfield Graphics,
    Fairfield, Pennsylvania

Designed by Jacques Chazaud

FIRST EDITION

Acknowledgments

———◆———

Very special thanks are due those who took the time to share their thoughts and insights with the co-authors through personal interview or by mail. The individuals who provided this invaluable help are:

Evelyn Bailey, Director of Special Education, South Central Satellite, BOCES, Pueblo, Colorado

Diana Bander, Ph.D. candidate, Harvard University; former Director of Learning Skills Center, Goddard College, Plainfield, Vermont

Marge Duffy, secondary school staff, Fairfield, Connecticut

Mrs. Beryl Kaufman, Executive Director, Connecticut Association for Children with Learning Disabilities (CACLD), 20 North Main St., South Norwalk, Connecticut

David Kaufman, student, Trumbull, Connecticut

Betty Lou Kratoville, parent, author, editor, and educator, Houston, Texas

Dr. Harold B. Levy, pediatrician, author, Shreveport, Louisiana

Lawrence Lieberman, Ed.D., psychologist, Newtonville, Massachusetts

Silvia Richardson, M.D., Associate Director, University Affiliated Program for Learning Disabilities, Cincinnati Center for Development Disorders, Cincinnati, Ohio

Ernest Siegel, Ed.D., Professor, Department of Special Education, Adelphi University, Garden City, New York

Carole Singer, Guidance Counselor, 7th Grade Team, Mineola Junior High School, Mineola, New York

Ira Singer, Ed.D., Superintendent of Schools, Herricks School District, New Hyde Park, New York

Genie Myer, student, mother, Great Barrington, Massachusetts

Marjory Zerin, M.A., and Edward Zerin, Ph.D., Co-Directors, Westlake Center for Marital and Family Counseling, Westlake Village, California.

The idea for this book originated in conversations with Walter C. Betkowski and David M. Brownstone. These two close friends of the co-authors, with Irene M. Franck, were also wonderfully helpful in providing subsequent suggestions and comments. Another friend, Fran Hawthorne, furnished expert professional assistance by conducting the research and doing the first-draft writing for Chapters 12 and 13. Barbara Veals did the typing of the final manuscript for several of the chapters. Mary Racette also ably assisted with typing the final manuscript. The largest part of the manuscript was typed with very special skill by Vaughan W. James.

Also generously helpful in supplying ideas and source material were the following:

Bruce Bennett, high school senior, Stamford, Connecticut

Joan Burkhard, Director, Riverbrook School, Stockbridge, Massachusetts

Dean Canada, Manager, Canada's of Vail, Vail, Colorado

Michael P. Christiano, Special Education Coordinator, secondary level, Fairfield, Connecticut

Aylett Cox, Director of Teacher Training, Dean Memorial Center; Assistant Director, Language Lab, Scottish Rite Hospital, Dallas, Texas

Lester Dinoff, president, public relations firm, New York, New York, and his class in Public Relations and Advertising at Pace University, Pleasantville, New York

Pat Eames, administrator and coordinator of educational and community services, Washington, D.C.

Howard Eberwein, Director of Special Education, Pittsfield Public Schools, Pittsfield, Massachusetts

William Ellis, Headmaster, Friends School, Baltimore, Maryland

Beth Fairweather, English instructor, Pittsfield High School, Pittsfield, Massachusetts

Danny Fleming, teacher, Plano, Texas

Hal Fleming, engineer, photographer, Plano, Texas

Daniel Gildesgame, Ph.D. candidate, Columbia University; publisher, Monterey, Massachusetts

Leon Gildesgame, industrialist and educator, Mount Kisco, New York

Ruth Gildesgame, parent, Mount Kisco, New York

Marta Gilmore, assisted with the manuscript for this book, Fayetteville, North Carolina

Jacob Harris, M.D., psychiatrist, Westchester Psychiatric Group, Yorktown Heights, New York

Louise Hullinger, parent, teacher, Chicago, Illinois

Jeanne Jaslow, parent, businesswoman, Shaker Heights, Ohio

Walter Jaslow, educator, counselor, Shaker Heights, Ohio

Carl Kline, M.D., child, adolescent, and family psychiatrist, Vancouver, British Columbia

Fred Lancome, sculptor, Monterey, Massachusetts

Joe Lasker, artist, parent, author of books for children, Norwalk, Connecticut

Lillian Lerner, District Supervisor, District 10 Board of Education, Bronx, New York

Josh Levy, sales manager, Stamford, Connecticut

Harry Lewis, Ed.D., Director of Program Development, Plattsburgh State College, and author, Plattsburgh, New York

Jeannette Marlowe, M.D., Deputy Director of Medical Services, Wassaic Developmental Center, Wassaic, New York

Paul Meyerowits, attorney, New York, New York

Jeannie Millar, teacher of special education, Great Barrington, Massachusetts

Skip Paddock, former advertising executive, teacher, Pittsfield, Massachusetts

Jean Peterson, Executive Secretary, National Association for Children with Learning Disabilities, Pittsburgh, Pennsylvania

Hon. Joseph R. Pisani, New York State senator, New Rochelle, New York

Fran Pollet, speech and language specialist, parent, Valley Stream, New York

Jack Pollet, importer and manufacturer, Valley Stream, New York

Ira Quint, President, Colonial Corporation of America, New York, New York

Nancy Ramos, education consultant, author, parent, Palo Alto, California

Tim Roberts, Department of Special Education, East Texas State University, Commerce, Texas

Myra Ross, Director of Guidance, administrator, Green Chimneys School, Brewster, New York

Samuel B. Ross, Jr., Executive Director, Green Chimneys School, Brewster, New York; President, Edwin Gould Outdoor Educational Centers

Jan Sennett, former diagnostician and learning disability specialist; presently wife, mother, and community volunteer, Chicago, Illinois

Ceil W. Tannenbaum, wife, mother, grandmother, Fort Lee, New Jersey

Eli Tash, former President, National Association for Children with Learning Disabilities; presently administrator, St. Francis Children's Activity and Achievement Center, Milwaukee, Wisconsin

Gerald Weinstock, business executive, Larchmont, New York

Alan Weiss, student, University of Massachusetts, Amherst, Massachusetts

Andrea Chase Weiss, assisted with the manuscript for this book, Avon, Colorado

Eric Weiss, student, University of Massachusetts, Amherst, Massachusetts

Ira Weiss, former proprietor, Monterey General Store, Monterey, Massachusetts

Jerry Weiss, student, Reed College, Portland, Oregon

Nat and Mae Weiss, parents, grandparents, and great-grandparents

Richard Weiss, paratrooper, 82nd Airborne, Fort Bragg, North Carolina
Ruth Wiedemann, parent, Richardsen, Texas
Spencer Witty, Chairman of the Board, Merchants Bank of New York, New York
Martin Wolinsky, President, Auto-matic Burglar Systems, Inc., Hamden, Connecticut.

Contents

———◆———

How to Raise Your Child
to Be a Winner

What a Winner Really Is—
and Creating One Home-Grown

Every child needs to be a winner.

Every child needs to know the joy of succeeding at life, gloriously.

Every child needs to experience this satisfaction often, at home and in school.

Every child needs to know what to do in order to win whatever is most important in life for that child, through each advancing phase of learning and growth.

Every child needs to develop the natural stance of a winner, with dauntless self-confidence, "heart" to face challenges, high energy and zest.

Every child needs to bring all the strength and spirit of a winner to full power through that slow but magical transformation into an independent, self-reliant, assured adult.

Growing up to be a winner in this sense is the birthright of every child. It's the birthright of *your* child.

As a parent, you have a crucial part to play in helping your child realize that birthright. What you do and say over the years has more impact on the child than anything else—more than friends, relatives, community, teachers, schools, colleges. When very young, the child literally sees life and the world through you. For the infant, you are the largest and most important part of the world. And while the child grows up, you provide the central vantage point from which your child views life inside and increasingly far beyond the home. Moreover, your actions first decisively shape the child's key capabilities. Your actions can then determine the kinds of schooling in which all capabilities might best develop.

It isn't easy to raise a child as a winner, though. All through your child's growing years, many powerful forces in American life today can act to undercut your child's natural self-confidence and sense of accomplishment. Put bluntly, they can act to make your child a loser.

Your most important job as a parent is to counter these forces, at every turn. You can defeat them—and all the bitterness and frustration they can inflict on your child. We've written this book to tell you how because we know of no other book that does so. We've designed it to help you meet your supreme responsibility as a parent, from your child's first years to full, free adulthood.

You Can Assure Your Child's Success

Your child will meet forces right in your home, community, and schools that can undercut a boy's or girl's ongoing success. In telling how you can recognize and counter these forces, this book serves as a broad guide to schooling, college, and career choice for your child, from the earliest value-forming years on into the twenties. It explains with many true stories and examples all the major things you can do to assure your child's success through those years.

Let us sample the essence of our advice on all the ways in which you can help build your child's success. This will give you an idea of how you and your child might benefit from the coming chapters.

Strong foundations come first. Your talking and reactions to the child play a fundamental role in shaping the child's basic attitudes. Unwittingly, you yourself may hamper your child's present or future efforts to succeed through things said and unsaid. We make clear what you can do and say, especially in your child's infancy, to foster basic attitudes for winning.

We explain how you can avoid either of the two main traps in parent-child relations: the trap of manipulative child and victimized parent on the one hand, and the trap of authoritarian parent and submissive child on the other. We also include:

More than twenty questions on major areas of possible misunderstanding between you and your child;

Sample conversations showing how you can avoid being manipulated by your child; and

Vital questions for you to ask your child's school when it reports an incident of allegedly serious misbehavior by your child.

Getting the Best out of School for Your Child

Very specific foundations needed for success in school must be built by you and your child in the years before school starts. They include vast ranges of essential skills so frequently acquired by five-year-olds that they go unnoticed, unless a child doesn't have some of them. The commonplace miracle of basic mastery of spoken language is an example; another is drawing ability good enough for starting to make the shapes of letters. More elusive skills concern precise vision and visual memory.

We explain:

How to help build essential foundations of readiness through the preschool years;

How to tell when your child is ready to start school, and also how to tell when your child is ready to face the different demands each step of the way up;

How to recognize distress signals that your child is *not* ready for some stage of schooling and hence is experiencing too much stress.

Readiness questions don't end with kindergarten and first grade. In a larger sense, readiness remains important even when your child nears age twelve and then grows on through the teens. We tell you why and how to be sensitive to your child's readiness. And we give you diverse examples of children in these older ages who buckled and went badly astray when thrust by parents into responsibilities or obligations for which the youngsters simply were not yet ready.

Many key ways in which you can help foster beneficial attitudes between your child and teachers are explored, based on our own personal and professional experience. You'll learn how to get good results from conferences with teachers. *It involves understanding on your part that teachers have feelings and problems, too.* In addition, we give:

Suggested points to cover in conferences with teachers to learn of your child's performance in school;

Actions that your child can take to generate more positive attitudes on the part of teachers;

Things teachers can do to generate more positive attitudes among students;

Ways in which you yourself can persuade the school to launch new kinds of programs needed by your child and other pupils.

The ability to get your child placed in the right kind of program and class in school can be decisive for success or failure. With lively examples, we illustrate how even very good schools can make placement decisions that lead some students to months of frustration and wasted effort. Vital ammunition is furnished to help parents prepare for conferences on new placements for the child—ammunition in the form of specific questions to raise, and information that will help you to determine and secure what's important for your child. Given too are alternatives that work very well for some young people—alternative techniques for spelling or math, or entire alternative programs for young people bored by conventional academic learning. Many ways in which schools can take the stigma off necessary remedial classes are also described.

Should all your efforts to get the right kind of schooling from public schools fail, private schools offer a wide choice of options for your child. We explain the variety of attractive and effective features available at private schools, and identify schools of unusual interest, such as those that have proven effective for children with learning disabilities. Also identified are many private schools that are regarded as "the best" or most exclusive, schools whimsically referred to in past eras as the "St. Grottlesex" variety.

A checklist of essential and desirable features for you to consider in selecting a school for your child is given.

Those circumstances in which a private school could substantially help your child win admission to a highly respected college are also discussed.

Meeting Challenges with a Learning-Disabled or Gifted Child

Meeting the needs of a child with a learning disability could pose a rather heroic challenge for you. As we explain, it is the parent who often carries most responsibility for detecting the first signs of a disability and for arranging help to overcome it. We provide:

Detailed descriptions of symptoms of learning disabilities, as they would appear in the child's reading, or writing, speaking, listening, or mathematics work, or attitude toward school;

Explanations of the main varieties of learning disabilities, and what you can do in the home to help your child win out over his/her disability; and

A detailed checklist of questions for you to ask concerning school services for the learning-disabled child.

You could face an even more heroic challenge if you happen to have

Winners in America Today

As you can see, we have very strong ideas about winners and winning in America today. These ideas and suggestions grew naturally out of our experience in raising a total of seven children collectively, as well as our experience as authorities and consultants in professional work with thousands of other children through many decades.

In addition, we enlarged our own thoughts about winners by interviewing more than 100 diverse friends and colleagues. In essence, we asked each of them ten questions about winners and losers in our society. Our large but informal survey was intended to be used descriptively rather than statistically. After all, one of our deepest beliefs is that, though the hallmarks of genuine winners are similar, the ways in which each individual can become a winner are necessarily and absolutely unique.

Winners are not just those who win out in intense competition to attain wealth, power, or fame. Individual self-direction, self-discipline, and high self-esteem typify a winner. Winners exhibit an aura of personal dignity. When challenges present themselves, winners indicate a willingness to take risks, accept responsibility, and persevere to overcome obstacles. Many of our respondents prized the individual who is in a position to make his or her own decisions, carry them out, and accept the responsibility for making them, without passing off possible mistakes on others. All of our respondents felt that as parents we need to help our youngsters to set their own values and make their own judgments, emphasizing the need for kids to learn to make decisions independent of the pressure to conform imposed by their peers.

Countering False or Unrealistic Ideas about Winning

Standing in sharp contrast to these views about genuine winners are false or unrealistic visions of success that constantly bombard all of us —and our children. Realistically we must face the fact that we are all battered by value judgments from the outside world as to what gives a person status in our society. Many people equate social status with superficial but necessary factors dependent upon personal economics. Like it or not, our kids are going to grow up in a world where money defines many of the values that determine status. Income often is overemphasized as the primary quality of success.

Having viewed an average of 5,000 hours of television even before entering kindergarten, your child may be brainwashed into believing certain things. The average child seeing television for even a few hours a day will be told that what it takes to be a winner is wearing the right sneakers, owning the right bicycle, moped, or automobile. As your child gets older, the advertising message comes through loud and clear. You are what you have . . . or . . . what you can buy. Our kids get a massive dose of propaganda from a highly competitive, materialistic culture even before they reach the ripe old age of sixteen.

Mass media would have us believe that the "good life" is available packaged at a few fine stores near our homes, where we can purchase trend-setting objects that make us feel like winners. TV, magazines, and newspapers suggest that the symbol of success is our home, its location, its size, and the number of amenities it contains. A Westchester County, New York, psychiatrist suggests that people even transfer their feelings about themselves to their homes. A home may come to represent someone's identity, ego, and status.

Super-hype ads try to convince us that winning comes *only* through financial success; that the degree of success we achieve is apparent in the way we dress, smell, eat, drink, brush our teeth. Winning by association is seen in the car we drive and the credit cards we carry. This attitude is confirmed by Lee Rainwater and Richard Coleman in their recent book, *Social Standing in America*.[1] Their findings underscore the widespread belief that financial standing demonstrates social standing and class. They quote one man who said, "Look around you. A man driving a Cadillac feels he can thumb his nose at me because I'm driving an old Volkswagen." (That was before the present gasoline shortage, whereas the Volkswagen now represents a reverse status symbol.)

In spite of careful monitoring, the media's message to kids is that the status game is based on money and possessions. The media subtly direct us and our kids into believing that the cult of materialism is the *only* road to "making it." Kids are told that they can look like winners if they dress in a certain way. Self-proclaimed experts suggest that wearing the right clothes for the part puts one ahead in the competitive race. Even ads in the venerable *New York Times* transmit the message that "She who would win must look like a winner." One ad suggests that wearing pro-clothes or having the pro tennis racket will make the purchaser play tennis like a winner.

We're told that reading certain magazines will help us win. Even adults are tempted by this kind of advertising. For example, one magazine announces that it is the *only* one specifically written for top executive officers, suggesting that buying and reading it may make us feel like a top executive officer too. So it goes, status by association; your child is constantly fed this message of the media.

It is not simple to counteract this kind of message. But parents can and must do it if they are to raise kids who are genuine winners. Such unrealistic messages about success can be highly destructive by putting us and our children under unnecessary and unreal pressure. Schools respond to the pressures in the community by overemphasizing the importance of academic achievement. Communities vie for the highest number of Merit Scholars, or entrants into the Ivy League or Seven Sisters schools. Socially, the adolescent world responds to undue pressure by absorbing these false standards, and accepting the kids who "have" while rejecting those who "have not." Suburban enclaves perpetuate a Camelot syndrome, creating a view of safe, tidy cocoons where life is straight out of a story about Barbie and Ken (of Barbie doll fame). As a result of all this, our children may develop values that are questionable.

Sometimes a youngster has difficulty in setting his or her own standards, and making decisions. Fear of being rejected by others and non-acceptance as part of the "in" group can pressure a child to allow himself to be manipulated by others. The story that follows is about Fred, a sixteen-year-old who made this kind of mistake for a while. It was the wise intervention of parents and a school counselor that put Fred back on track.

Fred spent much of his time trying to be liked by his friends at school. He wasn't particularly good at sports, nor was he the life of the party, the entertainer, or class clown. He was a shy, sensitive youngster, who loved animals, gardening, and working outdoors.

He tagged along with the "in" group, acting as everyone's "gofer." He was used by others, who sent him on useless errands and gave him unnecessary chores to do. They copied his homework, and he was the one who got into trouble when the teacher noticed identical assignments.

Fred wanted to belong. He craved acceptance so badly that he spent most of his time being the kind of person that others wanted him to be, but little or no time being the person that he wanted to be himself.

Fred was angry at himself. He didn't want to play this part, but didn't have the self-confidence to see himself making friends any other way. He feared losing his friends yet could not see that they really were not his friends. Fred was not working at winning, only working at being what others wanted him to be.

Fred's identity was absorbed by the demands of others. Fred was losing by hiding his own feelings under the layers of insulation. His friends were delaying their own growth by manipulating Fred and using him for their own needs.

It all came to a crisis when Fred was caught with drugs but released with a warning. Fred needed help; he got it through perceptive intervention on the part of a school counselor and the aid of his patient parents.

Through them, he began to understand that he had been running with the "pack" even though he often did not want to be involved with their activities. Drinking, drugs, and other experimentation were not Fred's choice but rather done to be one of the gang. Slowly, he worked his way out of the box and moved to a more mature, independent handling of his own decisions.

When kids are pressured by constant demands to be the *best* at everything they do, they are put under a lot of stress and strain. A schedule overloaded with activities and lessons may keep a child busy but leave him or her with little time and few resources developed on his own.

Fortunately, a number of suburban towns recently awakened from their head-in-the-sand attitude to find that the demands of their social academic pressure cooker were causing many bright, gifted adolescents to break down, turning to alcohol, drugs, and even attempted suicide as a solution to the enormous stress they felt. Perhaps the children of some super-achiever parents know something that their parents have not yet faced. They may sense that they will not be able to make it as their parents have done before them, that there can only be a small number of chief executive officers in this world. These kids know that their parents are a tough act to follow, and many of them don't want to follow that act anyway. However, they don't understand that they can be winners even if they don't follow in their parents' footsteps, but opt for alternate lifestyles. Kids who cannot handle stress may not have developed the kind of inner self-confidence that would insulate them against unrealistic demands. Their painful cry is a *cri de coeur* of resounding strength.

Bill was seventeen years old, an achiever in school, son of an ex-Marine turned corporation executive. He was locked into a lifestyle in which success was measured by the number of beers you could hold down, the size of your car, the grades you earned, and the number of teams you were on. Bill was unsuccessful with an attempted suicide, but his story spread and his affluent suburban community was shocked to find a total of five reported suicide attempts among teenagers in one year. The stress of needing to win, the obligation of having to win, and the demands of continuing to win may have been too much for Bill and other youngsters like him. Statistics tell us that the number of college students experiencing symptoms of depression has grown. Suicide is a major cause of death among the young adult population—and still society pressures them.

To become winners, children have to be helped to develop a resilience that allows them to evaluate their efforts as separate from themselves. They need to feel OK whether they achieve or fail, so that they do not confuse their product with themselves.

Being a winner takes more than just an isolated event. Rather, it is an *attitude,* a feeling that pervades all that we do and say and feel about ourselves. The child who knows that what she says and does pleases those around her, and therefore reflects a sense of optimism and approval, gains a sense of self-esteem and importance that pervades all the things she says and does.

Being a genuine winner means *feeling* like a winner because you have learned a new skill, conquered an inner fear, faced a new obstacle, or met a new challenge.

Examples of Genuine Winners

A few examples of genuine winners illustrate how much true winning differs from the false and unrealistic ideas about winning that are all too common in our lives today.

For eleven-year-old Joey it was conquering the fear of falling while bike riding. He managed to climb back on his bike after an accident because he had received the kind of direction from his parents that gave him the inner strength to face something he must overcome. Joey's parents knew that walking away from any negative experience is a trauma that can predispose a child to walk away from other lesser obstacles repeatedly.

Joey had hurt himself badly, and the pain of a sprained ankle was something he'd rather not repeat. He would do anything rather than risk putting himself in physical danger. His mother argued that there were many sports that Joey could enjoy; why place him in a fear-producing situation that might only cause him further bodily harm?

Joe's dad was understanding but firm, saying: "You've been through a painful and disappointing experience, Joe; but a lot of things in your life may be upsetting and even cause physical pain. When they occur, are you going to walk away from them as well? Joe, there are times when you'll need to know that you can face physical pain and deal with it."

"But, Dad, I know I can get back on that bike if I want to. I just don't want to!" Joey said, his eyes brimming with tears.

"Joe, I can't force you to do it, but I'm certain you will want to know that you can do it even though you are afraid," Joe's father said, hugging him at the same time. "And we'll talk about it again when you're ready to."

Needless to say, it took Joe quite a while to get back on that bike. But he did it, and the confidence born of that experience may carry him through many other physical demanding situations in later life. Joe was learning to be a winner.

For Eric, a delightful seventeen-year-old, one experience of winning was a positive lesson. Eric had received as a gift from his parents a seven-year-old VW convertible with over 100,000 miles on it. He spent the whole summer between high school and college earning the money to buy the parts to rebuild the engine.

As those of you who have learned Murphy's law can well attest, "Anything that can possibly go wrong, will"—and it did. Eric had served his internship assisting in the repair of a friend's car. He learned a great deal and felt equipped to do the job, yet the completion of it proved so unnerving and demanding that it nearly caused him to give up in total frustration. Along the way, he developed the drive to complete a task, the inner confidence to know that given enough time any problem can be solved, and the determination that we all need in life to stick to something. Perhaps his success was just luck, but we think that much of it came from the attitude his parents had taken with him throughout his life.

He told us that he recalls his dad telling him never to give up no matter how discouraged you get. And when he could not solve a problem, his dad would say: "There's no shame in not knowing something, but there is in not trying."

Alan, another young acquaintance, has a C+/B— average in his second year at college. However, the grades alone are not the real measure of his success. His math instructor calls him, "One of the friendliest people in the class, a real contributor to making an 8 A.M. class one of the most enjoyable on my school schedule. A solid worker who could use some work in basic skills but learns well."

His English instructor noted, "Writing doesn't come easily to Alan, but he has worked admirably and made good grades." And his science instructor, "Continued work on writing skills and organizational skills will improve his grades. He is an enthusiastic and conscientious student, a pleasure to work with."

"It doesn't come easy to me," said Alan, "but I know I'm making it in class. Maybe I appreciate their comments more because I know the amount of work and effort that achievement requires. Sure I feel like a winner, because I know that my efforts are appreciated and recognized. My teachers seem to understand my problems and though my marks aren't the greatest, I know I'm producing better results every day."

Joe O'Brien, a real estate broker turned land speculator, had successfully turned unwanted land parcels into major acquisitions for supermarkets and shopping malls for the past twenty years. He had made it! Or so it seemed. Joe lived in a beautiful suburban community (in a house purchased for $40,000, now valued at $140,000), had a wife, three teenage sons, a boat, and a three-car garage. Joe's eldest son, Tim, a great basketball player, had earned many awards for his athletic prowess; but Dad had *missed* all of these occasions in Tim's life because of business obligations.

As Joe tells it, he missed almost every important event in his son's life. On graduation day, Tim had offers from four colleges to grant him scholarships and had won the Athletic Medal as well. Joe missed that one too. He had been called to Dallas in a last-minute conference on a piece of property his firm was putting together for a sports center.

"I decided that I'd had enough of giving my life to others and wanted to get to see and know my family again," said Joe. "I guess I suddenly realized that the best part of my boys' lives was passing me by, and I hadn't taken the time to notice."

Joe went to graduate school, then started on a teaching career working with problem kids whom nobody else seemed to want to teach. He went on to excel in his new profession just as he had in the first one.

"But I'm back home after school and my boys see me on weekends as well," he said, "and this is the kind of life I really want."

Winner or loser? Joe's son, Tim, says of his father: "My dad is a winner, because he'd rise to the top in any job he did. And he cared enough about all of us to give up that money he'd been making."

Joe says he still wakes up at night and thinks about how closely he had become identified with his job, and how little he was identified for himself.

"I wondered who I was without my business card. I even forgot my phone number without it. There are times I think I was my business card, not really myself! Now I can look at those workaholics and 'white knuckler' friends of mine who are always waiting for someday to live and I know that I'm a winner! My kids have learned something too— that life is made up of a lot of difficult choices, and you set different priorities. I think what they saw me do was better for them than all the words I could have used to explain my actions.

"You know," he continued, "I have a friend who has a beautiful thirty-two-foot sailboat called *Someday*. When he bought the boat, he told us that he was going to retire and live on it for half the year down in Florida. He has plenty of money, a retirement plan that can easily support him, and he's been qualified to retire for two years now. You know, he doesn't even spend ten days a year on that boat! His family tells him he's worked hard enough to retire and enjoy the fruit of his labor. But he's afraid of taking the risk, so he's still waiting for 'someday.' You know what, 'someday' may never come. Is he a winner? Financially maybe, but he's locked into a security trap that prevents him from continuing to grow. In my book he's a loser now because he doesn't have the personal security to take a risk; he's lost his nerve!"

CHAPTER

2

How You Talk and React to Your Child Sets the Foundations

How Do You React to Your Child?

Do you often wonder how effective your communication with your child is, and whether or not it can be improved? Take a few moments to read these questions and jot down your responses on a separate piece of paper. Answer either: Yes (often happens); No (never happens); or infrequently happens.

1. Do you think that your support, encouragement, and discipline have helped your child to become a winner?
2. Are your child's grades in school important to you?
3. Do you reward your child for good grades, punish him/her for bad ones?
4. Do you become upset when your child fails an exam, doesn't make it on a team, or is rejected in some way?
5. Would you like your child to follow the same career pursued by you or your spouse?

If you have answered Yes to three or more of the five questions above, your answers suggest that you place a good deal of stress on your function as a role model for your child. You probably feel that his or her success in school is important to success in later life, and have an important personal stake in your child's performance.

6. Do you feel that your child can manipulate you into getting his/her way, despite your objections?
7. Do you have to constantly remind your child to do his/her homework, household chores, etc?
8. Do you and your spouse disagree concerning your child's discipline at home or in school? Does it often lead to arguments?
9. Do you have one child who angers and upsets you more easily than the others?
10. Do you feel angry or threatened when you think your child is attacking your parental authority?
11. Do you feel guilty when you have to say No to your child?
12. Do you have physical symptoms that you attribute to tension and stress?
13. Do you think your child is experiencing physical symptoms that might be attributed to tension and stress?

If you have answered Yes to four or more of the eight questions above, your answers suggest that you are a very sensitive person. You are probably a highly conscientious parent, who feels that discipline is important in a child's early years. You take your child's behavior quite seriously and you place high value on his/her success. You will probably benefit from many of the ideas that this book offers to help you steer your child through the system as effectively as possible. The suggestions given here will help you to allay your feelings of guilt and anger, and to put your child's behavior into a clearer perspective.

14. When your child is experiencing difficulty at school, do you find yourself thinking that the child is at fault, that he/she should study harder, or pay more attention in class, or do more homework?
15. When you go to school for a meeting about your child, do you assume that the school authorities are always right and your child is probably wrong?
16. Do you wait for the teacher or school administrator to call a meeting concerning your child's behavior or performance at school?
17. Do you feel that the education of your child is primarily the responsibility of the school and that you need not follow up because teacher "always knows best"?
18. When the schoolteacher or psychologist calls you to arrange for a meeting about your child, do you find yourself feeling guilty, or getting angry at your child?

If you have answered Yes to three or more of the five questions above, your answers suggest that you may be leaving too much responsibility for the proper handling of your child to school authorities. Despite good intentions, many schoolteachers, psychologists, and principals are overworked. Decisions often must be made with attention to large group demands or budget considerations rather than to your child's individual needs. Parents have to become actively involved in the educational process. There are times when they must take the initiative in calling attention to their child's difficulties. Often they must ask questions that may appear to challenge the authority of school personnel. Further on in this book you will find information about the kind of questions to ask when working to get the best educational program for your child. Without such information, a parent may not be able to handle the complex problems that arise in a child's daily life at school.

19.   Do you feel that the "care and feeding" of children is the total responsibility of your husband/wife?
20.   Do you feel that your husband/wife stays relatively uninvolved when it comes to your child's problems?
21.   Do you feel that your husband/wife undermines your consistent handling of your child because he/she is too lenient or strict?
22.   Do you feel that your husband/wife does not spend enough time with your children?

If you have answered Yes to three or all of the four questions above, then you and your spouse need to sit down and work out a more cooperative arrangement in sharing the management and disciplining of your children. If you are carrying the burden of responsibility without support, you are bound to feel overworked, overtired, overpressured, and even angry. These are not healthy feelings for anyone. When children know that they can count on their parents agreeing, they are less likely to test authority. When they expect disagreement between the two most important people in their lives, children experiencing problems may cause friction to divert attention from themselves.

It is important that both parents read this book. If you are going to raise a child who is a winner, you will need to share the same background of information.

The preceding list of questions is designed to encourage you to reexamine your attitudes toward parent-child-family communication. There is no correct answer sheet to score you as a "good" or "bad" parent. These questions are not intended to evaluate you. They are designed to evoke thoughts concerning the way you talk and react to your child and his or her actions.

Parenting is a responsibility unlike any other that we undertake. For a period of approximately fifteen to twenty years, we accept the responsibility for nurturing, directing, regulating, and even molding the life of another human being. Although our obligations vary both in degree and quality, the pattern of communication between parent and child, established early in life, may be either constructive or destructive for that child. Your feelings as a parent will affect the way you talk and react to your child.

Parental Attitudes that Help Mold Children

"Parents have all to do with contributing to a child's self-love." This seemingly obvious observation was made by Genie Spear, a former student of ours, at her son's third birthday party. Many parents seem less aware than Genie as to how much they can contribute to their child's development.

"A child should be helped to feel good—just for being, and not for doing," says Diana Bander, director of the Learning Skills Center at Goddard College. As parents we get so involved in the achievement and accomplishments of our children that we may begin to display them as the "ultimate status symbol."[1] We can't wear our kids on our lapel or show them among our neighbors like a mink coat or a condominium in Vail. Yet we may fall into the trap of doing so unconsciously.

Equally dangerous is the habit of seeing one's children as an extension of oneself. If we cannot brag about our children, then what is left for many of us to talk about?

It is especially difficult for some mothers to avoid developing the Mother Hubbard syndrome. In this situation, the mother actually perceives that her reason for living is based in her children. When they mature and leave home, she becomes lost, lonely, and without function. This is the natural extension of seeing one's children as the total function of life.

Parents mold children through their unconscious attitudes, with little or no overt communication. We grow up in certain kinds of families and we receive messages via the family script. Where parents do give generalized encouragement and set higher expectations, the message is: "We know that you can do it and we will help you."

For children who are given early opportunities to explore their neighborhoods, do things for themselves, the message is: "We trust you and want you to become independent and self-sufficient."

When our children disagree with us and we respond without rancor, we are saying: "We appreciate your positive thinking, we like to hear your ideas, but we just don't agree with you."

On the other hand, the constant reminder of danger lurking around every turn may tell our children to be anxious and frightened. It may imply that you cannot trust people around you, and you cannot trust yourself. Little Peter was lifted by the seat of his pants and hauled upstairs by his father as the exploring eighteen-month-old tried to maneuver his way up very slowly. Without meaning to, his dad was telling him that he was incapable of learning how to climb a staircase. Later, Peter let his anxiety be known when he learned to sit at the bottom step, crying and screaming repeatedly for someone to carry him up. It was as if he was saying: "Take me up, I'm helpless. I've learned that from my dad!"

Messages are incorporated into the lives we lead, the comments we make, and the facial and body language we exhibit to our children. We tell them in various ways to get an education or else!

- Knowledge is important!
- Wisdom is a kind of power!
- Be my son the doctor!
- Become an engineer like your father!
- Get a job that offers security; then you won't have to worry!
- You just can't pass any courses!
- You're a winner!
- You're a loser!

Parental Expectations

Often we are not satisfied when our children perform with only moderate success. In a competitive middle-class community, parents are pressured to set expectations that may be too high.

Jimmy, a seventeen-year-old student of ours, claimed that no success ever satisfied his parents. "They're like junkies when it comes to getting good marks. The more you give them, the more they want."

Unfortunately, even those parents who have learned to accept the differences and limitations in their offspring are victims of a social system that cultivates a kind of élitism in society.

Mrs. Ryder, a mother of five, was quite proud of her brood. Her oldest son, Ricky, had experienced great difficulty in academic areas and transferred to a part-time vocational school program for the last two years of high school. At a cocktail party in her suburban neighborhood, she was questioned by another mother about the activities of her children. She recounted the various schools and activities, adding proudly that Ricky was in a carpentry program at the local technical school. The inquisitive neighbor condescendingly replied, "Don't worry, Barbara, Ricky might go to college anyway."

Barbara Ryder was a sensitive and thoughtful mother. She admitted to having had some difficulties in the earlier years in dealing with the fact that her oldest son might not make it in the traditional mold. "As a parent," she observed, "even if you come to terms with your children's limitations or alternative goals, there is always another person to rub salt in what may still be an open wound."

It is difficult for a parent to avoid feeling devastated when a child does poorly in school. However, when we recognize that the abilities connoting success in school are only those involved with learning letters and numbers, and we broaden our view of what success really means, we can better handle lack of traditional academic success. Schools only give kids gold stars for reading, writing, and arithmetic. What of the student such as Ricky who can take a raw piece of wood and make something useful and beautiful out of it? As Mrs. Ryder grew to recognize that Ricky had many strengths other than academic ones, she was able to feel proud of his accomplishments in vocational school. It mattered less and less that others seemed to care only for school success and measured winners only by their grades.

How Kids Manipulate Parents

In addition to this, Dr. Larry Lieberman, a psychologist in Newtonville, Massachusetts, says that parents unwillingly put themselves in a position to be hurt and manipulated by children if they invest too much of themselves in their child's success or failure.

"Whenever you want something from someone, you are in a classic position of being manipulated! Teachers and parents want something from a child in school, and the child learns quickly that adults want something from him. The child may learn to comply by manipulating." This is the way kids get into power plays with parents and teachers.

If we allow ourselves to be put in the position of being manipulated by our children, then we have only ourselves to blame. Before we criticize our children, we must pause for a moment to remember who raised them!

Unless children internalize positive attitudes without needing to manipulate others, they will not truly see themselves as winners. Feeling like a winner is fundamental to success at school, and to good interpersonal relationships. The following story of Billy illustrates this point.

Billy was a bright, articulate eleven-year-old who was experiencing some difficulties at school. He had also learned the art of manipulation quite well. Billy was quick at math and he enjoyed the challenge of solving problems. However, when it came to reading or writing, Billy had developed a conditioned response of avoidance. He would get his work done, but there was a nightly battle over starting and completing homework.

Billy was the second child in a family of four, cooperative in most ways, but had so much difficulty in the reading and writing tasks that he would avoid doing them until the last possible moment. Each night Billy and his mother had a talk about how he would schedule his work, and each night he whined and complained, setting up so many obstacles that she was worn down to compromise by the dinner hour. He had learned that his mother could be manipulated because she was so anxious to see him get his homework done.

By the time his mother arrived home from her job as a receptionist in a local doctor's office at 5:30 P.M., she had already put in the equivalent of an eleven-and-a-half-hour workday. She rose at 6:00 A.M. to do some laundry, make school lunches, prepare breakfast, and set up dinner so that the dinner hour would be less hectic. She was tired, had much more to do, and got little or no help from her husband.

Billy would beg for one TV program before starting homework, and if his mother didn't watch the clock, one half hour stretched into two or three before she knew it. Billy's father would then walk in after a hard day and the sparks would fly.

"Have you finished your homework, Billy?" he would ask querulously. His father was ready for a fight because he could predict a negative answer.

"Mom said I could just see this program, Dad," Billy would respond with calculated innocence. Billy knew that Dad's next words of anger would be directed at his mother. He wanted to be as uninvolved as possible.

"Marion, how many times have we said that Billy should do his homework before he watches any TV?" his father said with irritation. "You just let this boy do anything he wants when he wants to do it. No wonder he can't read or write on grade level. He gets away with murder around here!" The argument escalated.

Billy sat motionless in front of the TV, not daring to say a word for fear of getting the brunt of his father's anger, but feeling a bit guilty for producing it.

His mother would say something like, "If you had to get up at six, do housework, cooking, car pooling, and carry a full-time job as well, you might understand how hard it is to keep kids on an 'office schedule.' You're just used to telling everyone what to do and they have to take orders!"

Billy would feel smaller and smaller, digging his knees into the carpet and wishing that he could vanish into the flooring and reappear somewhere else.

Variations on this theme were happening nightly at Billy's house, and his parents had become so involved in his homework problems that they were arguing more and more frequently. Mrs. Winchell began to believe that her son's manipulations were a result of their arguments rather than a causal factor. Billy's father believed that his wife's permissive attitude and lack of scheduling were causing the problem. Neither of them could see that Billy was avoiding taking responsibility for his own work, procrastinating about meeting demands, and was highly sensitive to their Achilles heel, his homework. They hadn't noticed that they both made little fuss over Billy's manipulations and stalling techniques at other times of the day.

For example, when Billy did not make his bed, his mother simply subtracted 5¢ from his 30¢ weekly allowance. She would say, "No work, no pay, Billy. That's the way it goes in my office!" Billy's feeble protests would fall on deaf ears. On Saturdays, Billy's complaints about having to clean up his room were handled amicably. His mother was relaxed, a bit less pressured, not feeling the stress of her weekday job, and Billy could not get her to overreact or give in to his complaints. Unfortunately, daily homework was a completely different matter. His parents did not notice the specific nature of Billy's complaints or they would have visited his teacher and principal in short order: Billy was having an unusual amount of difficulty in work involving language skills.

Billy didn't feel like a winner when it came to reading and writing. He knew that he would avoid the pain of trying for as long as possible and then accept it when he could stall no longer. Somehow he had tried this technique at dinner hour and found his mother nervous, overtired, and inconsistent, and it worked. Billy didn't enjoy playing the "plunger." Dr. Larry Silver, a specialist in adolescent psychiatry with the National Institute of Mental Health, tells us that some children survive by taking on the role of "plungers" and "exploders." The "plunger" is likened to the man who sets off the dynamite charge, and the "exploder" is the one who "blows." Billy was the "plunger"—and his parents did the exploding. It wasn't fun for him, but it was one approach to survival.

A child who is conditioned to be the "plunger" in the family frequently causes minor crises by getting others sufficiently angry to react. These kids may create chaos as the spider spins a web, entrapping his victims. Billy was prone to this kind of behavior, especially at homework time. He used it as a tool to extricate himself from the chores connected with writing and reading. If his younger sister was nearby playing quietly with her dollhouse furniture, he would come barreling through the room at full speed, mowing down the fragile furniture in his path. Joanie was left crying hysterically, trying to mop up the debris. When his mother arrived, Billy always had a plausible excuse for the disaster; but it had served his purpose. He was distracted from doing his homework and he acted as if he were the victim, not Joanie. Like so many children, when Billy could not meet the demands of schoolwork, his tension overflowed, causing him to act out his anger with his parents or his brothers and sister.

As parents we often have to help kids direct their feelings through the appropriate channel. If your child is worried about reading and writing, you may have to tell him not to take it out on his baby brother or sister.

If a child needs practice in this kind of communication, the parent may have to express these thoughts for him at first, to verbalize the things that may be troubling the child. Something like the following might be tried:

"Billy, why don't you bring your books in here and I can help you get started on your reading and written work? Perhaps there are things that you don't understand that I can explain"; or, "Let's talk about what the teacher has asked you to do, Billy, so that you will have a better idea of it before you start."

Billy might start his homework a little bit earlier, before everyone in the house reaches the witching hour and is short-tempered and tired.

When Mrs. Winchell is tired, she might say to Billy, "I think I'd better have some cheese and crackers now, Billy, before I help you so that I won't be too hungry and get angry easily. Why don't you have some too?" She probably should have some ready for her husband as he walks in the door, to deal with his immediate hunger and fatigue.

Expressing our own feelings is not a sign of weakness for our children; rather, it is a sign of strength. The parent who can admit to being moody, overtired, or even wrong has told a child that he too has permission to be human and make a mistake. If we have feelings and they must accept them, we will need to accept theirs as well.

Our children often do things that make us uncomfortable. We can show anger at their inconsiderate or unkind actions without attacking them as people. Sarcasm does not belong in communication with children. The child has no fair way to respond. He is at a disadvantage because he has not yet developed the kind of language skills that adults have, and he cannot respond in kind. Dr. Haim Ginott, the late child psychologist, and author of *Between Parent and Child,* suggests that a parent can criticize his child's acts without criticizing the children.

Hearing a child described as a "monster" or "Dennis the Menace" because he has expressed the normal curiosity of a three-year-old is not in the best interests of that child. One mother was banned from the local supermarket if she arrived with her five youngsters, two of whom were hyperactive. Children will touch, wander, explore, and take apart everything in reach. This is Murphy's law of childhood.

Becoming angry and annoyed is a perfectly acceptable outlet for parents; however, it is a lot healthier to explain to the child what he or she is doing wrong, or how you feel about it as a parent, and to avoid attacking the child as a person.

Labeling kids as "good" or "bad" is not helpful. A youngster who is touching things she should not touch needs to be told, "Those little cups belong to Grandma. They are not toys to play with. They break very easily. Let's go into the kitchen and find some metal things that are not as breakable." That is far more constructive than labeling the child a "bad girl."

A parent might feel embarrassed when her little boy acts up or has a temper tantrum in a supermarket demanding that she buy a toy for him. However, sarcastic or angry comments are lost on the child. Quiet control and consistent handling will go a long way in solving this long-term problem. Perhaps Mother can bring along a long forgotten toy in her pocketbook, retrieve it, and distract the child from the other things on the shelf. If he persists in having temper tantrums, it might be best to arrange for someone to stay with him for an hour or so while his mother shops in peace, rather than having a persistent conflict in the public market.

Billy's mother might have tried one of the following ways to get him to work.

MRS. W.: Remember when you didn't know your multiplication tables and you didn't want to do your math homework, what did we do?

BILLY: We practiced them to make it easier.

MRS. W.: What could we do to make reading easier for you, Billy?

BILLY: I guess . . . we could practice it, too.

MRS. W.: Why don't we get your books and practice?

or

MRS. W.: What do you have to write tonight for school, Billy?

BILLY: Aw, I have to write a book report.

MRS. W.: Can you tell me a little about the book?

BILLY: Aw, Mom! Do I have to?

MRS. W.:   What was it about?

BILLY: Abraham Lincoln.

MRS. W.:   When did he live? Do you know what was happening in our country that was important at that time?

BILLY: Well, there was a war to free the slaves.

MRS. W.:   That's good, Billy; what else do you remember about Lincoln?

Sometimes getting youngsters to give answers about schoolwork is a frustrating task for parents. "It's a bit like pulling teeth," said Billy's mother. "He responds only when he's confident that he knows something about the subject, and I may have to do a bit of probing and give him a lot of clues before I can get him talking. However, I found that the first question may not get an immediate response, but I can talk to him about the subject and then get him to respond. The important thing is not to give up after the first try just because he only grunts or says, 'I dunno'!"

Parents must often "prime the pump" by giving kids a lot of background information on the topics they may be discussing at school. They may have to do a bit of homework themselves to have some of that information. However, talking about a subject repeatedly gives a youngster the confidence to talk about it in class, to ask questions, and even to write more than he or she might have without such background information.

A youngster like Billy is not always sure of the important things to write in his report. Mrs. Winchell had primed the pump and set him on the track. Children often will avoid their obligations because they fear failing, and it may take much patient effort for a parent to get them back on the track.

How Kids Frustrate Parents

Our first response to our child's expressions of self-doubt and inadequacy often is impatience. Why shouldn't my child be able to do what the others seem to do with ease? However, it is when a child is feeling strong negative feelings about himself that he most needs our positive reassurance of his self-worth. Billy was backing off from obligations because he did not think he could handle them. His mother's anger and impatience would have made the situation even worse. Her handling of the situation in a patient, positive, and encouraging manner did not allow him to turn sour about himself.

As parents, we need to provide the pluses when kids see only the minuses. We must see the cup as half full even if our children see it as half empty. If we don't "accentuate the positive and eliminate the negative," we too fall victim to self-doubt.

Another mother, Mrs. Gray, had experienced so much frustration in the handling of her seventeen-year-old son, John, that she felt he was her "personal crown of thorns." She was angry, embarrassed, and hurt by his actions both at home and at school, and she felt that the school authorities oversimplified her problem by constantly blaming it on her recent divorce. By the time we saw her in consultation, she would tighten up even at the mention of John, and show anger in both voice and body language. When we pointed this out to her, she seemed surprised, and told us that she had not realized she was having physical reactions to her problems. Yet whenever she was put on the carpet about any school crisis, her body became so tense that she often had painful muscle spasms in the shoulders and neck.

She expressed some guilt when we described John as her personal "pain in the neck," but seemed relieved at knowing that other parents often felt that way too. We went on to explain that difficult children frequently create an uncomfortable environment for the adults around them. Their idiosyncrasies bring out the worst moods in those who must live with them, and *they are often most unlovable when they need love the most.*

We all use those around us to mirror our behavior, and therefore the response of those around us reflects both positive and negative attitudes and vibrations. We pick this up through voice tone and body language as well as the words that are spoken.

An Exercise in Communication

We frequently try a little exercise with parents to illustrate this form of communication. We ask them to say similar words to their troublesome child in a variety of ways.

> *As a direct statement:*
> "John, you did a great job with the yard today!"
> *As a question:*
> "John, why didn't you do a decent job with the yard today?"
> *Enthusiastically:*
> "John, I'm really delighted about the great job you did in the yard today!"
> *Sarcastically:*
> "John, what a job you did in the yard today!"

Angrily:
"John, you call that a job you did in the yard today! It was terrible. What a mess!"
Lovingly:
"John, dear, you certainly did a wonderful job in the yard today."

Mrs. Gray was quite surprised at how many messages could be conveyed by the way she said one simple sentence to John.

John was one of those students who "looked like trouble" the moment he walked into a classroom. He was a well-known visitor to the school guidance office, attendance office, nurse's office, psychologist's office, and even principal's office. His mother smiles now as she reminisces about his high school days, commenting: "For a while I felt like renting a room at the school, I was there so often!"

She reacted instantly when she heard the assistant principal's voice on the phone by saying, "All right—what did he do this time?" or, "Don't even bother telling me what happened, I'll pick him up in twenty minutes!" With some help, she began to understand how her negative attitude led her to expect John to be wrong all the time.

John had been referred to us by the school for tutoring in reading and math. At one of our consultations with John present, in a moment of truth he blurted out his feelings: "Mom, you wouldn't believe me even if I offered to take a lie-detector test!"

"I never realized that he felt that way," she said. "I realized that I had no faith in him anymore and that there might be some truth in the things he was saying, but I never even gave him a chance to get to first base.

"As things at school occurred, I asked a lot of questions. I decided there were a lot of things I didn't know about why John was getting into so much trouble. I found that John was not completely wrong! Often he was blamed for things he had only known about just because everyone else expected him to be wrong, just as I did. I couldn't blame the school personnel completely because I was guilty of the same kind of kangeroo-court techniques as they were."

We suggest that all parents ask questions before they are ready to blame their children for things that occur in school.

Questions a Parent Might Ask about Acting-Out Behavior in School

1. What does the school consider acting-out behavior?

Acting-out behavior is any kind of behavior considered disruptive or inappropriate at school. However, it is important to note that actions considered disruptive vary from school to school. What might produce suspension at one school could be handled in a conversation with a guidance counselor at another. It is important for parents to be aware of these variations in attitude and to be informed as to just what the behavior of their child has been.

2. *Does he/she act that way only in class? If so . . . why?*

3. *How do the different teachers handle him/her when he/she acts out? Is there consistency in the school's handling of the child?*

4. *What provoked this particular incident?*

5. *Have there been other incidents just like this one? If so, how many?*

When we overreact to school communications that notify us of our child's misbehavior, we are acting as if our child is guilty until proven innocent. Mrs. Gray and other parents who are experiencing this kind of problem often need to recognize that their negativism further reinforces their child's anger and frustration. Sometimes we have to let our children know that we might have been wrong in jumping to conclusions about their behavior without giving them a chance to respond. We suggested that Mrs. Gray might discuss the problem with her son John and be quite frank about her misperception by telling him something like this:

"John, you must feel as if it's you against the world when we all get after you for things that happen at school. It's rough to feel alone when you have a problem. If you let me help, maybe we can work out some of these problems together."

Another mother in a similar situation, Mrs. Saunders, commented: "I had been making things worse for my son without realizing it. I decided to tell him that I felt embarrassed when the school called me to tell me about his actions. I explained that I became nervous, and when he finally came home, I'd have worked my anger up to such a pitch that we were both bound to blow off steam at each other.

"Much to my surprise, Jeff, my sixteen-year-old *enfant terrible,* responded with more understanding than I had shown for his actions," she admitted.

"He said, 'Don't feel bad, Mom, you're only human and I know how angry you can get.'

"You'd be surprised how much the sulkiness dissipated when he knew that I too could admit to being wrong," she added.

The response of kids like John and Jeff when questioned as to how they made it through some of those rough times at school is usually, "Well, I knew my parents cared," or, "My mom was willing to support me if I made mistakes." When asked about their successes in spite of school and social difficulties, kids seem almost unanimous in indicating parents as the primary support system that helps them make it.

John Gray is now an executive trainee with a large corporation, and Jeff Saunders is an apprentice engineer with a building company. Ten years have passed since John's first tough days in high school. We often wonder where John would be today if his mother had not showed him that she was there when he needed her most, despite the guilt, frustration, and aggravation he might have caused.

As parents, we must learn to handle our kids and their problems without attacking the child and making him or her feel like less of a person along guidelines like these:

1. Describe what seems to be causing the problem.

Mom: "Joe, when you leave all of your homework for the last minute you are bound to have difficulties in completing it. There are just so many last minutes."

2. Describe to your child what you feel when your child exhibits inappropriate behavior or does not handle responsibilities and obligations.

"Joe, I feel very confused when I get only negative comments from you when I ask perfectly open questions. I would feel a lot better if you would just give me direct answers, like Yes and No."

3. Describe what needs to be done to help the child through a situation.

"Joe, we need to get you some help with your reading so that you won't dislike reading work so much. We might be able to arrange to get some help at school, or even outside of school with a tutor if that is what you would prefer."

4. Avoid attacking the child for his/her actions.

"Joe, I don't like the way you spoke to Mr. Hardy in English class. The language you used might be appropriate to a locker room with your friends, but should never have been used to a teacher in class.

"You know someday when you have a job you will have to be aware that the people with whom you work just don't appreciate that kind of language. Your boss won't be happy with it and it could cost you a lot more than a job. School and the working world just aren't the place for that kind of language. It's especially hard for kids to be able to tell when such language is not appropriate because movies, books, and even TV programs have scripts that include many four-letter words. But that doesn't make it right."

Preaching is just not appropriate, nor is saying, "I told you so." When a person is drowning, that's no time to try to teach him how to swim!

Helping Kids to Show Their Emotions Honestly

Many children have difficulty in showing their emotions openly because they have learned from their parents to keep them bottled up inside. As children, we were told that adults should act "brave, grown-up, unemotional." Kennedys don't cry. Maybe Smiths and Browns don't cry either. How can children learn that emotions can be experienced and shown freely if they don't see the full range of emotions in their own parents?

Children need permission to show their emotions without fear or rejection. If one can't give vent to feelings, they are repressed and cause stress-related symptoms and other tensions that can appear as any one of a whole range of psychosomatic disorders.

Permission to express emotions is given when parents make it all right to vent anger safely, when home is a safe place for the blowing off of excess steam caused by frustration experienced in the outside world.

During our adult lives we know that disagreements in personal and business matters can escalate to become full-blown arguments unless we are prepared to appreciate the difference between "give and take" in a discussion and "intolerance" on the part of one person for the viewpoint expressed by another.

The script might go as follows. Tommy, age eleven, arrives at dinner, unwashed and disheveled after baseball practice and with his baseball cap still perched on his head:

MR. SACHS: How many times have I told you to wash up and comb your hair before coming to dinner? And take off that filthy damn cap and those dirty jeans.

TOMMY: I washed up an hour ago, and what's the big deal about wearing old jeans and a baseball cap anyway?

MR. SACHS: Don't you dare question me! How would you like to go without dinner?

TOMMY: Big deal! I don't give a damn about having dinner. It just tastes like * # @ ¢ anyway!

MR. SACHS: That does it—I've had enough of you and your foul mouth! Go to your room. Can't I ever have a peaceful meal in this house?

Mr. Sachs could have changed the level of discussion after Tommy's first insult by saying, "You know, Tom, when I saw you with those dirty pants and that cap at dinner, I became annoyed. It's just not proper to look like that at the table; but I probably shouldn't have used the word 'damn.' " Some real communication can follow when both parties are not just trading angry words as Mr. Sachs and Tommy were.

In order to deescalate such arguments, a parent must be willing to give up a portion of parental authority for the sake of continued open communication. Many parents feel a great need to be BOSS. However, we need to be the BOSS only when we are anxious or afraid of something and need to establish our authority in the face of a child's challenges. Some children are expected to give parents instant emotional gratification through their constant obedience. It is easy to see that any challenge to that obedience may be perceived as a threat to many parents.

Having reached the sublime position of parenthood, we must always remember what Thomas Gordon wrote in *Parent Effectiveness Training:* "Parents are people, not gods. They do not have to act unconditionally accepting, or even consistently accepting. Neither should they pretend to be accepting when they are not. While children undoubtedly prefer to be accepted, they can constructively handle their parents' unaccepting feelings when parents send clear and honest messages that match their true feelings. Not only will this make it easier for children to cope, but it will help each child to see his parent as a real person-trans-parent, human, someone with whom he would like to have a relationship."[2]

"In my day, an eleven-year-old would have gotten a licking if he said what Tommy said to me," commented Mr. Sachs. "Children listened to their parents back in those days," he continued.

That is a tenuous argument for parents to use to support a return to earlier methods of child rearing. Today, both children and parents are confronted with many kinds of pressure that make discipline a complicated subject.

Recalling the good old days does little to improve our present relationship with our children. Perhaps if we think back, the "good old days" weren't so good after all. But neither insubstantial threats nor harkening back will change the things our children are exposed to, nor will they clear avenues of communication.

Deescalating arguments is the first step in problem solving. Problem solving is the key to success. Success is the basis of feeling like a winner. If we would help our children feel like winners, we must take them through the paces of constructive, open communication without manipulating others, allowing a healthy show of feelings by parent and child.

It is important to show a child that you can handle his or her anger and disappointment without either giving in or erupting in anger. It is destructive to allow guilt to enter into the situation. Complicating the job of raising children are the overwhelming feelings of guilt that many parents feel if they have some sort of problem that may affect the child's life. It is extremely important to put one's guilt feelings in perspective.

The parent who is alcoholic, ill, unemployed, divorced, or under great emotional strain is victim of this debilitating guilt, and may attempt to overcompensate for problems he or she feels he has caused in his child's life. Children are resilient. Divorce itself is not necessarily destructive to children (according to Louise Despert, psychoanalyst, in *Children of Divorce*); nor are the other disabilities of adulthood. The tired, irritable mother or the depressed, unemployed father have problems that a child can understand, given time and patience.

In the case of separated or strained relationships between parents, it is most important that the child not be allowed to use one parent as a lever to get special treatment or special favors from the other.

Jimmy, an eight-year-old adopted child, could bring his mother to tears with: "If you were my real mother, you'd let me do that."

Sally, a twelve-year-old, was looking for extended social privileges by saying: "Betty's mother *always* lets her do it."

And Billy, a nine-year-old, would torture his mother with comments like: "If Daddy were here, he'd let me do it."

Children need to know that their feelings are important to their parents. As they experiment with the expression of feelings, they will learn by trial and error what is acceptable and what is not. A well-timed temper tantrum aimed at getting a toy in a store may coerce Mother into submission through embarrassment. Having given in once, that mother will be subjected to "TTs" again and again until she reaffirms her consistent application of rules.

It is much more difficult to respond to a child's feelings sympathetically without giving in to his or her demands. But this can be done, in ways like the following:

MOTHER: I know that you would like to have that toy, Jay, but I am not going to buy it.
JAY (*sobbing pathetically*): Bu-bu-bu-but I want it.
MOTHER: I can tell that you want it.
JAY (*sniffling and howling*): I want it!
MOTHER: I know, Jay, I know that you want it, but I'm not going to buy you any toys today!

Too often we see mothers taking their children's actions or problems as their own personal responsibility. Mrs. Gray aptly described her son John as a "personal crown of thorns"; others have told us that they find themselves feeling as if they *own* their children's problems themselves. This tends to make the mother even more angry if the father remains uninvolved with the disciplining, nurturing, and tending of children's needs. However, many fathers still rarely climb down from their seat of indifference except for dinner or Saturday afternoon football.

Susan, a charming young lady now attending college, claims that her father absentmindedly gave her allowance payments three times on the same day because he was so mesmerized by the football game he was watching he didn't even notice her requests. "It was usually like that in my house on Bowl days," she said. "But during the World Series, I could only get my allowance twice in one day!"

The Problems of Modern Parenthood

"Motherhood is too important to be left for women . . . it has to be shared," declares Jessie Bernard. "Parenting is truly a full-time job for both parents, not just for mothers. Fathers often get so caught up in their jobs and careers, offering them easy excuses to remain uninvolved. It is not the quantity but the quality of time spent with children that is important."[3]

Formerly, the roles and responsibilities of parenthood were embedded in an enduring tradition. Women knew what was expected of them as mothers—cooking, sewing, nurturing children, and keeping the home fires burning. Fathers were responsible for funding the process, offering economic security, and providing discipline to the family. There were relatives available to fill in for mother when necessary, and children seemed to grow up with some sense of continuity.

No longer are the roles of mother and father clearly defined. Consequently, the job of parenthood is far more complex. Extended families live apart, grandparents are separated from grandchildren by distance as well as segregated social worlds. Both parents often are away from home working twelve-hour days, leaving kids to bring up each other. Many families are basically one-parent families, with a nonresident mother or father as a periodic visitor to kiss and run.

"Do all parents have to get a divorce?" asked Terry, an eight-year-old student of ours. "All my friends are having divorced parents. Do I have to?"

Experiencing the divorce of parents need not mean "losing" for a child. Certainly it brings trauma, insecurity, and conflict into the life of a young child. But it may also bring a sense of self-worth, independence, and emotional growth as well, as many responsibilities are assumed earlier than they might have been in a two-parent family.

Most single parents experience an enormous sense of guilt, feeling that they are depriving their children of the healthy adjustment of a two-parent family for their own selfish reasons. The single parent may feel an enormous sense of loneliness and isolation, and this in turn can complicate the problem of readjustment for both parent and child. There are a number of pitfalls for the single parent in this complicated task of raising a well-adjusted child who is equipped to become a winner.

One single parent told us that she found she was overcompensating for the absent father by letting up on consistent discipline. She was denying herself a normal social life to spend her recreation time with her kids. She said that she only realized how harmful this was when she had the opportunity to spend a weekend away at the shore without her kids. She felt restored and relaxed by the new-found friendships and came back home a much happier person. Her sixteen-year-old son commented in an offhanded way, "Mom, you're almost your old cheerful self again. You should get away more often."

The same mother told us that her thirteen-year-old daughter probably recognized that she was trying to be the "perfect mother" by giving too many gifts with her hard-earned money. She presented her daughter with an expensive sweater from a boutique near her office, spending twice as much as she should have. That night she overheard her daughter telling a friend on the phone: "Mom brought me *another* present, but I don't know why."

In trying to make up for the absent parent, she was doing things that her kids knew were out of character for her. Her kids had become more sensitive to adult feelings and were better able to understand hers.

Single parents also have to be on guard against the kind of manipulation that can occur when their kids find ways to use one parent's emotions against another. Manipulating parents is a child's earliest vocation. However, when a parent is alone, the things that kids say assume greater importance and traumas seem more serious. For generations kids have been saying to Mommie, "But Daddy always lets me do it," or to Daddy, "If you loved me as much as Mommie does, you'd get it for me." Kids in two-parent homes often utilize the communication gap for their own gain. Dr. Lee Salk, psychologist and author of *What Every Child Would Like Parents to Know about Divorce,*[4] points out that children cannot manipulate parents in such situations once the parents have become emotionally divorced as well as legally divorced from each other.

Parenthood is probably one of the most important and creative jobs we will encounter in our lifetime. No career offers less training and preparation, no vocation is so demanding of our wisdom, patience, and creativity, yet receives so little time and attention in school.

When asked whether Harvard University had truly prepared him for the world of medicine and life, a prominent psychiatrist, author, and educator, Shepard Ginandes, is quoted as saying, "It was a superb education but it did not prepare for two major areas of life: one was how to balance my checkbook and the other, how to be a father!"

"God has given me this sensitive, creative child, but He forgot to include the manual of instructions." This feeling has been expressed by many parents in many ways. We bring our own perceptions into the job of parenting. These are gained through our own experiences; we have some warm, comforting memories and some strong dissatisfactions with our own upbringing. We may perceive our parents as having been loving, warm, and tender, or harsh, punitive, and intolerant. Our feelings concerning the effectiveness of their performance as parents help us to set our own goals and values.

Letting go of one's children is a key to raising kids who can make choices and feel independent. Unfortunately, knowing when to let go is as important as when to hold on, and the timing of these is a bit like walking on eggshells. No child can feel valued or successful unless he/ she has the confidence born of independence. Sometimes the process of gaining independence from parents is like wresting a red balloon from a three-year-old. Dr. Thomas Szasz, a noted psychiatrist, and professor of psychiatry at SUNY Medical Center, Syracuse, New York, observes that "you should not bite the hand that feeds you, unless it prevents you from feeding yourself."

As Nancy Friday views the mother-child relationship in her book *My Mother My Self: The Daughter's Search for Identity,*[5] getting unstuck from even a good mother is a difficult task. Sometimes the child needs an ally, a father or grandmother. These people may act as role models to help us broaden our choice of vocation. They are less subjective than our parents, and often see us as bigger, more important people than our parents do.

Children need to have the experience of making decisions for themselves—even if they are the wrong ones. Decision-making is a process learned through experience that is developed after many years of trial and error. This criterion for maturity was stressed by many who responded to our questionnaires. There is nothing quite so characteristic of the loser as the incapacity to make decisions affecting one's lifestyle. The need to develop decision-making skills is especially crucial in an increasingly demanding and conflict-ridden world. Winners are autonomous, independent people, who develop the equipment to function on their own when they must. Learning to function apart from parents is a slow, demanding, developmental task, achieved only after long years and much practice.

One of the co-authors of this book, Helen Weiss, tells it this way: "As the mother of five sons, I've found that letting go by allowing my children to make their own life choices was probably the most difficult stage of development for me. It was especially demanding the first time and has grown easier every time since.

"My oldest son, Richard, was an extremely overactive youngster, constantly in motion, exhibiting all the typical patterns of restlessness and distractibility throughout school years. Richard was also a seemingly fearless child, sensing little or no danger in situations that might cause terror in any other child of his age.

"When it came to making decisions about education and vocation, I tried to temper his impracticality with hard facts and the realities of life, and to keep him on an even keel. At the age of twenty-one he moved south from New England, shared a house with friends, and struck out on his own. When he found it difficult to get work as a carpenter, he took a job packing parachutes for a local company.

"It was just a matter of time before my fearless acrobat decided to learn to parachute as well. Excited with his new-found skill, he called home on my birthday to tell me of the hobby.

" 'Hi, Mom, happy birthday!' he said excitedly. 'Guess what?'

"My naïve response was that I was pleased to hear from him on my birthday, and what was the great news?

" 'I've just taken my first parachute jump and I'm planning to join the Eighty-Second Airborne,' he said.

"My voice was muffled, and tears streamed down my face.

" 'You think it's a good idea, don't you?' he asked.

" 'Have you considered the dangers?' I said, trying not to show how upset I was.

" 'Yup, and it's what I want,' he said. 'You don't mind, do you, Mom?'

"After goodbyes had been said, I put down the receiver, still crying, and turned to Marty to tell him about Richard's decision.

"Marty said, quite calmly, 'Well, it's his decision to make—and at least you know that when he jumps now he'll use a parachute!' "

So much for one positive example of the way a hyperactive youngster can direct his energy.

John Gray, the young man mentioned before, experienced a positive reaction when his mother supported him through those trying situations in high school. John developed a strong sense of loyalty to his mother, based upon her commitment to him. Children learn through what we do rather than what we say. They model their behavior from what they see as meaningful in the lives of their parents.

Harry Chapin, a balladeer and musician, sings about a young man growing up, wishing to have his father spend more time with him. The father has little time for the son, and so the boy grows up modeling his life on Dad's. "Cat's in the Cradle" suggests that we learn from our parents through their doing. Too late, the father realizes that he has, in truth, produced a son who has no time for him either. So it goes. Parents help kindle the spark or smother it through their actions and reactions to their children.

Raising children is a little like cliffhanging. Being a winner as a parent means perching constantly on the edge and not falling off.

For the child, the process of decision-making often involves making mistakes. It is tough for a parent to stand by and let those mistakes happen. Yet how is one to learn, if not through personal experience? If we do all the thinking for our kids, they may lose the skill to think for themselves.

The process of maturity is begun quite early in a child's life. As the child moves into preadolescence, the parent is faced with a normal prodding by the child for the granting of more freedom. The parent in turn expects a show of more responsibility on the part of the child. An informal contract is entered into as the child is granted more freedom and the parent gives up control. Youngsters need time to test our lessons in personal responsibility in a series of small manageable steps.

Often this training can start with a simple daily task such as choosing the clothes to wear to school the night before, to enable the child to make the bus on time the next morning. For Mary this was difficult to learn and there were many late arrivals at school because of the early morning scenes she had caused. Mary's brother Tommy, age nine, was learning to assert his personal freedom by spending his allowance the way he wished. His parents didn't always approve of Tommy's purchases but they felt that he would only learn by experiencing the repercussions of his own decisions. The cheap toys broke quickly, and Tommy was learning to save to buy things that would last. In another family, eleven-year-old Barry was responsible for feeding and walking the family dogs. Their health and well-being depended on Barry and he was held responsible by his parents. All of these youngsters and their parents had entered into personal contracts to practice the skills essential to developing independence. When the transition to independence is not smooth or the contract's terms are not met, imbalance sets in and we have either an authoritarian parent exerting too much control, or a manipulative child who is granted too much freedom. This is the "problem child," as seen by David Elkind, author of *The Child in Society*. The problem child gets much freedom but shows little personal responsibility.

The child who shows little responsibility in turn also shows little loyalty to his or her parents. If we ask loyalty of our children, we owe commitment as our part of the bargain. We commit ourselves to supporting them through bad and good times, and they in turn will respond with loyalty and trust.

Much of the pattern of acting and reacting that we engage in with our kids is a result of the way we were treated ourselves as kids. Those of us who felt good about ourselves during our growing-up years are better able to communicate that sense of competence as parents. A person who has felt valued is more aware of his or her own strengths and weaknesses, and exhibits a solid sense of self-worth, spontaneity, and creativity.

Open communication must be the goal between parent and child. It is far too easy to fall into the trap of authoritarian parent versus submissive child, or manipulating child versus victimized parent.

Our attitudes as parents do affect our children. Kids are quick to recognize our pride in their accomplishments as a reflection of their personal worth, and our goals for them often become their own goals, even if they are unrealistic ones. If our children do not feel free to show us their honest feelings at home, they may role-play to fool us and close the door to communication.

If we encourage prolonged dependence upon us, our children may lose the motivation and self-confidence to become free of us and make their own decisions.

How you act and react to your child will contribute to whether or not he or she becomes a winner. So:

—You should act as a strong role model for your child.
—You should take responsibility for the proper handling of your child, and not relinquish this responsibility to teachers, school administrators, or psychologists.
—You should assert yourself with school authorities whenever it becomes obvious that your child is having some difficulty or being inappropriately handled in school.
—You should listen to your child attentively, and try to understand that his/her problems are important to him/her although they may seem trivial in the adult world.
—You should act directly to help your child solve his/her problems.
—You should accept the primary responsibility for nurturing, directing, structuring, and supporting your youngster—if you want to help him/her become a winner.

CHAPTER

3

Building Readiness from Earliest Years

Your child cannot feel like a winner if he or she is not ready to perform the many tasks expected at home or at school. Readiness is a complicated process, dependent on both the internal forces of maturation and the external environment in which a child grows. The readiness factor is a subtle variable, because a child may exhibit differing levels of readiness for the performance of different tasks.

Readiness for learning is the sum total of life experience that a child brings to school from kindergarten on. It relates to his or her physical, emotional, and cognitive development. But it also relates to learning at home that helps growth in personal responsibilities, decision-making ability, and the capacity to relate well to other children and adults. This chapter explains what you can do as a parent to develop such essential readiness in your child.

Recent studies like those of Dr. Stella Chess, New York psychoanalyst and author of *How to Help Your Child Get the Most Out of School,* suggest that the temperament of most children is fairly consistent as they mature to adulthood. Dr. Chess reported her findings based on observation of children over a period of twenty years, stating that children who are born "difficult" seem to have ongoing difficulty in relating to others throughout their growing years. These children appear more negative in response, slower to adapt to new situations, distractible, and withdrawn. This difficulty pervades their emotional, social, and physical growth, and all these negative factors feed into what may become "unhealthy dynamics" between the child and the parent or teacher.

Dr. Chess's findings suggest that personality and behavioral traits evidenced in infancy tend to persist throughout at least the first twenty years of a child's lifetime. If children are to learn to accept themselves, they must feel accepted by their parents. Parents need to be aware of the fact that the reticent, quiet, passive youngster will probably remain so, while the overactive, disorganized world-beater may exhibit many of the same traits at twenty that she did at twelve. Parents will do themselves a grave injustice if they try to change a child into another kind of personality type to satisfy their own personal goals and standards. Patterns of temperament, attention span, and behavior will continue in a generally predictable manner. The parents must learn to accept their "tiny tornado," quiet "Caspar Milquetoast," "Glad-hand Charlie," or "plain vanilla" offspring for what he or she is. If the parents are unaccepting and disappointed, the child will surely read the signs. To feel out of synch or unacceptable in one's own family can only bring on serious emotional maladjustment.

Why It's Vital to Start as Early as Possible

Children need to be helped to be ready for their first important job, that of school. This is a vocation that will last for at least twelve years, and possibly four to eight years more if your child attends college or graduate school. Critical to the learning experience is the child's readiness. This readiness breaks down into many subskills, and without these skills the child will probably be frustrated by his or her initial experience in school. The frustration and the negative feelings it causes may remain with the child long after the first days of school.

For most children, "headstarts" begun at home can help a lot. Recent years have seen much research concerning early development programs at home and in school. In 1961, J. McVicker Hunt, a professor of psychology at the University of Illinois, pioneered this research and described his findings in his book *Intelligence and Experience*. Dr. Hunt's evidence suggested that intelligence was not fixed but depended on the earliest environment one was exposed to and the kind of stimulation encountered there. His findings stressed the preschool experience at home and in day care and preschool centers. He believes that development comes from a child's attempt to cope with his early environment, to affect things and people around him. Development is stimulated through the response of those early caretakers of the child.

Research in a day care center in Mount Carmel, Illinois, suggested positive results from early attention, language development, and other stimulation using a handbook on infant education developed by educator Earladeen Badger, entitled *Teaching Guide for Infant Learning Programs*. In a highly successful program at the Pediatric Department of the University of Cincinnati Medical School, mothers were recruited on the day after giving birth to their first infants. Teaching these mothers to respond to their infants on their level of development with toys and game activities has had an extremely positive effect upon the development of these youngsters as measured by periodic testing. Federal funding has promoted Headstart programs aimed at early intervention to close the social and educational gaps in the development of disadvantaged children. This and other evidence suggests the advisability of helping infant, toddler, preschooler, and kindergartener with structured play learning. These programs reach back earlier and earlier in the developmental process, to the infant in the crib—possibly to the day after he or she comes home from the hospital! But cultivation as early as possible is important. An infant is conditioned to have certain feelings toward life through the kind of care and attention it receives from its earliest moments on earth.

From infancy on, a person's brain and central nervous system represent a complex processing and communication system essential to the learning process. Various sensory inputs enter the system through the eyes, ears, nose, skin, and mouth. Correct learning occurs only if the inputs are processed accurately. The brain must categorize, translate, and comprehend these inputs. Only then can the child produce something meaningful through speech, action, or writing. Figure 1 illustrates these elements in the learning process.

Educational research suggests that much of the child's attitude toward problem solving and learning is set during the first five years of life. Learning skills and habits can change after that time, but *the pattern established in preschool years often deeply influences the kind of learning that follows.*

Support for this theory concerning the significance of patterns of learning set in the early years comes, among others, from Dr. Jerome Bruner, Watts Professor of Psychology at Oxford University, in his two books *The Process of Education* and *Towards a Theory of Instruction*.[1]

It is Jean Piaget, however, former professor of developmental psychology at the Sorbonne, Paris, whose writing has given the clearest picture of the way children think and learn. The child learns in his own home long before he ever comes to school. He has learned to deal with basic physical needs, to laugh and cry, watch and listen, and even to experience profound feelings of love and hate. Piaget, known as "Mr.

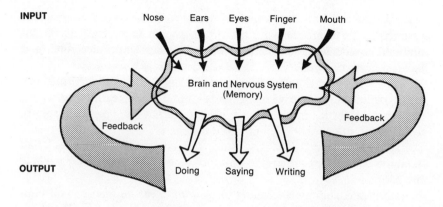

FIGURE 1. **Elements in a Child's Learning Process**

Child Psychology," has been an observer of the physiology and biology of child development. He set up stages of development that help us to analyze a child's readiness for learning within these stages. And Molly Brearley, a leading British educator, in *The Teaching of Young Children,* reinforces Piaget's belief that it is the knowledge, skills, and enthusiasm with which a child arrives at school, rather than any specific educational method or book, that matters most.

Children probably absorb information more rapidly during the relatively short preschool period than they ever will again in an equal period of time. And it is the parent who is the teacher of supreme importance during these years—a parent teaching with little or no help from any educational system. These years give parents an unmatched opportunity for fostering the basic self-confidence and delight in learning that characterize a winner.

Building a Winner through Infancy to Age Two

You can better understand how to cultivate your infant's development by knowing the generally accepted stages of development from birth through the age of two that have been defined by Jean Piaget. Let us follow one little boy, Tommy, through these stages.

Tommy, a month-old baby, is at the *reflex* stage. He grasps at everything in his reach. He swings his pudgy little fist in space like a punchy prizefighter.

As Tommy grows to the ripe age of three months, he will enter into what Piaget calls the period of *self-investigation.* He will reach for his fingers and place one or more in his mouth. He will find his left hand close to the right and clasp them. He will explore anything in range. He will take his cue from the response of others. If they use a stern voice, irritated at his finger-chewing, he will know that there are negative vibrations around him. Infants read body language and voice tone, and have no need of words.

Tommy at about the age of seven months is in the *reaching-out* stage. He is pulling down the whirling birds over his crib, eating the wings, and reaching for his mother's hair, glasses, and beads. Positive response to his explorations will let him know that he is "Good Tommy," while a slap on the hand or angry word will convey the message, "Bad Tommy." These are often the entrance lines that can direct a whole life-script.

Later, little Tommy is learning to *coordinate his muscles* to pull himself into a sitting and standing position at the side of the crib. He is about eleven months old and our world explorer wants *out!* His demands are punctuated by loud cries when he has exhausted the supply of toys in the playpen and thrown them onto the floor. Then there is only one thing that will satisfy him, and that is his freedom. Keep him penned in constantly and you will thwart his natural need for *crawling, walking, throwing,* and other *gross motor activities.* Let him out even though this puts you on the run, constantly on guard against disaster.

An eighteen-month-old Tommy has learned that objects on tables are to be *fingered, handled, and dropped.* He doesn't mean to break them but down they come. He will push anything with wheels. He will even push things without wheels—chairs, lamps, books—so better be aware of the things in his reach.

Tommy will need to pass through each of these stages with positive encouragement. Constant "no-no's" will turn him off. He may ignore them and become defiant, or obey them and stop exploring. He will learn trust from those around him if he feels accepted at each stage of development. He will not learn trust if he feels his normal needs are thwarted. His mother and father are the all-important persons in his life at this time. Their attitude is crucial to his mastery of each developmental stage.

Having successfully mastered the previous stages, Tommy at age two moves on to face more formal learning in the area of *problem solving.* Now he will find that objects have uses, and he must be able to master them. A stick and a ball become a kind of toddler golf game. A shovel, pail, and sandpile may lead to the construction of California freeways or a leaning tower of Pisa. A cup filled with milk may lead to the Hoover Dam, an ice-cream cone to a lesson about liquids and solids. At times he will smile and at times he will cry. The early preschool child is an "enigma surrounded by a riddle." For parents, there is a need to understand that all of this is normal. To become a winner, Tommy needs nurturing and encouragement, and his mom and dad may need the patience of a saint.

Just as Piaget tells us that there are stages of development common to all children, so Dr. Arnold Gesell, founder of the Gesell Institute in New Haven, Connecticut, and others have acquainted us with the generalized expectations for children as they move up the ladder of development. Children from varying environments, high and low on the socioeconomic scale, can be expected to master skills at roughly the same chronological age.

Schools take their cue from these outlines of expected performance and set their norms for achievement (see pp. 55–56 for a listing of expectations). The inability to perform some of these tasks is considered to be a developmental lag.

A number of years ago, research was completed on an evaluation of factors of development in what was conceived of as a child's Development Quotient. This measure focused upon memory, perception, intelligence, initiative ability, and other important behaviors of learning. The research found a strong correlation between high scores in Developmental Quotient and intensive nurturing of children in the early years.[2] Other studies by noted psychoanalysts compare the importance of nurture and human caring to the growth and development of young children. Infants and young children crave togetherness, love, and approval. If deprived of it, they may waste away and even show physical symptoms of withdrawal.

Dr. Terrell H. Bell, former U.S. Commissioner of Education, emphasizes the importance of teaching the basics at home for the average preschooler.[3] Dr. Bell feels that the kind of input resulting from early intervention is crucial to the readiness exhibited by all children. He equates success in school with early readiness and preparation. The checklist below provides a means of making a rough estimate of the individual child's strengths and weaknesses in the area of some of the skills important to reading readiness. From this it is possible to plan learning experiences, beginning with the present level of the child's success, which will increase the skills he or she needs for reading. Many of these skills may be observed informally at home or at play. On a separate piece of paper, rate your child's skill as "poor," "fair," or "good."

Checklist of Skills Important to Readiness

1. *Motor Development* (Large and small muscle)
   Can the child hop?
   Can he skip?

        Can he jump with both feet off ground?
        Can he catch a ball?
        Can he throw a ball with one hand directly at target?
        Can he walk a straight line without losing balance?
        Can he walk up and down steps without holding on?
        Can he tie shoes, cut with scissors, use a pencil?

2. *Directionality*
        Can he determine right and left?

3. *General Information*
        Can he identify the parts of his body?

4. *Visual Perception*
        How developed is his eye-hand coordination?
        Perception of space?
        Figure-ground perception?

5. *Visual Discrimination*
        How well does he match socks, chips?

6. *Visual Memory*
        Place key, coin, and pencil on table.
        Remove one; can he guess which one?

7. *Language Usage*
        Articulation—Do many sounds cause the child difficulty?
        Can he verbalize picture content?
        Can he understand verbal directions?
        Can he interpret relationships between ideas that are presented verbally?
        Can he interpret relationships between ideas that are presented visually?
        Can he solve simple problems?
        Can he repeat sentences?
        Can he understand simple statements?

8. *Auditory Discrimination*
        Can he rhyme words?

9. *Auditory Memory*
        Can he repeat simple directions?

10. *Time Sense*
        Can he put events in logical sequence and tell a story?

Early readiness has a marked effect upon the child's attitude about himself and the attitude of others toward him. Harvard sociologist Dr. Christopher Jencks, author of *Who Gets Ahead in America*,[4] suggests that those who have academic ability often succeed because they are selectively encouraged to have higher aspirations. They are pushed to remain in school for a longer period, and it is the positive attitude of those around them that helps them sustain motivation and goal orientation. Dr. Jencks believes that, as early as the sixth grade, youngsters may be identified as potential academic winners and are actively encouraged to do well in academic studies.

Toys and Sympathetic Talk Help Boost Readiness

Toys and books that are commercially available were used to marked effect in a twelve-year research project on how toys can enhance preschool skills, conducted by Dr. Phyllis Levenstein, a research psychologist at SUNY Stony Brook. In the project, the toys and books served to enrich the educational preschool preparation of youngsters through interaction with their mothers. The project had the combined effect of providing readiness activities for disadvantaged children and enhancing the interaction between mother and child in the learning process.

Dr. Levenstein and her co-workers produced evidence that these youngsters performed significantly better in reading and math at the third-grade level than the control group in the project.

Conclusions from the study suggest that conversation between mother and child concerning books and toys, instruction in basic readiness skills, and active participation by both, all contribute measurably to giving the child the headstart characteristic of a winner. Trained "toy demonstrators" in the project went into the homes of the children. They demonstrated the use of the toys and accompanying activities with language appropriate to the demonstration. Parents learned effective ways to talk to their children, using both concrete and abstract words, by following the example of the counselor. Mothers are *shown* what to do, not *told* what to do.

For example, as two-year-old Tommy matures, there will be many opportunities for his parents to utilize such concept-building and language-enrichment techniques.

Tommy and his father are on the bedroom floor playing with cars and a truck. The car is broken, and the truck is to *pull* the car *into* the garage. In order to introduce the concepts of color, size, and motion, Tommy's father might say the following things to Tommy, while maneuvering the toys:

> "We must *pull* the *red* car *into* the garage" (a shoebox).
> "The truck will *push* the *red* car up *onto* the lift" (two empty matchboxes).
> "*Push* the *red* and *blue* cars *out* of the garage, Tommy!"
> "Now we have *two* cars, *one red* car and *one blue* car" (introducing concept of quantity).

Language and Communication

Communication with your child does not just mean issuing orders; one can observe many families together on a train, bus, or in a restaurant making no real contact with each other. Real communication is not:

"Pick up your napkin."

"Wash your hands!"

"Stop pestering, Willy!"

"Sit down."

"Be quiet or I'll smack you!"

Unfortunately, most of us do not make the most of such times together. Children feel that we care more when we solicit their opinion about their feelings, and about things that are important to the family group. A key part of developing readiness is helping children learn ways to say what's on their minds.

If communication with children is to be effective, it must be a two-way street, a give-and-take dialogue in which they do not feel that they are being ordered about, but rather that their feelings and rights are being considered.

Often giving reasons for our requests will open the door for some give and take. Instead of: "Wash your hands!" try: "Germs cause disease and we don't want you to get sick from those germs. It is important to wash your hands before eating."

Or, instead of: "Be quiet or I'll smack you!" you could say: "You know your brother and sister are trying to do their homework, and they would appreciate it if you would go outside if you are going to make noise. You will have to go outside for noisy play when everyone else needs the house to be quiet. We'll ask that they do the same for you when you need quiet time."

Sometimes opportunities for open family communication have to be made. The average family is in motion most of the day and everyone is on a different schedule. When both parents work, time to communicate may be limited to dinner hour or evenings. Yet there are other periods available, such as car trips, bath time, just before bedtime, shopping trips, and so on. In a single-parent household it is even more difficult to find time to communicate, especially if there is more than one child. Yet children only learn to express their feelings and opinions openly when they have experience in doing this—experience that is best gained in a nonthreatening and accepting home environment. Single parents with more than one child can trade off days with a friend who has a child of the same age in order to free themselves up for a day alone with the other child.

Decision-Making Practice for All Ages

In particular, decision-making is a developmental task that requires practice and training. We all have to make our share of mistakes before we learn to have confidence in our ability to make decisions. Our children are no exception.

The boy who has his clothes laid out every morning will have a lot of trouble learning to decide what to wear when alone. The girl whose day is so scheduled that there are no options allowed her will not learn how to plan her own time when called upon to do so. We have seen many youngsters who have not developed the ability to use their play and study time appropriately because their mothers always have handled the scheduling of their lives.

When youngsters must always do what you want them to do, when you want them to do it, they do not learn to set priorities. Deciding what must come first and what can be delayed is important in dealing with chores at home, part-time jobs, and long-term homework assignments.

When it comes to making serious social decisions involving teenage after-hour activities, kids often face decisions that can have very serious consequences. Although we might prefer to avoid thinking about it, our naïve thirteen-year-old well may be exposed to youngsters offering "pot," alcohol, and sexual encounters at a much earlier age than we were exposed to these things. To overprotect children is to be the proverbial ostrich, sticking our heads in the sand and hoping that the problem will go away.

Open discussion of problems and gradual release into freedom is healthier. By constrast, Jessie, a seventeen-year-old girl, went off to college after years of overprotection, like a canary let loose from her cage. Two years of wild acting out took place before Jessie landed from her "flight" and began to settle down. Unfortunately, the voyage was made at great emotional cost both to Jessie and to her parents. She had experienced failure, a broken love affair, and even an abortion before she straightened out her life. Overprotection of a child may lead to far greater heartache in the long run.

How to Tell When Your Child Is Ready to Start School

Most children show unevenness in their development in different areas. Parents have no need to worry when a child cannot perform a few of the expected tasks at each age level. However, the greater the number of tasks failed, the greater the probability that the child will experience failure and frustration in school.

Overplacement is a frequent and serious cause of early school failure. If your child is immature, you should consider delaying his or her entry into school, possibly for a year. For example, the child who reaches the age of five in November might be chronologically ready to enter kindergarten (and the competition of some six-year-olds), but might be better off waiting a full year to do so.

The successive stages of development are listed on pages 55–56. Use them as an informal guide to determine whether or not your child has passed these milestones on schedule. This is an informal observational guide for parents, and should not be considered as a substitute for professional advice.

Overplacement is especially hard on boys, who seem to mature at a slightly slower rate than girls in these early years.

Barry Wilson, as an example, is a verbal, dynamic five-year-old who is the right age for entrance to school. His birthdate falls within the last month permitted for entrance. Barry has fairly good gross motor skills and can crawl, walk, hop, run, and skip quite well. He has a good deal of difficulty, however, with eye-hand coordination and throwing a ball.

Barry might be tested on the following for readiness:

(a) Match colors of cutout felt pieces
(b) See likenesses and differences in colors and name them
(c) Recognize the constancy of shapes no matter how they are arranged
(d) Express himself in full sentences and follow simple directions
(e) Bounce and catch a large ball
(f) Have established a right- or left-hand preference for holding eating utensils, pencil, crayon, etc.[5]

If he could not handle these tasks, the school might suggest letting him stay in nursery school an extra year to give him time to develop the necessary readiness. Barry's mother might also be encouraged to play developmental games with Barry at home to help him build these skills. Feelings of failure due to lags in development can make a child feel like a loser from the very first days at school.

The following outline gives only a limited group of activities that you can do at home. Much more can be read and done if you wish to purchase source books of activities for children. Try to draw upon the resources that you have at home without having to go out and buy expensive learning materials.

You may be surprised at the amount of things available for learning that are already present in most of our homes.

Learning in the Kitchen

The kitchen is a fine place for learning to take place. Simple jobs help promote fine motor coordination. For example: rolling out cookie dough or cracker crumbs with a rolling pin is fun and promotes co-ordination of the two hands; using a cookie cutter to cut out shapes is a lesson in simple form perception and form constancy; learning to peel potatoes and use an egg beater or hand mixer is helpful and requires coordination. Following a recipe is a way of learning to sequence activities in a logical step-by-step progression:

1. Assemble all ingredients
2. Gather all the tools you need
3. Open all cans and boxes needed
4. Grease your pot or pan
5. Heat the oven
6. Measure (a mathematical exercise)
7. Mix the ingredients (if left-handed, stir clockwise; if right-handed, stir counterclockwise)
8. Pour into the pan
9. Time the cooking . . . watching the clock
10. When cooked and cooled, cut into pieces (fractions)

So-called clumsy, "disorganized" children often don't get the chance to measure, pour, stir, or slice when their mothers cook because they make such a mess. They need to handle such tasks more than other so-called normally coordinated children.

Taking Walks

Games can be utilized when going for a walk or taking a bicycle ride. Leaves can be picked up and categorized in a scrapbook. Sorting nuts, screws, and bolts into jars can be utilized as a visual perception and categorizing exercise, too.

Games of Places

Never take for granted that because a child travels with you, he is gaining all the experience he needs. He must have things *explained* to him. When going to the grocery store, *explain* what happens in grocery stores. At the post office, *explain* where the letters go. At the bank, *explain* where his money is going. Teach him important addresses and phone numbers.

Organizational and Motor Tasks

There are many other aids in a home that can be utilized to encourage your child. The reading of labels can be a helpful reading practice. He can learn to identify words repeatedly by having to search out certain boxes or pans from the pantry shelf. The dusting of a room requires coordination when little objects are removed from the table. The tidying of a room requires visual perception to spot things that are out of order and need to be replaced correctly. In order to do this, he must recall where they were in the first place.

Many tasks can also improve motor skills. Clipping laundry onto a clothesline with clothes pins, mopping and sweeping the floor, helping to move furniture, helping to push a lawn mower, and raking leaves are all jobs that require motor coordination.

Directionality

Practice of left and right discrimination can be done in the home. When a child sets the table, he must observe that the fork goes on the left and the knife and spoon on the right. As he goes around the table, he must reverse his image in space and still put the fork on the left and the knife and spoon on the right.

Sorting and separating pairs of things gives your child experience both in examining the quality of the things he is sorting and in learning how to multiply by 2. If he sorts shoes or boots or a row of socks in pairs, he can then use those as multipliers of 2.

Games of Holidays and Calendar

Teach him the days of the week, the names of the months, and the seasons of the year. If you have difficulty, relate them to holidays or specific times that he can recall, such as Christmas in the winter when there is snow, and Easter in the spring when there are flowers. A special TV program that is on Friday night may help him relate to days of the week. Display a calendar large enough for him to circle and color in important days as a reminder. He will learn sequencing of numbers, the days of the week, and the dates from the calendar.

Kinds of Measuring

Teach him to observe speed on a speedometer; time on a clock; distance on a yardstick, ruler, or mileage gauge; temperature on a thermometer; weight on a bathroom scale. (All of these things cannot be taken for granted with a learning-disabled child.)

As we move away from the things that are found in every home, we enter into the discussion of very basic specific play activities that parents can do at home and teachers can use at school to encourage learning in a child.

Learning Directionality

Why is a directional sense so important to your child? Directional sense is defined as an understanding of his own body in relation to right and left, forward and backward, up and down; in other words, all the various directions a body will face. How does this relate to dominance problems? If your child indicates symptoms of mixed dominance, it is quite possible that he may have difficulty in orienting himself in space and in understanding direction. The right and left directional clues may be quite difficult for him and may require extra reinforcement. If this seems obvious in your child's case, try some of the following exercises.

In order to determine right and left consistently, it sometimes is necessary to use a magic marker to write R and L (right and left) on a child's hands or sneakers for a period of time.

Simon Says: Playing *Simon Says* daily might be appropriate. For example:

> Simon says raise your *right hand*
> Simon says raise your *left hand*
> *Put your hands down*

When "Simon Says" does not precede your directions, the child should not follow the command.

Handprints: A plastic sheeting is placed on a table. The child's hands are laid palms down on the plastic sheeting and an outline drawn with a magic marker. The tracing of the right hand and the left hand can be pasted to your child's desk or wall until he has learned to match up his right and left hand and can clearly discriminate between them.

Footprints: Take red and green construction paper and set it on the floor, a piece of red paper under the child's right foot and a piece of green paper under the child's left foot. (This is better done without shoes.) Draw bare footprints of the right and left feet, in the appropriate color, and arrange ten red right feet and ten green left feet in a pattern of steps across the floor. The child must walk on the feet, identifying right and left as he goes. As his ability to recognize right and left improves, have him do it with one right foot omitted and one left foot omitted alternately; remove every second right and left foot so that he must hop from right to right and then left to left, while naming the foot he is using. This can be developed into an amusing and interesting game for children.

Readiness tasks are the foundation of later learning skills. Without this firm foundation, a child may feel that climbing the ladder of learning is like building a pyramid on quicksand. Mastery of each stage of development is required before moving on to the next stage. Without such mastery, children are memorizing trivia but understanding little. The basis of mastery in learning is that each child has an individualized schedule of skills and moves through the system at his or her own rate.

Most educators agree, however, that certain tasks of readiness are necessary in any preschool screening. They have found that there is a high correlation between success in school-related tasks and the ability of the preschool (kindergarten) child to do the following:

Self-control   The child should be able to:
Manage his/her behavior without excessive distractibility, hyperactivity, or poor impulse control.

Gross motor patterning   The child should be able to:
Balance on one foot with eyes open without falling
Hop on one foot at least three times consecutively
Throw a ball at a target (underhand or overhand)

Fine motor exercises   The child should be able to:
Place pegs in a pegboard within a limited time span
Tie a knot
Hold a pencil or crayon correctly

Body representation   The child should be able to:
Make a human figure drawing with some basic body parts included

Laterality   The child should have developed:
Some tendency to right preference (or left preference), using eye, hand, foot and ear

Visual to motor or copying skills   The child should be able to:
Copy certain basic forms, such as line, circle, square

Auditory skills   The child should be able to:
Understand simple language
Recall three or four words in a sequence and repeat them

Unfortunately, most schools are not geared to individualize to the degree that mastery education requires. Many children are shortchanged in their education. Parents need to be aware of this as their children move up through the system.

Major Developmental Areas

Children develop the skills basic to learning by moving through six major developmental areas. They are as follows:

GROSS MOTOR SKILLS—birth to two years
Large muscle development, like rolling, sitting, crawling, requires some muscle tone and strength.

SENSORY MOTOR SKILLS—birth to two years
Child begins to integrate fine motor muscles and large muscles, gains balance and rhythm; becomes aware of direction out from body and body in space. Begins to develop right- or left-handedness.

PERCEPTUAL MOTOR SKILLS—two to seven years
Child is now learning basic listening, looking, and writing skills; recalls sequences, and has ability to make meaningful associations with spoken words and letters that he sees.

LANGUAGE SKILLS—eighteen months and up
Dependent upon prior listening and speaking skills. Words must be associated with things as we think and communicate with words.

CONCEPT SKILLS—two to seven years
The ability to generalize from what we have learned in order to solve problems, make meaningful judgments, understand and classify information in math and reading.

SOCIAL SKILLS—two years and up
Skills involved in relating to people and acting appropriately.

Human beings are extremely complex animals. We move through predictable stages of development, but we tend to forget that we must move through stages of social skills as well.

In his book *The Origin of Intelligence in Children,* Jean Piaget suggests that it is a great mistake to suppose that a child will acquire math concepts only from teaching. The child develops such concepts quite independently through growth and maturation. Thus, much of the failure experienced in dealing with difficult concepts may result from unreadiness in the child. We may be teaching, but he is not learning.

Now, let's pick up again with the story of Barry Wilson. The five-year-old's parents had decided to let him move into kindergarten rather than have him delay entrance for one year, as was recommended. Later, Barry had some difficulty when reading and writing were introduced in grade 1 and the grades that followed. His overplacement simply made his problem slightly more complicated.

Barry was well able to remember the shapes of letters and to identify them, write them, and remember them in sequence as words. However, he had great difficulty in recalling the sounds of those letters, and recalling rhymes and words in groups. The pressure of being in a group of pupils more advanced in language abilities made his difficulties more frustrating for him during the first few years of school.

Dangers of Pushing Children Too Early

All of us develop skills at different rates. We must march to the beat of our own drum, accepting our individual differences. When it comes to the education of winners, readiness plays an all-important role. Readiness is the lubricant that oils the wheels of our personal learning machines. No amount of tutoring is a substitute for developmental readiness. This is especially true in this world where our "hurried children"[6] are pressured to achieve more at each stage of development. Such pressures complicate scholastic, social, and even sexual development.

Any observer of children will notice that there are things that seem impossible to teach at one stage yet are easily taught a short while later. How can we explain this, even when it happens with the same child and the same teacher? The most obvious variable is the factor of readiness. Stanley Martin, a mathematics teacher whom we know, recognized this when he said: "You know, if only the curriculum guide didn't require the teaching of fractions, decimals, and percentages in grades 4 and 5, my students would have less failure and more success. When I teach this material to the same kids two years later, they understand it so much more easily. It's truly a piece of cake then."

His comment illustrates how often children are boxed into a curriculum that doesn't take readiness into account.

When kids are pushed beyond their readiness level, they will signal parents of their stress. They send messages, although they often can't tell of their discomfort with words. Parents have to be constantly attentive, "listening with the third ear," in the apt words of Theodore Reich, to pick up the vibrations.

Again, in the story of Barry Wilson, Mrs. Wilson said that she began to recognize that Barry was in trouble about six months after he entered school. She commented, "I felt like a detective trying to enter into his world and uncover the reasons for his strange behavior. The distress signal seemed to go off whenever he had any written work to do from school. As the years went on, it repeated itself again and again at homework time."

She went on to describe Barry's actions. They ranged from angry outbursts over homework to bedwetting whenever he had a test at school. Barry's father also thought that Barry should join Little League's junior teams at the age of eight. The father had played baseball since boyhood and wanted his son to enjoy it as much as he had. Unfortunately, Barry's poor eye-hand coordination combined with his outbursts of temper kept him confined to the bench a good part of the time. It wasn't until Barry's outbursts began to occur with regularity after he came home from the baseball games that his parents recognized the amount of strain he was experiencing. When they asked about his baseball, he at first did not want to talk about it; they kept on with gentle prodding. Barry sobbed, but continued to say that nothing was wrong. Finally, he muttered: "I mess up the games for everybody. I can't hit the ball when I'm up at bat and I always throw it wrong."

Mr. Wilson recognized that his positive motives had led to a lot of negative feedback for Barry. The boy simply was not ready to handle the stress of competitive sports. His coordination problems made the development of appropriate skills a tedious process. Mr. Wilson recognized that Barry needed more help to develop his coordination, without the stress of placing excessive demands on him. A less sensitive father might have blamed the child for his incompetence and set up a vicious cycle of failure.

The father started working out with Barry in the early evenings and on weekends. Mr. Wilson played catch with him, and put various throwing games strategically around the playroom and in the backyard. He installed a regulation basketball backboard in the yard with the hoop only a few feet higher than Barry's head. He taught Barry how to walk while bouncing a ball, then run and bounce it. All the games they played were aimed at building Barry's skill and confidence. The unexpected dividend of this time and attention was a strengthened relationship. Kids crave time alone with a parent. In our present era of stress and rushing, the moments of "mothertime" or "fathertime" are often the best remembered.

Terry, a rambunctious nine-year-old with whom we worked, valued his "fathertime" more than any other reward. He spoke with great pleasure about the hours he had spent with his dad during the acute gasoline shortage in the summer of 1979, waiting in the gas line on days for cars with odd-numbered license plates. Terry felt that this had been his time alone, and treasured these moments of talk and jokes with his dad. He was actually disappointed when gas became more plentiful and they didn't have to sit in long lines anymore.

Academic achievement is often determined to a large degree by the accuracy with which children can handle processing of letter and number shapes. If a child misunderstands their meaning or cannot reproduce them accurately on paper, he or she may be experiencing a delay in sensory motor integration. Individual readiness to perform complicated written tasks can vary from six months to as much as four years. One of the primary causes of failure is difficulty in the area of written performance. Parents can help children to handle the tasks by providing them with the kind of fine motor experiences mentioned above that encourage the development of small motor muscles.

For example, games including pegboards, mosaic tiles, and plastic chips can afford parents with opportunities to provide constructive fine motor tasks. Building sets such as LEGO, Lincoln Logs, and small blocks assist the child in developing a sense of eye-hand coordination, as well as balance and structural design. The handling of a large crayon, large pencil, or thick magic marker gives the child an opportunity to grip a writing tool correctly before he is given a thin pencil or pen to work with. Coloring books, dot-to-dot drawing activities, and sewing cards are also activities that are enjoyable as well as instructive. The early use of simple tools—such as screwdriver and hammer, and peg games—combines eye-hand coordination skills with instruction in the use of fine motor muscles. Bear in mind, though, that young children often do not have the fine motor finger dexterity to push buttons and keys on musical instruments. They may become frustrated early and turn away from these skills with displeasure if they are presented with musical activities too early.

Parents can assert themselves on their youngster's behalf and insist on appropriate testing and followup in school for a youngster who is experiencing these kinds of difficulties.

One important factor for parents to keep in mind is that failure, once experienced, can become a self-fulfilling prophecy. Having been rewarded in certain efforts by the experience of "pain" rather than "pleasure," kids will tend to avoid that kind of performance. To write and fail leads one not to want to write at all. To read and make errors makes one avoid reading. We cannot achieve skills that we avoid. If we are not ready for a task, we can only fail at it. Unreadiness leads to failure and may contribute to making a loser.

How to Judge Readiness and Relieve Stress as Your Child Grows Older

As children mature, the expectations of their parents and other adults grow as well. Contemporary society places great emphasis on earlier and earlier achievement, regardless of whether growing young people are ready for earlier achievement or responsibility. As the psychologist Dr. David Elkind suggests, children are simply not given the degree of support that they need to handle these demands. Children who yield to unrealistic expectations without being given a highly supportive structure in which to grow will become stress-ridden kids. They often experience a sense of failure, either in school performance or in their sense of self-confidence and social growth.

If unrecognized, the danger signals may lead to further anxiety. The child may go into a downward spiral and have great difficulty in turning things around to regain success. The child who performed early as a winner but loses steam in the middle grades and goes on to fizzle out in early high school years may be a victim of this kind of pattern. Kids handle these problems in a variety of ways. Some direct their anger outward and get into trouble with the school authorities or the law; others turn their anger inward, and may experiment with alcohol, drugs, or sex.

For example, Randy, an attractive eighteen-year-old, came to us for help. She had dropped out of school at fifteen. Through the months until her sixteenth birthday, she had lived in a tent in the woods so that she wouldn't be picked up by school authorities. Both of Randy's parents had worked full time since she had been ten years old. For a while she had handled the responsibility given her like a winner, keeping house, doing homework, meeting her parents' expectations. But at the age of thirteen this compliant little "goody two-shoes" had begun to show her anger at the excessive load. She stayed out late. Her parents never knew where she was after school. Often, she did not arrive home until long after they had cleared away the dinner dishes. Randy offered no explanation.

By the end of the eighth grade, Randy's marks had plummeted. She had begun to experiment with drugs and was often out all night with the local bar-hopping crew of boys. Her parents were beside themselves but continued to rationalize Randy's behavior as a stage of development. They didn't recognize the seriousness of the situation until she had been out of school for over a year, was unable to hold a regular job, and talked about life as "not worth living."

Randy accepted counseling and was in therapy for about six months when things began to turn around. She had met Peter, an eighteen-year-old engineering student at the local state university. Peter began to help her rebuild her feelings of self-worth. By this time she had been out of school for two years, was far behind academically, and needed a lot of support to help her finish school.

Kids like Randy give out a lot of early warning signals to parents and teachers, but often there is no one available to recognize the signals. Usually, major danger signals are identified late. What might have been a relatively simple problem may become very serious. A useful reference is *Signals: What Your Child Is Really Telling You* by Paul Ackerman, Ph.D. and Murray Kappelman, M.D.

Listening for Messages of Unreadiness and Stress in Your Child

If parents want to learn to "listen with the third ear" for early messages of stress due to unreadiness telegraphed by their children, they may find the following suggestions helpful.

1. Try to listen to your kids aggressively. Be sure that your child knows that you have been listening carefully by restating what he/she has said in your own words.
2. Try to set a special time to spend alone with each child regularly. This time needs to be relaxed, without distraction from radio, TV, or other activities.
3. Try to get the family together as a group regularly. The children of the Kennedy clan recall their father's rule about the dinner hour: the evening meal was a sacred time when the family was

brought together. Each of the children was required to bring some topic to the dinner table for discussion. It became the focal point for communication and no subject was barred.

We know families that do try to set aside the dinner hour for this purpose, but it is rare for the members of a family to get together to eat dinner. Everyone has activities, meetings, rehearsals, and all too often dinner is a short-order meal *à la* McDonald's.

4. Try to know your children's friends. They give you a lot of insight as to how your child feels about himself. Include his friends in family meals and outings. Don't bombard your child with questions and criticisms about a friend; some kids get the impression that their parents would give their friends an IQ test if they had the chance! Try to keep your questions to a minimum and your "radar" tuned up at maximum.

5. Always acknowledge the helpful things your child does. Don't be too quick to mention the things he/she forgets without giving the same weight of importance to the things he/she remembers. Kids stop listening to their parents if all they hear is complaints and criticisms.

6. Be aware of repeated signals of distress, the circumstances surrounding them, and the frequency with which they occur. Heed the signals and your own intuition. You probably know your child better than anyone else.

There are many behaviors that might signal stress. However, it is the sudden change, and the degree of change in behavior, that is the most obvious clue to a parent.

Anxious, sullen, unhappy children do not learn well. The punishment for not learning well in our system is failure. And failure turns a winner into a loser.

Signals that Your Child May Need Help

Children who need help with readiness skills or adjustment difficulties send out signals. Their acting-out or acting-in behaviors will tell a parent that trouble is brewing. Some of these behaviors might be the following:

1. The child is experiencing problems sleeping.
2. The child is experiencing problems eating.
3. The normal ups and downs of mood have become extreme.
4. Schoolwork shows a marked downturn from previous quality.

5. The child shows a change from his/her normal good nature.
6. The child appears quiet, reticent, even depressed.
7. The child cries more than usual.
8. The child appears to be angry all the time.
9. The child fights excessively with siblings, friends, or parents.
10. More incidents occur at school.
11. The child becomes balky about doing schoolwork.
12. The child avoids social contacts.
13. The child becomes extremely secretive about his/her activities.

There is no infallible formula for setting realistic expectations that will predict success and make a child a winner. However, a parent needs to tune in closely to the child and his/her responses.

Overscheduling a child's life can be especially disastrous. So can boredom. When the week is filled with music, sports, and religious lessons, and little time remains just to be a child, how can any youngster develop independent resources? What often follows is the plaintive complaint, "I have no one to play with and nothing to do"—the conditioned helplessness that drives a parent wild.

What might be done instead is to provide the child with the tools and raw materials to draw, paint, construct, cook, repair, read, throw, bat, catch, dig, and plant. The parent should also provide the "thinking time" for planning these activities early enough.

Helping Teenagers with Readiness

Sometimes children of any age need substantial amounts of continued close help from their parents. But often parents find it extremely difficult to work with their own children in any kind of instructional situation. It is frequently very hard to remain uninvolved and objective when working with one's own offspring. It's especially difficult to keep your emotions in check when trying to assist your child.

If you are a parent who finds it almost impossible to work dispassionately on readiness tasks with your child, you might set up an informal "student exchange" plan with a neighborhood friend of yours who's in the same boat. Quite a few parents do this because it's much easier for them to work patiently with a friend's child than with their own. Such plans often work best when your child is simply swapped for the other on a regular, equal-hours basis several times a week. You and the other parent doing the tutoring will, of course, want to talk together periodically about how the children are coming along.

At least for the time being, you'll have to go to some trouble to work out such an arrangement in a voluntary, free-form way. Few schools as yet help organize parents for such swap-tutoring. Perhaps, some day, the rent-a-car people may take on the job through a new "swap-a-child" division.

On the other hand, many parents find working with their children on readiness skills perfectly easy and natural. But however such extra help is provided, it can prove vital to your child's confidence and self-respect. Especially in the upper grades, public schooling rarely provides enough readiness help for children who may need it badly.

Help like this may be needed even into your child's teenage years. Kids don't invariably grow out of unreadiness all by themselves. Unreadiness may still exist in a gawky six-foot son in football shoulder pads, or in a maturely rounded, fair-haired, blue-eyed Barbie doll of a daughter.

Frequent or extreme shifts in trying out roles like sports star or glamour girl, along with other evidence of still unstable personality in adolescence, can make it all the harder for us as parents to diagnose and give the necessary help with readiness lags to a teenager. All of us can remember the emotionally unstable time of our own adolescence, with its wildly exhilarating flights of fantasy followed by troughs of moody blues.

But, running below the stormy emotion and fast-changing interests of the typical teenager, are deepset developing attitudes toward life. The adolescent with the winner's attitude feels basically confident about his or her parents, capabilities, and life in general, whether or not the child is hugely successful just now. In particular, the teenager who is a winner develops increasing strength to face and deal constructively with challenges, boredom, disappointment, and failure.

By contrast, the adolescent with the loser's attitude frequently feels helpless at being far behind others in schoolwork, sports, or social life. He or she often belongs to a fringe group or no group at all. Maybe she is a passive youngster, who just can't seem to find herself and doesn't even seem to know where to look. Her uninvolvement reflects feelings of impotence in the face of overwhelming pressure.

Such a teenage loser appears unwilling to take responsibility for his or her actions, avoiding forward momentum out of fear of failing. Small spurts of success come at random times, but a child like this doesn't "pick up the ball and run down the field for a touchdown," frustrating the parent even more. As one mother of four teenagers described such a child, "With Rick, my seventeen-year-old, I sometimes feel the need to spur him on the way I might do with a racehorse. He comes so close to making it in so many ways and then he just gives up, goes back to the safety of his protective cloak of uninvolvement."

She went on: "Rick seems to lack confidence in himself. He avoids competitive situations even when he can compete successfully. He has always seemed less mature than his friends in many ways, unready for things that came to them easily in sports, studies and friendships."

Clearly, Rick had not learned that in order to change and grow, one must take chances in life and risk making decisions that might be wrong. Such chances and risks can often be frightening to a youngster like Rick. Yet the most important factor in his learning the habits of venturing, so critical in growing up, can be the steady, strong encouragement of his parents.

Backing like this was thoroughly familiar to another seventeen-year-old, Jerry. Jerry told us of his father's favorite remark, one that the boy carries with him through thick and thin: "My dad just says, 'Don't just stand there—do something.' Then, when I do happen to flop, I don't get any 'I-told-you-so's!'—Dad instead gives ideas about other things I might have taken into consideration. And when I get something right, Dad will say, 'Wow! That's great!' or, 'That's terrific!' and I get a pat on the back."

Lee Buscaglea (whose research on "Development Quotient" was mentioned earlier) declares that "Birds don't sing in caves, and neither do people." Children even through their teens need to be listened to when they sing, and recognized not only for their good voices but their cacophony. Without recognition and approval, we don't exist.

As parents, we must be aware at all times of the adolescent's need for our acceptance and our bolstering of the child's self-respect. The difficulties experienced by your teenager don't loom as large if the child feels he or she always has your basic approval and respect.

Many middle-class parents have grown up with a tremendous drive to become winners. It is especially difficult for a parent to whom success comes easily to empathize with a child whose motto seems to be, "If I don't try, I can't fail."

Trying to keep up with the lifestyle of one's parents is often beyond a youngster's reach. If this is true of your child, it's essential for you to go out of your way to give the youngster approval and respect for doing what *is* within reach.

You may have to be understanding and patient in this way on into your child's twenties. The youngster who exhibits lack of readiness for fairly normal responsibilities and social experiences of the early years may continue to be unready for many kinds of experiences throughout the teenage years. Parents are often told that kids "will grow out of it." But however much a grandmother and a pediatrician may assure you of this, they never seem to be able to give you any really reliable date or timetable. The parent continues to ask, when, *when* will I be able to expect him to keep his room clean, complete his homework, train for his future vocation, support himself and be on his own?

However, with the right kinds of encouragement and help from you all along, it finally does happen, on the child's own inscrutable timetable. With one young man, it wasn't until he was twenty-two. "I began to care for my things when I had to pay for them," he said; "and when you spend two days sanding and varnishing a floor, you don't let anyone scrape it up with their boots."

4

School Putdowns and Halos: How Kids, Teachers, and Parents Interact

Education should be a personal discovery of what is interesting and worth learning. Teachers must enchant, direct, and lead into learning. Unfortunately, the opposite is often true. Students have little or no say concerning their schooling in grades 1 to 12 within most public school systems; during those years, education often becomes the forced feeding of a lot of trivia. Much of learning follows the "fill-'em-up" system. It is sad when youngsters find themselves bored before they have learned to love learning for its own mind-expanding sake. An old truism that's all too often correct is: "Education is too important to be left only to the teachers."

Why Kids Hate School

"My boy does not want to go to school at all on days he has gym. (Or public speaking. Or knows he must make an oral report or read a written one.) He has gym three days a week; he worries about gym three of the other four days. Saturdays he takes off. One-day school holidays afford no surcease. Unless they fall on a day he has gym. Then he is ecstatic."[1]

The boy whom novelist Joseph Heller describes is fictional, but the emotions are not. Youngsters spend twelve years or more of their lives in school. It is their only vocation during that period of time. Yet many feel as if they are "serving time" rather than enjoying an educational experience.

Why do so many of our kids hate school? For many, school is a constant battering of insults and sarcasm against which they are impotent.

Twelve-year-old Johnny told us: "I was in a class where all the kids who couldn't do the math sat in the back of the room. The teacher called it the lumberyard, because that's where she put all the *dead wood!*" What happens to an enthusiastic twelve-year-old when we put him in a humiliating situation in which he cannot fight back? He either represses his feelings or starts acting out.

"School is often a defeating experience. It presents itself to the child with the unspoken challenge . . . this is the place where you will be either a winner or a loser. There is no middle ground," offered Genie Myer, young mother and college student. "In order to go back and finish school, I had to realize that education was not the Hope Diamond and that I could be a winner, not a loser," she added.

So many youngsters feel like victims of the educational system. For some, the pressure of competition is simply too much from the first day. One youngster told us that he had a reading problem and was always placed in the "vultures" reading group, but never with the "bluebirds"!

Middle-class youngsters in homogeneous schools are constantly subjected to peer pressure to achieve. They crave a sense of belonging, especially during the preadolescent and adolescent period. They cringe from adult sarcasm and putdowns in order to save face before their friends. They pass through the system subjected to pressures that may seem insurmountable.

Kids hate school when school does not meet their individual needs; when arbitrary standards are applied, not allowing for developmental differences; when their individual progress is constantly measured in a competitive curve; when the system makes them feel like losers instead of winners.

"The system seems to be designed to put kids down," said Tammy, an articulate sixteen-year-old. "They always mark what we do wrong, never what we do right! When I take those standardized tests, I feel as if they're out to catch me, trick me or fail me! How can anyone feel accepted and worth something in a situation like that?"

Most teachers seem to view kids from the perspective of their own traditional backgrounds. They have definite preconceptions concerning the qualities they value in the classroom. They describe the classroom *winners* as "well-groomed, quiet, obedient, studious, enthusiastic, creative youngsters." These are the pint-sized grown-ups who are eager to please adults and have little or no trouble making it in the educational system. They describe the classroom *losers* as "untidy, disorganized, noisy, impulsive, immature, authority-testing, troublesome children." These kids are the "square pegs in the round holes"[2] that just don't seem to fit in.

Salesmen will tell you that they don't enjoy negotiating with a complaining customer, or one who doesn't buy their product. Teachers are the salesmen of education. Education is a multi-million-dollar industry mass marketed throughout our country. Teachers don't enjoy complaining or nonlearning customers either. Kids who don't act or learn the way others do need more time, attention, and a unique sales pitch; this puts additional demands upon a teacher who may already feel overworked.

Teachers Have Feelings Too

Lest we forget, teachers are also the victims of a system that they did not create. The boredom, passivity, or hostility exhibited by some secondary students recently provoked an insightful letter on the Op Ed page of the *New York Times,* entitled "Parting Shot from the Teacher," in which Thelma Johnson poignantly described her feelings to her departing tenth graders, saying: "I guess your anger makes me angry, and I resent wasting time that way. It's unproductive. You are interfering with my ability to do the job I'm trained to do. . . . Teaching isn't any fun anymore. . . . You have been raised by a television set and your credo is on your tee shirt. . . ." Many teachers experience these feelings of anger, frustration, and impotence when students do not respond to their efforts.

Discontent and apathy in school seem to be "contagious like the measles. They seem to overcome us in waves, related to the season, weather, and general malaise of our society," said one secondary school teacher and counselor whom we interviewed.

"What frightens me," she continued, "is the breakdown of student discipline, the increased damage to school property, and the general decline of student interest in the learning process."

A growing distrust of authority pervades our social system, and it has filtered into the school systems as well. Kids question the credibility of a system that seems to be based upon excessive competition, busy work, and tired tradition.

High schools report increasing damage due to vandalism; statistics for assaults on teachers and other students have risen. Despite school authorities' good intentions, they are squeezed in a budget-cutting, inflationary-spending vise. Communities turn down school budgets and teachers strike unlawfully. What are kids to think of a system that produces these kinds of problems?

"School, who needs it? That's what I think," said Todd, a seventeen-year-old high school junior we know. "If I didn't have my friends, I wouldn't have anybody in school to talk to. It's a lonely place. If you get into trouble it's a 'Mickey Mouse' routine. You know, they tell you to go to your guidance counselor, but he's so busy he hasn't got time for you. He's busy with the kids going to college. I think that's all they give him time to do anyway. By the time I can see him, I've failed the exam, flunked the assignment, or been suspended. Boy, when you get suspended, then you get a lot of people interested in your problems. They're like firemen coming to put out a fire then. But why do they have to wait until the fire starts burning?"

"Teachers used to be more understanding," said Joe, a lanky, muscular sports superstar. At sixteen, Joe had been on three teams at high school, succeeding athletically, but he said it was very tough for him to handle his academics without a lot of help. He didn't want to give up sports because he was hoping for a college athletic scholarship. But his grades went down and he couldn't get the kind of help he needed.

"You know, when I was in elementary school," he commented, "I just loved to play ball. I couldn't sit still in class for very long, you know, 'hyper,' so I looked forward to recess and afterschool ball games. My fifth-grade teacher used to punish me by making me sit on the bench throughout recess and watch all the other kids play because I couldn't remember my multiplication tables. Why did they take away the one thing I was good at to punish me for things I couldn't do no matter how hard I tried? After I started to get tutored and you taught me how to multiply and divide on my fingers, I would remember the answers. Why didn't my fifth-grade teacher do that?"

Learning—A Highly Individual Experience

One way of handling the realities of individual skill differences is to help kids to understand that learning is a highly individual experience. Some of us learn some things more easily than others; some are more musical, athletic, or artistic. Individuality is what makes our world so interesting. Kids cannot be stamped out like cookies with a cookie cutter to make the schools' job easier.

Our adaptation of a charming fable suggests that children need to be educated in a system that recognizes individual learning styles, strengths, and weaknesses. The story tells of the animals' experience in establishing an activity curriculum to modernize their educational program. (We have taken the liberty of modifying it.)

Once upon a time, the animals decided they must organize a school. They adopted an activity curriculum consisting of running, climbing, swimming, and flying. The curriculum was standardized, requiring each animal to learn each subject.

The duck was a super swimmer, but failed running miserably and was a bit "klutzy" at flying. This made him a candidate for remedial running, and he felt the sense of failure keenly when he had to stay after school for extra instruction. The rabbit, a super runner, was put in a remedial swimming class. Poor rabbit, he nearly had a nervous breakdown due to his intense fear of the water.

Climbing was definitely the squirrel's forte, but he couldn't fly exactly the way the instructor expected, so he needed extra help. Being a diligent learner, he tried repeatedly to overcome his handicap, but the overexertion nearly killed him. Poor squirrel, he developed so many physical and psychosomatic problems that he was a candidate for the special education class for the emotionally disturbed. The defiant eagle refused to do anything the way the others did. He was a terrible discipline problem and spent a good deal of time in the adjustment counselor's office learning to mend his ways. Last but not least was the eel, who, though only fairly good at everything, won the general excellence award.

The situation of children placed in an inappropriate setting parallels that of the animals. They undergo daily frustration and a bad educational experience.

Successful educational programs should help children to discover their individual skills, to develop them, and to utilize them productively. Schools should encourage individual differences among children and help kids to learn from each other. Unfortunately, many schools seem to be trying to stamp out individuality, to isolate and punish kids who act or learn differently. The movement toward mainstreaming of youngsters with handicaps has certainly been a progressive step in the right direction. However, for many youngsters the school is transmitting a message that reads either: "You are good at reading and math, therefore, you are what we call a winner," or, "You are not good at reading or math, too bad, you are a loser." No school personnel would transmit this message intentionally, but it underscores the tough, highly competitive, grade-oriented culture that we live in.

The System Must Change

Appalled at the injustices of the educational system, Alfred North Whitehead in his book *The Aims of Education* reminds us of the significance of this problem. "When one considers in its length and in its breadth the importance of the question of the education of the nation's young, the broken lives, the defeated hopes, the national failure which result from the frivolous inertia with which it is treated, it is difficult to restrain within oneself a savage rage."[3]

Kids are the victims caught in the trap. They need information, and support; they know that a curriculum that is boring and inappropriate traps the teacher as well as themselves. Ironically, the word "curriculum" means racetrack in Latin. Within an inappropriate curriculum, kids can see themselves running around and around in a circle, akin to the mouse on the treadmill.

Understanding How Children Do and Do Not Learn

Children dislike school when they feel that they are not learning new and challenging things there. Understanding how children learn is basic to an understanding of how they do *not* learn. Youngsters learn to behave and react in certain ways because they are recognized and rewarded for doing so. We become conditioned to feel good about ourselves by the positive responses of those around us. We become conditioned to learn new skills by experiencing previous success. One successful learning experience primes us for the next one—we expect success the next time we try something new. Thus, by reacting with encouragement and rewarding a child's learning behavior, we can get him or her to try again and again. Success feeds success; but failure also feeds failure.

The child who is deprived of positive feedback may develop negative feelings about himself and the school experience. If his life is filled with "no-no's," warnings, and "Fs" for failure, he will probably feel negative about new learning.

One busy Saturday morning, Mrs. Tatum's day off from her job, she was trying to keep track of Jeremy while doing the housecleaning. Jeremy, age four, was learning how to tie his shoes. His mother had taken an apron and wrapped it around the back of a kitchen chair. Jeremy faced the back of the chair, taking the two ties of the apron in his hands and trying to tie a bow. His clumsy fingers fumbled with the material and somehow he succeeded in tangling the two strands each time he tried. Mother, observing Jeremy's increasing frustration, put her arm around his shoulders, saying, "It's hard to do the first few times, Jer, but if you take one hand and put it this way the string will be easier to tie." Slowly she unraveled his latest tangle, gently leading his right hand and the strand of fabric over the left and through the loop. "Good job, Jer," she said, as he pulled the two strands tight. "Now let's try it again." She assisted him, making deliberate movements with the fabric, moving his hands in large, gross movements, exaggerating the motion. Each time she reassured him with, "Nicely done," or, "That's it"— words of positive encouragement.

Despite a few false starts, his stubby little fingers were soon tying knots and bows, though slowly and with great effort. Never once was a negative or critical word said by Mrs. Tatum. Jeremy got a very positive message: "You are trying hard, and though it's difficult, you will soon be able to do it."

On the other hand, learning also accounts for our negative feelings and our bad habits. We keep doing things that are negative because we are misled into feeling that we are getting rewards when they occur.

If a child feels that he/she is only getting attention from his/her parents when he/she misbehaves, he/she will continue to misbehave. To stress good behavior, we must constantly recognize and reinforce it by giving a child the approving responses he craves.

Little Jeremy might have learned another lesson if his mother's responses had been different. This time Jeremy is working on his shoelaces, having a terrible time with the knots and frazzled ends. His mother, busy vacuuming the room, turns around, and observing the scene, offers help. "Let me show you how to do that, Jer," she says. With nimble fingers, she ties a bow knot on both laces. Giving no more time or attention to Jeremy, she returns to her work.

A normally curious youngster finding strings to pull will pull them. Jeremy stares at his tied shoes for a moment, then with a flourish grabbing both loop ends in his stubby little fingers, he unties the bows. This maneuver leaves a tight knot and long strands of shoelace dangling about to trip on. As any self-respecting four-year-old will do when faced with an insurmountable problem, Jeremy grabs the ends, attempting to retie the shoelaces. Now his fingers become even more entangled in the strings. Three tries later, overwhelmed by his frustration, Jeremy starts to cry, beating the floor with the heels of his shoes. Finally, he pulls off both the offending objects, tossing them across the room. With no response from his mother, he becomes more angry and starts running about the room.

His mother, annoyed at the repeated interruptions, switches off the vacuum cleaner. She turns to Jeremy, and seeing him galloping around the room uncontrollably, she scoops him up harshly, setting him down with flailing arms pinned to his sides. "Stop that screaming this minute!" she yells, spinning him around and spanking him hard on the behind. "Jeremy, you have been a very bad boy. Just wait until your daddy comes home!"

In this version of our scenario, Jeremy has experienced learning, but it's the wrong kind. He learned that mothers can do things and little boys cannot; that his negative behavior got attention from Mother when his positive behavior was ignored; that yelling, screaming, and throwing things lets parents know you are alive and kicking.

On the other hand, Jeremy might grow up to find that passive behavior will induce others to become so uncomfortable about his problems that he can get them to solve the problems for him. If Jeremy finds that helplessness gets his mother to tie his shoes, why not try it for buttoning, zippering, bed making, household chores, and even homework?

On another occasion, Jeremy and a friend had been playing in his room all afternoon. Every toy in the toy chest was strewn across the floor by the end of the afternoon. When his mother arrived home from work and the other youngster had left, she insisted that Jeremy pick up his toys and put them back in the chest. Jeremy stalled the dinner hour away and by the time bedtime arrived, the room still looked as if it had been visited by a tornado. Mother again told him to pick them up, but he became involved in playing with one of the toys, forgetting all the rest. "Look, Mom, how this truck dumps logs," he said.

Mother began to pick up the toys one by one. Jeremy observed her quietly. If it was so easy to get her to do these things, why should he bother? If this kind of interaction continued night after night, his mother would probably become increasingly more irritated at herself and at Jeremy. Parents can induce passivity in their children by such conditioning without realizing the repercussions of their actions. The passive personality, no matter how talented and creative, cannot become a winner for fear of handling the responsibility for his own life. At maturity he has had woefully little experience in dealing with his obligations, but a great deal of success in getting others to work for him.

Initiating Positive Interaction with Teachers

Teachers play a crucial role in the way youngsters respond to school experiences. A positive relationship between child and teacher is probably one of the most important factors underlying ongoing success. Many research studies undertaken in the past ten years have suggested that no teaching method is as significant in student success as is the positive reinforcement of a good teacher/student relationship.

In school, children must develop the independence and self-sufficiency to take responsibility for their own work. The child who is ready for school must be ready to undertake problem solving and complete tasks deemed appropriate. Schools set levels of expected performance, and the child who would win in the school world must be able to meet these levels.

Kids will learn to hate school if they are placed in an environment that expects too much from them, or if they are unready for group expectations. Parents must be reasonably sure that their children are ready for the demands at school, or it may become a chronic frustration. Overplacement in school represents one of the most important causes of the failure syndrome.

Parent organizations are growing increasingly concerned about the quality of education. They have become actively involved in making suggestions concerning curriculum and teaching approaches, as well as providing such supportive services as tutoring, typing, and fund raising. Parent groups have been responsible for the setting up and funding of in-service training workshops for teachers throughout the country. When such workshops are organized, parents can often expose teachers to suggestions that they might not ordinarily be able to present in another context.

The following list of suggestions for teachers was one of the materials handed out to teachers in a workshop concerning communication. The workshop members were parents and teachers, and the discussion that followed was constructive for both parents and teachers:

1. Try to manage kids through pats on the back such as verbal praise, approving nods, smiles, or an affectionate touch on the shoulder from time to time. Reward work completion with some special treat whenever possible.
2. Don't use threats and punishment because they just turn kids off. "I'll send you to the principal's office" is not a threat. It's the busiest, most interesting room in the school, with telephones, copy machines, water fountains, and other excitements.
3. Try to define limits clearly and keep them reasonable. Active kids are bound to defy unrealistic limitations, so keep the rules basic and simple.
4. Try to avoid sarcasm even if the student seems ready to fight. "Hey, blockhead," was the label given to one teenager we know as he was chided for rattling a locker outside a classroom. He responded with an unmentionable word and was suspended immediately.

5. Kids will simmer and burn when embarrassed in front of their friends. That's where they have to make it—with their peer group. To challenge them before their friends means they have to save face and respond in kind. Then they get into trouble.

6. Let the kid who has been absent know that you really "missed" him/her. Often kids feel that the teacher considers it a bother to give them make-up tests or assignments. They feel that they have to pester a teacher to make up work and they just don't bother.

7. Look at the kids as they speak, let them know you are really interested in what they are saying. Sometimes teachers are so busy they don't even look up from the exams they are scoring or the books they are reading to talk to a student.

8. Always make personal comments on papers handed back to students. There is nothing more frustrating for a student than not getting papers back after working on them, or getting them back with little more than a low grade. If kids have taken the time to write work, you owe it to them to make the time to write important corrections and suggestions. So many teenagers tell us that they don't get reports back after they have spent hours on them. Some say they get them back with red marks on the page and they feel that it is their "blood on the battlefield." Red pencils cause kids to react the way red capes cause bulls to react. Try to avoid using them too much.

   Attitude is the name of the game. Treat a kid as a winner and he/she will respond like one.

A Few Words about Teacher Incompetency

If teachers play a positive role in student success, is the converse equally true? Are there negative vibrations when there is static between teacher and child? Obviously a poor relationship can be extremely destructive in the child's feelings about him- or herself.

Just as we are not talking about "bad" students, we are not talking about "bad" teachers. There are inexperienced teachers, poorly trained, with inadequate exposure and perhaps highly traditional attitudes that may no longer seem appropriate or relevant to youngsters' learning.

A concerned student advisory committee made up of 500 high school students selected from across New York State reported to State Education Commissioner Gordon Ambach recently with their concerns about being taught by competent teachers. Student sensitivity to bad teaching has become a primary concern as a result of new state minimum competency tests. If we test students for minimum competence, what then of the qualifications and deficiencies of public school teachers?[4]

Parents have to make their wishes known to their boards of education as well as to state legislators. If we expect to train winners through the educational system, they need to be taught by qualified professionals. Tests are needed to set minimum standards for teachers as well as for students. Teacher licensing is as important as licensing in any other profession. Teaching is a craft, demanding skills, resources, and appropriate attitudes.

At present, the lack of teacher certification at the statewide level allows poorly trained teachers to enter the profession without an exam or even an interview in most areas of the country, with the exception of some major cities such as New York.

"Johnny can't read because his teachers don't like him," read the headline of an article from United Press International. Dr. Floyd Sucher, professor of education at Brigham Young University in Provo, Utah, says his research indicates educational discrimination against boys. Despite the fact that his observations suggest that boys try to respond in class at least eight times as frequently as girls, teachers are less patient with them, more troubled by them, and often feel they are disrupters or misfits. Society's expectations of appropriate male behavior and the expectations of behavior in the classroom just don't jibe. Aggressive independence, prized in the outside world, is considered disruptive in the schoolroom.

Recent articles tell of burned-out teachers giving up their profession after years of trying because the conditions of employment make teaching impossible. If a teacher feels like a loser, he or she cannot educate kids.

"The individual teacher has to feel that he is a winner. He has to feel that he is capable of bringing about change, growth, and learning in the child. When the teacher feels like a winner, he can transmit that feeling to the child and doesn't feel threatened by children's misbehavior." These are the words of Evelyn Bailey, author and teaching supervisor. She adds: "Teachers and children must not be in competition in the classroom. If they are in competition, invariably the teacher wins and the student loses. If we are not in competition and I as a teacher feel OK about myself, then I am going to start building success for my students, because that way I can be even more of a winner." Mrs. Bailey feels that teachers need support groups to help them deal with their gripes and complaints about kids and administrative problems. Without a constructive way to vent their anger, she suggests, their energies are often depleted before they reach the classroom.

Parent-Teacher Communication

When faced with poor communication between teacher and child, parents need to take aggressive action in handling the situation. If you feel that your child is experiencing undue frustration because of a teacher's inexperience, it would be helpful to intervene on the child's behalf by providing the teacher with some sources of alternative strategies and materials. Many teachers may resist accepting suggestions from a parent. However, most will be interested and sensitive to a child's problem. If you get no satisfaction from a direct conversation with the teacher, the suggestion can be routed through a diplomatic principal, director of special education, school psychologist, guidance counselor, or some other administrative person.

Attend school board meetings and support the expenditure of funds to provide teachers with in-service workshops, training sessions during school hours, and release time for attending conferences and conventions. Teachers get exposure to new techniques, materials, and ideas through these educational experiences.

If you have questions about the appropriateness of methods used by your child's teacher, be prepared to ask them, and don't give up until you get answers that satisfy you. We have found it helpful to advise parents to go to school armed with specific questions. Being unprepared only leaves a parent feeling inadequate. When our children experience problems, we are often reduced to anxious feelings similar to those we may have experienced as young children ourselves. Preparation helps to avoid these feelings and provides focus on the problem during a parent-teacher conference.

When a child is experiencing any sort of adjustment difficulty at school, parents become anxious. It is extremely important to keep the channels of communication between home and school open. Antagonism and anger on the part of parents and teacher are unproductive and certainly don't help the child. Emotional outbursts don't help a parent, child, or school in dealing with a problem. When you want to solve a problem, attack it!

Questions to Ask the Teacher about Your Child's Performance

1. How much time does my child spend in your class (one period or the whole day)?
2. What do you think my child's strengths are?
3. What do you think my child's weaknesses are?

4. Have you specific suggestions concerning ways my child can improve weaknesses?
5. Do you have an opportunity to give my child any one-on-one help or small group assistance?
6. Have you talked to my child about his/her weaknesses? How did he/she respond?
7. What specific suggestions for improvement did you make?
8. Will my child need help to follow through on these suggestions?
9. Is it appropriate for us to help at home? If so, how would you suggest that we do so? If not, why not?
10. Do you notice any specific physical symptoms that might give us information, e.g., red, watery eyes, runny nose, need to get closer to the blackboard, need to have instructions repeated, mood swings, excessive fatigue, overactivity?
11. When my child is resistant to doing a task, is it because he/she won't do it or can't do it? How do you ascertain resistance or inability to perform?
12. Does my child have friends in class? If not, why do you think he/she is experiencing social problems?
13. Have you tried any strategies to help my child improve his/her social skills?
14. When my child is tested, do you feel that he/she knows the material but has difficulty writing the answers?
15. Have you ever tested my child orally to separate the knowledge of information from the writing task? How did he/she do?
16. Does my child do better on tests when there is no time limit?
17. Have you any suggestions for services outside of the class that might help my child?

Problems Outside School

Parents are often in the position of being the primary people involved with their child's education and development during the twelve years of public schooling. They are in the unique position of observing the child at work, at play, at rest; and this offers them an insight into extra-educational problems that may be a causal factor in preventing a child from becoming a winner at school. We have found it helpful to direct a few questions to parents to have them focus their attention upon the kind of physically and emotionally based difficulties that may be causing problems at school.

According to ophthalmologist Maurice Tannenbaum, M.D., attending physician at Westchester County Medical Center, parents should observe their preschool children closely for signs of visual problems. Among the behavior patterns he notes as suggesting possible difficulties are the following:

1.   The inability of the child to focus both eyes straight ahead. It is important for parents to observe whether or not one eye drifts out or crosses in. This symptom is most obvious when the child is tired or not feeling well.
2.   A drooping eyelid may suggest some kind of muscle problem interfering with a child's vision.
3.   Children who are experiencing double vision may rub one eye repeatedly. They do this to compensate for the double vision by shutting one visual image out.
4.   Repeated squinting of one eye when a child is exposed to bright light may suggest that the child is having a difficult time keeping both eyes working together. In order to compensate, the child may squint, closing one eye to help stabilize the visual field.
5.   Any family evidence of crossed eyes or drifting eyes should lead a parent to observe a child quite closely.
6.   Premature youngsters, those of low birth weight despite full-term development, and those who had been placed in an incubator, also show a higher incidence of some visual difficulties.

Dr. Tannenbaum goes on to say that the symptoms that may be more obvious in older children might not indicate a visual difficulty but should be checked out in any case. Look for the child who sits too close to the television set. Many youngsters will hold material quite close to their eyes. This may indicate a problem, but often is a result of the child's need to concentrate and block out distraction from his or her field of vision.

Ask yourself these questions about your school-age child's vision:

1.   Does my child avoid close work?
2.   Do my child's eyes appear red and watery at certain times of the year, or all the time?
3.   Does my child complain of frequent headaches after reading, close work, or movies?
4.   When writing, does my child tilt his/her head at an awkward angle or hold it very close to the paper?
5.   Does my child seem to be straining his/her eyes or scowling or frowning when doing close visual work, or watching TV?
6.   Does my child seem very tired after doing any sort of reading or close work?

7. Does my child use his/her finger as a marker when reading, lose the place frequently, reread passages again and again?
8. Does my child choose picture books over those which are all text? (This is appropriate over grade 4.)

If you find your child experiencing some of these symptoms of visual strain, it is extremely important to get a visual examination performed by a qualified specialist. The child who has difficulty in seeing may find success in school impossible. Our friend Susan, mentioned before, told us that she is convinced that she failed three years of math at high school because she could not see the blackboard. Her problem was not picked up through the standard school Snellen Chart Test, yet her astigmatism and poor convergence caused many number-form confusions and double vision at times. When asked why she had not complained to her parents and gotten glasses, Susan responded: "What, wear glasses? I was chubby and I had no friends. I didn't need glasses to make it any worse!"

Numerous physical factors other than visual acuity can affect the child's success at school. Remember the winner was described by teachers as compliant and cooperative; a number of children exhibit mood swings and excessive activity that may respond to medical management. There are two questions you should ask about your child's behavior:

1. Does my child appear to be more active than his/her peers, need to move around touching everything? (up to age ten)
2. Does my child get excessively fidgety and wriggly in situations that demand quiet sitting, listening, or patience?

Nervous, anxious kids need help. Such behavior may be indicative of many things: hyperactivity, stress, or depression. The symptoms may also be situational in nature and the child's tension may diminish as the problems are handled or solved. It is important for a parent to seek advice from a medical practitioner who is familiar with the biochemical causes of behavioral difficulty. Good medical management is helpful in keeping fidgety kids under control.

Creative, Curious Kids in "Trouble"

Creative, curious kids are anxious to explore every avenue of learning. They do this with or without the approval of school authorities, and can get into trouble.

Billy Lewis and his friends all met at his home on Saturday morning. It was Billy's birthday party, and he and his sixth-grade friends had their fill of hamburgers, ice cream, and cake, then scouted the neighborhood for a good baseball game. It was a holiday weekend and the schoolyard was locked up tighter than a jail. There they were, a group of healthy, happy thirteen-year-olds equipped with bats, balls, and gloves and ready for action, with no place to act.

One by one, over the schoolyard chain-link fence they went, ignoring minor scratches and ripped pants along the way. Once inside the fence, they spread out on the field engrossed in their game, taking little notice of the police car passing on the street nearby. They had made it into four innings, 3 to 3 tie score. Billy the Kid was up at bat when it all hit the fan. Into the schoolyard came two police cars, the school caretaker, the principal, and other assorted onlookers.

Billy and the boys protested that they had done nothing but climb over a fence to play; but their words reached deaf ears. The twelve frightened, confused youngsters were herded into the four cars and taken down to the police station, where, hours later, they were delivered into their parents' hands for an assortment of lectures, punishments, and good stiff lickings.

Billy's parents were faced with a different task. Billy, an articulate and outspoken youngster, had never been in difficulty either at school or out of school. A gifted child, he had a strong sense of right and wrong, and felt that public schoolyards should not be locked up against kids who wanted to play. He did not feel that he and his friends had broken a law or regulation, though he understood that they did not have permission to come into the yard and should not have vaulted the fence.

Explaining the contradictions that exist in our social worlds and school worlds can be extremely difficult. But there are times when we must tell kids that society's rules may be arbitrary and unfair, and when they are, grown-ups can either change them or obey them. Children, however, cannot change them, but must accept and obey them.

The principal mandated three days of suspension from school, and Billy and his parents felt that the punishment did not fit the crime. Why keep a child who loves learning away from school as punishment because he used inappropriate social judgment?

Mr. and Mrs. Lewis felt that Billy had to be taught to obey rules despite the unfairness of those rules; but they also felt that they had to work to change those rules if they believed they were applied unreasonably. They went through the channels of authority—principal, school superintendent, and school board—to get the suspension dropped for all of the boys involved in the incident. They enlisted the aid of all the parents in the group, seeking to change the regulation with regard to schoolyard closing on school holidays. They convened a group of parents to become actively involved in raising the funds necessary to safeguard the schoolyard and provide supervision for kids on weekends. Their active involvement developed into a role model for Billy and his friends. Rather than sitting at home and complaining of unfair rules and regulations, they became involved in changing those limitations on their kids. This experience taught Billy and his parents something else: "You can fight City Hall!"

Suggestions for Parents to Help Change Schools

1. Parents must stop feeling guilty for getting involved on their child's behalf.
2. Parents must find out what they are entitled to by law.
3. Don't apologize to school board or administrators for demanding your child's rights.
4. Patience and time don't help your child. He/she has just so much time at school, and once lost, those years never return.
5. Lack of funding is often cited as a reason for program lags. Don't accept that as an excuse. Money is often spent on less relevant things.
6. The squeakiest wheel gets the grease. The whispering parent cannot be heard amidst the roar. Speak out!
7. Don't fear social disapproval or political disagreement. Your child gets only one chance of making it through the school system.
8. Assume a positive attitude that you "can fight City Hall." United parents, parent associations, special committees, all have power. In unity there is strength.
9. Always remember your child's welfare is on the line.[5]

Children's Rights

At the present time, children have few rights that they can count on. They are in fact considered to be the private property of their parents, or of a legal custodian who has the same parental obligation and right to manage and control the child. Corporal punishment is used extensively in homes and schools throughout the country, and children have no right to protest or appeal its use. Children are no one's constituency, and adults do not vote on their behalf. They suffer from this lack of representation and have no voice in legislation that affects them. Children can be imprisoned for acts that would not be considered a crime if committed by adults. They are the victims of a system that is often arbitrary and cruel. In their book *The Children's Rights Movement,* Ronald and Beatrice Gross have provided parents with a resource handbook of material concerning their rights with regard to their children.[6]

When it comes to school discipline, youngsters are often the victims of inappropriate methods. The boy who does poorly in school will frequently act out in class to distract the teacher from his academic performance. He may succeed in getting himself put out of class, or even out of school for a period of time. This is, in fact, what he wants. He is so unhappy at school that he will do any and all things to get out. On the other hand, this is the child who probably needs to be present in class much more than other compliant youngsters.

The child needs to be told that such behavior will not get him out of class, but that it may call attention to his difficulties, and we will help him with those problems.

Creative, gifted youngsters also find themselves getting into constant difficulty because their unconventional ideas and idiosyncratic thinking are a constant challenge to authority. The characteristic behaviors of the gifted are exactly those which appear to be defying traditional school values. These children are often loners, daydreaming the hours away when their peers are occupied with athletics or busy work. They appear naïve, even gullibly open-minded about all kinds of ideas and problems, producing apparently bizarre responses to simple questions. They are freethinkers, sometimes seeming tangential in their responses. They perform poorly in a rigid, oversupervised environment, will even appear to be learning-disabled to the untutored observer. These kids are the "square pegs in round holes," and to lose them is to lose a creative source of future innovation.

These youngsters are sophisticated enough to understand the need for rules and regulations, but adamant in their challenge to any administration that sets arbitrary standards bolstered by "Mickey Mouse" rules. Reasonable rules are accepted with challenge, but unreasonable ones are discarded.

These children are a valuable resource for our educational system, but a demanding challenge to teachers and administrators in that system. More of this later.

Our young friend Billy of the schoolyard incident found that it led to some other repercussions in his life. One mistake caused him other problems. In Billy's own words:

"The worst part about school is that once you get into trouble, they expect you to be in trouble again. They watch like a hawk and every little thing you do you've got to answer a lot of questions. Ever since we went into the schoolyard that day, I get questioned. It's like the FBI every time I'm out in the hall. I feel like a criminal, like they just can't wait to catch me at something else!"

Billy had recognized the rule of the "self-fulfilling prophecy" clearly etched on his file. Not only was he expected to be a troublemaker by some, but his parents had become the center of activities to change certain rules existing in his school. School programs develop inertia. Once established, the rules are hard to change because "We've always done it that way." He who is ready to make waves had better be careful when and how he does it.

Kids are quick to learn about the "self-fulfilling prophecy." In one school in which we worked, the "special progress" class for poor readers would introduce themselves: "We're from the dummies' class, we can't learn nuthin'." Groups of kids relegated themselves to the dung heap. They wore the badge of loser and it became the rallying cry that gave them strength.

"Each year I start out with brand-new children and I am a brand-new teacher," said Eli Tash, administrator at the St. Francis Children's Activity and Achievement Center in Milwaukee, Wisconsin. "It is up to me to achieve trust in that child by accepting him the way he is that day, that week, or that month," he added. Kids need to know that they won't have to carry the burden of their mistakes with them throughout their school career. Only the teacher or administration of the school can convey that message.

Parent-School Communication

When dealing with problems of parent-school communications, it becomes apparent that both parents and school personnel may suffer from selective auditory perception. By this, we mean that two people hearing the same words spoken may perceive different meanings. We often hear what we expect to hear and allow unconscious preconceptions to color our viewpoint. It is important to keep our minds open.

Joey Brown's parents wanted Joey to handle his own battles when it came to school problems. Mr. Brown felt that his wife had a tendency to overprotect Joey and assume responsibility for obligations avoided by the twelve-year-old boy. Yet, if his parents did not come to school, the teachers might infer: "His parents don't care. They punish him for any little thing that he does. Perhaps that's why he balks at doing his schoolwork."

We can see the puzzling position of parenthood. Parents are often criticized and evaluated by those who have not "walked in their shoes."

David, an articulate, talented ten-year-old, had a severe reading problem. He had difficulty in remembering letter forms, often rotated them, and misread words. His mistakes slowed his reading and made it difficult for him to understand what he had read. When David was in the third grade, his teachers noted on his report card: "He never does any reading on his own. This is one reason why he can't read." Through private tutoring and extra reading help at school, David overcame his earlier difficulties, becoming a voracious reader. Sometimes his reading took precedence over other school activities, leading his seventh-grade teacher to say: "He keeps his nose buried in a book and hurries through everything else just to get back to the story he is reading." Kids may have problems, but the severity of those problems may be related to the way parents or teachers perceive them.

When Jerry Woods arrived in the tenth-grade history class at Spofford High, he had been preceded by his legendary older brother. Willy Woods had been in and out of trouble and had left an indelible mark on the memory of Miss Sutton, the tenth-grade history teacher.

One open school night, Jerry's parents met Miss Sutton and commented on how pleased they were to have another of their boys in her class. She looked puzzled and said, "I don't have one of *your* sons in my class this year. I don't know where you could have gotten that idea." Mr. and Mrs. Woods checked with Jerry, only to find Miss Sutton's name on his program card.

Jerry, indignant at this questioning of his credibility, responded with annoyance: "Well, I know who my teach r is . . . I ought to . . . I go to her class!"

Miss Sutton had also fallen into the trap of "self-fulfilling prophecy." Because of her preconceptions, she believed that all siblings would be alike in temperament and learning style.

She had known Willy very well and her experience convinced her that this new serious, intelligent, academically oriented youngster could not possibly be related to the infamous Willy. Miss Sutton simply did not want to believe that these two youngsters could be brought up in the same family. Her embarrassment was obvious when she found that Jerry and Willy had the same address, phone number, and mother and father listed in the records.

Children are just inexperienced people, trying to make their way and survive in the system. However, whether or not teachers perceive their behaviors as *winning* or *losing* is often a product of preconception.

Teaching Kids How to Talk and React to Teachers

Many kids need to learn how to handle adults more effectively. Children could glean much from popular psychology books if they could understand and apply the principles. If they can't understand them, we can help them to comprehend the basic rules of psychology in dealing with adults.

It might be a simple situation involving words that are appropriate in school as distinct from those that a teenager might employ in the locker room. Or it might be some simplified public relations concerning "how to win friends and influence people." Then there are times when parents cannot effect any change in the teacher's attitude toward their child. At times like this it is necessary to teach the child how to understand and handle the teacher.

In an article entitled "Little Brother Is Watching You," psychologist Dr. Paul Graubard noted that kids who are always in trouble don't recognize negative response in adults and haven't learned the basic rules of positive reinforcement.[7] Adults are equally susceptible to encouragement, a pat on the back, or nod of approval; but kids don't know this unless you tell them so, and show them how to use these strategies in their communication with adults.

"My history teacher is always bugging our class," said fourteen-year-old Sam. "He says we're the worst class he has, and he seems to pick on us for everything that happens in the hall."

"I'm sure that you feel he is being unfair to all of you, Sam," his mother sympathized. "That's too bad. It must make you feel very angry at times to be held responsible for the acts of others. Are there any things that some of the kids do that might be unfair to him, too?"

"Well, some of them make a lot of noise slamming lockers outside his room. They come in late and interrupt the class after we've started. But it's not all of us who should be taking the punishment."

"That's a real problem, Sam," said Mom. "You wouldn't want to tell on your friends, but you're taking a lot of punishment that you and the rest of the class don't deserve."

"If I spoke to Mr. Harvey," Sam responded, "and told him that very few kids are responsible for bugging him and that the rest of us really like his class, without mentioning names, do you think he might appreciate that?"

Sam's mother was delighted at the way Sam was learning to handle adults. Youngsters need to understand that adults have feelings too, and that a teacher who feels unappreciated will respond with anger, even misdirected anger.

"You know, Sam, teachers are only human. How would you feel if you spent a lot of time preparing interesting things for classes and then a small group of kids took advantage of the situation to spoil the lessons you had planned?"

Things Kids Need to Know about Dealing with Teachers

1. When you like the lesson or find something especially interesting, tell the teacher. It helps him or her to find other activities that are just as interesting.
2. When there are classroom chores to be done, offer to be helpful, don't just pick up your books and run after class if you have a minute or two of extra time.
3. Try to look at the teacher when he or she is speaking. Teachers feel that you are not interested in what they are saying if you always keep your eyes averted and are doodling airplane pictures on the desk.
4. Try not to slouch down in your seat all the time. Sit up and appear alert.
5. Ask questions from time to time so the teacher will know you are awake and breathing. Asking questions is a good way to get involved and stay attentive so the class won't drone on.
6. Act like a winner in class and you may begin to feel like one.
7. When you receive a mark on a test, especially on an essay exam, you should question the mark you receive if you don't think it is appropriate.
8. Ask the teacher to put a permanent schedule on the blackboard as to when reports are due, when major tests will occur, and so on.

Sometimes youngsters who have had unpleasant school experiences meet someone who seems to change their attitude. If a teacher enters a child's life at a crucial time, that child may experience success. Initially, if that teacher accepts the child for what he is without making any effort to change him, the child may learn to trust him. Eli Tash suggests that "you cannot succeed in teaching a child until you have performed this vital first step of accepting him." Through this process the teacher confirms the child's potentiality. Tash continues: "The child must believe that he can learn, and that the teacher accepts him the way he is. Then child and teacher move on together to learn a new skill." When the child feels this trust and success, he becomes a winner.

Teachers tell us that they feel that kids respond best to constant positive thinking on the part of a teacher. One junior high school teacher said: "I simply won't accept negative thinking on the part of my students. I believe that no child is unable to learn something if the teacher has enough time and patience."

Jean Brown, a high school English teacher, added, "The only way to

get students to like themselves is by showing that you care for them."
She felt that secondary school students are trapped in a grading system
that creates unfair pressures and excessive competition. "Kids need
constant reinforcement that they are worth something." Mrs. Brown
found that kids need evidence of their success demonstrated visually.
She uses charts and graphs extensively, having each student keep a
record of progress. She feels that these constant reminders tell a child:
"You are good—each time your work improves." Individual progress
charts help a child see his or her own improvement without being constantly compared to the group through grades on a standard class curve.

When asked to describe their best teacher, youngsters tell us revealing
things about the way they would like to be taught. They learn best from
dynamic, enthusiastic teachers who enjoy the subject matter. Humor
and personal experience ranked high in making classes interesting and
relevant. Kids expressed feelings of boredom when classes involved lecture and a lot of talking, but interest when audio-visual materials, lab
work, fieldwork, or shop work were included. They showed a marked
preference for learning by doing, rather than learning by listening.

One youngster who had experienced profound difficulties in developing early verbal skills told us that her father was probably the best
teacher through her years of school. When asked why, Jenny, a second-
year student at Simon's Rock Early College, said: "When I couldn't find
the words to explain things I wanted to say, he gave me a chalkboard
and told me to show him what I meant. I would draw or write something on the board. Then he would explain it to me, using pictures,
things, or any real demonstrations he could find."

"Teachers who help you the most are the ones who always seem to
have time to help you when you need it," said Becky, a thirteen-year-
old.

Ten-year-old John, a former student of ours, wrote of his feelings
about teachers and their reactions to clowning about at school. He had
been told by his teacher that "there were three things in him, a jester, a
knight, and a wise man." The process of education and maturation
would teach him how to keep these three elements of his personality in
balance.

John wrote: "It seems that in school whenever I bring the jester out,
I get into trouble. When I bring out the knight, I get into trouble. Most
children are in school until they are seventeen or eighteen years old.
And they are in school most of those years more than they are out. So
when can we bring the jester out? If we can't bring the jester out at
home and we can't bring him out at school, then where in the world can
we bring him out? As one poet said, 'Life is but a dream,' but school is
a nightmare."

This perceptive youngster saw himself constrained by the lack of joy in the learning process. He felt that his jester was put "out of business" for twelve years. Love of learning is a necessary part of any successful educational process. Joy in learning is an indispensable adjunct to any educational program. Success in learning is the key to joy. But success can only come when one feels like a winner.

Every winner has had experiences of failure along the way. One top-level corporate executive told us that his way up the executive ladder was marked with failures. He said, "If my sons could see the path I've seen, it would look like a minefield after the battle. But I've been allowed to learn by my mistakes. I figure that my kids should be allowed to learn from theirs."

For some youngsters, it may take a lot of support and even outside counseling to get them back into a positive frame of mind. Every winner experiences losses at some time in life, and it often helps if we, as parents, share our own "minefield" with our children to help them identify our clay feet.

Winners often feel like losers when they exhibit poor judgment or experience bad luck. But they seem to keep the attitude of seeing the glass as half full, rather than half empty.

Little Jimmy, aged eight, saw the world with a positive winner's perspective. When he arrived at our offices, he was wearing only one sneaker. One of us looked at the bare foot and asked: "Lost one shoe, Jim?"

Jim replied: "No, Mrs. Weiss, found one!"

5

How to Get Your Child Handled Right by Schools

If Schools Place Your Child in the Wrong Program or Class

Many suburban and urban parents have mortgaged their lives to provide their children with the *right* kind of education in the *right* school in the *right* town. These parents are well aware of the importance of school and class placement to the future of their children. Unfortunately, the expense and the family sacrifices to meet that expense still do not guarantee that children will be placed properly each year of their school career. Class placement may be arbitrary or inappropriate, and often is a result of administrative expediency. Every school administrator must juggle budgetary considerations, state mandates, declining class enrollments, teacher tenure, and union contract requirements. In this potpourri of economic problems, he must find the appropriate place for your child. Sounds easy, doesn't it? But it is not. One local administrator of a district of 20,000 youngsters likened his job to dancing barefoot "like a cat on a hot tin roof. No matter who I satisfy," he said, "there will be at least three others who will scream foul."

Much high school programming is done through rented computer time. We all know how "easy" it is to get an error corrected on the computerized billing of the local electric company. It is often necessary to "fold, spindle, and mutilate" the billing card to get a human response to our inquiry. What does the average high school student do when he/she falls victim to the computerized program system and needs an individualized program? He suffers, and it is often the student who ends up feeling folded, spindled, and mutilated!

Proper Programming and Placement for Your Child

Proper programming and appropriate class placement are probably the two most important factors in student success or failure. We sat at a meeting concerning Lou Bowman, a thirteen-year-old, and observed the teachers discussing his performance. One teacher, Mrs. J., observed that "Lou is restless, unable to concentrate, doing poorly in my class because he has not completed much work." Another teacher, Mr. C., commented, "Lou has done most of the lab work in science, though he has some difficulty writing it up. I've got him working with a partner so that he gets some assistance from a stronger student. I wouldn't mind having a dozen more like him in that class. He's enthusiastic, energetic, and no job is too much for him to tackle." Poor Lou. If only he could have had a dozen teachers like Mr. C., his school career would probably have been a succession of positive experiences. In one class Lou no doubt felt like a loser; but in the other, he was feeling and behaving like a winner.

Is it magic? No, just a matter of the teacher's attitude and expectation, appropriate materials, and a youngster who feels comfortable and at ease with himself. Researchers have found that teacher attitude is extremely significant in the way youngsters view themselves. The findings of Dr. Robert Rosenthal, professor of social relations at Harvard University, and Lenore Jacobson, an elementary school principal, suggest that youngsters respond positively or negatively to a "self-fulfilling prophecy." They become the kind of students that the teacher expects. The positive teacher who sees their problems as "difficulties" treats them like a winner. The negative teacher who has trouble in tolerating their level of restlessness, inability to concentrate, and poor written work may treat them like losers. It is interesting to note that when asked, thirteen-year-old Lou agreed. "I'm doing good in Mr. C.'s class. He likes me." He didn't want to talk about his experience in Mrs. J.'s class at all. If you want to estimate your child's success-failure index, just ask him. He is probably the best judge of the situation.

Public/Private School Placement—No Guarantee of Success

Unfortunately, the additional $4,000 to $6,000 per year you may spend for private school doesn't guarantee you a proper class placement for your child either. Sally, an articulate seventeen-year-old, attending the "best" private school for girls in New England (one of the "St. Grottlesex" variety, as explained in Chapter 6), was forced to take and fail freshman algebra three times before some appropriate testing was done. Sally was a B+ student in English, a B student in science, yet she was allowed to fail math three times before someone woke up to ask pertinent questions. By the time she came to our office, she was describing herself as a "failure" and was almost ready to give up her final year of school. When she was tested, it was found that Sally was a youngster of superior intelligence, though it took a good deal of convincing to persuade her that math presents a highly specific kind of problem. Sally suffered from dyscalculia, the inability to recall basic math processes and facts. After years of failure on math exams, she panicked and performed very poorly. Her feelings of inadequacy were compounded by the fact that she did well in the classwork, but simply fell apart when tested.

Sally had been taught math in the traditional abstract way, memorizing the steps and facts necessary to perform computation. Whenever she could not remember facts, we helped her to develop ways to compensate. Like most educational difficulties, dyscalculia requires alternative educational approaches if it is to be avoided as a major handicapping condition.

When Sally forgot math facts, we taught her how to make an approximation in numbers to judge the answer as correct or incorrect. Forgetting the multiplication facts was overcome through the use of a simple system of finger math multiplication (discussed later in the chapter). Understanding fractions was taught with the use of plastic fraction pies, and rectangular fraction blocks. Thus she developed a visual understanding of every problem, using concrete hands-on tools before being allowed to manipulate abstract numbers. In high school, a small calculator was added to her battery of math tools, and she was then able to handle basic business math and finish her school requirements. "I felt like a mental case," she said anxiously, "until I understood what was wrong." This same young woman had a straight B+ average at college in her major field, English.

At the beginning of her senior year Sally wrote to us, once more complaining that her graduation might be held up because she was unable to pass the required one year of basic college math. Again, intervention was necessary. Sally had been afraid to communicate her problem to the authorities; she had avoided this, hoping that the trouble would go away before graduation year. Her fear of being different prevented her from facing up to a very real obstacle. Like many young people, Sally had hoped that some mystical power would eradicate the problem. Unfortunately, there is no simple cure for dyscalculia and this did not happen.

After the completion of college, Sally took a job as a copy girl for a local newspaper in a small town in the western part of New York State. She moved up the ladder of success to become a reporter on that paper. Her last letter informed us that she had become interested in the town's educational system through an article she had written, and was involved now in getting a parent-teachers educational committee going to develop regional in-service training for local teachers. She says that her awareness of her own feelings and frustrations as a student helped her to write about the subject of special needs in education, and she believes that she has passed on some of this insight to others.

She still has some difficulty balancing her checkbook, handling her financial affairs, and reading maps and timetables, but she is not ashamed to ask others for help, explaining her confusion. She says she has found new friends through her openness and no longer fears to disclose her problems. Sally has faced her difficulties honestly and continues to progress.

Many adolescents and young adults have difficulty in facing their problems squarely and realistically. Their need to be like their peers and belong makes them acutely aware of their inadequacies. Parents often have to intervene on a youngster's behalf despite protestations of "Let me do it myself!" Making it through the system often requires as much muscle as one can swing, and parents are the reinforcements when a kid is winning the battle but losing the war.

Mary, a student at the "best" public high school in New York's northern Westchester County, was locked into a similar administrative "Mickey Mouse" routine. Having failed Spanish three times, she was forced to take French as a substitute, despite the fact that she did not need a foreign language to enter her chosen field of animal husbandry at the state college.

Eddie, a bright eleventh-grader at the same school, was told he must take a second foreign language in his senior year, despite the fact that an outstanding university had already accepted him for early admission. The university had indicated that it would waive the second language requirement since he was going to be an art major.

Jerry, a student at another school, was told that his entrance into an Early College Program at the end of the tenth grade would prevent him from getting into graduate school. He spent two years at the Early College, moved on to an Ivy League school for his last two years, and was accepted at two fine law schools.

Counseling to Develop Communications Skills

Much guidance work at high schools is designed to assist students in gaining training and placement in appropriate vocational fields. However, the number of misinformed students is too great to overlook. School policies change, and many schools are willing to make some modification for a student's individual needs and interests. Before your child is locked into a mass-produced program designed to meet the needs of students twenty-five years ago, be sure to ask a lot of questions.

The role of good guidance in the matrix of school services should amount to much more than just college and vocational placement. Mrs. Carol Singer, former instructor of communications at the University of Hartford, sees the guidance function as that of helping kids to perceive that they are capable, setting realistic goals, and practicing the achievement of those goals through role playing. Guidance means working with teachers as well. In her present role of guidance counselor for the seventh grade at Mineola Junior High, Long Island, New York, Mrs. Singer sees her job as helping students to relate to adults by giving them experience in testing out their responses in an adult frame of reference. Kids will be well placed in a class when there is open communication between teacher and child, and when each has a better perspective, or an understanding of where the other one is.

In order to get along successfully in any class situation, kids need to be helped to understand that neither their parents nor their teachers always know what they mean from what they say or the way they act. When misunderstanding occurs between parent and child, or teacher and child, it is often an uneven contest, and the child will lose. However, we should teach youngsters to listen to parent and teacher with careful attention, to try to understand what their parent or teacher is feeling: anger, annoyance, pleasure, and so on. The child can learn to frame his responses with care, avoiding an escalation of anger of the person to whom he is talking. We need one small "Jiminy Cricket" to sit on the shoulder of each child, whispering: "Tell the teacher you really appreciate the extra time she took to explain the math when you were late to class . . . don't just grunt!"

It isn't easy to train a full-time "Jiminy Cricket." But the purpose of this kind of training in personal communication is to help kids decide to take a few important things into consideration: how certain people like to be spoken to, that they really want the other person to know what they mean, and that they care enough to make the effort to communicate openly. Mrs. Singer also feels that youngsters who are poor at relating to adults turn teachers off without realizing it. They need training in expressive skills, or how to use their voices to assert their ideas; "kinetics," or how body movement indicates how you feel about yourself; and "proxemics," or body distance in relation to other people.

For example, the sarcastic tone of voice habitually used by a teen-ager is guaranteed to "tick off" his parent or teacher and escalate a needless power struggle. The sloppy-slouch position at the desk in class will certainly let the teacher know she is putting you to sleep and bring about a rebuke. Crowding people too closely, invading their body territory, may cause them enormous irritation, and they may try to avoid you or put you off with a rejecting comment. All of these things can be avoided when kids become more aware of good communication skills.

In his book *Between Parent and Teenager,* psychologist Dr. Haim G. Ginott notes what he considers to be the most fruitful steps in communication. He feels that it is the parent's or teacher's responsibility to demonstrate these steps rather than simply telling them to a youngster.

1. Listen with attention. This means making eye contact, stopping what you are doing, and focusing your attention on the person speaking.
2. When you respond to the person who is talking, repeat the gist of what he/she is saying, putting it in your own words so that you understand it clearly.
3. Even if you disagree with the person talking, avoid name calling and criticism in your response.
4. Give your own point of view without making value judgments or being derogatory about the other person.

In a real-life situation, this translates into a constructive interaction between child and parent or child and teacher. It is also helpful in assisting youngsters to interact with others their own age.

If we can't change the class, school, or program to make it more suitable for the child, at least we can teach the child to handle the adults he or she will have to meet in a less than suitable situation.

Good schools are already teaching good communication skills. Any corporate personnel director will tell you how often he has hired someone because of the poise with which he presented himself. Winners present themselves well and display their success through their good communication skills.

Middle School—A Change of Life

Youngsters who have often breezed through school in grades 1 through 5 may experience problems in middle school and high school.

Some students are simply unready for the demands of departmentalized programming that usually begins at sixth grade. These kids are often disorganized, fragmented, and unstructured in their approach to academics.

Dougie, a pert, blue-eyed, freckled-faced twelve-year-old, was having difficulty adjusting to the demands of the sixth grade. He had had no obvious difficulties in the past, yet his sixth-grade teachers found that he was always giving excuses for incomplete assignments and lost papers, books, sneakers, and gym shorts. Dougie was late getting from one class to another, often missed the bus to school, and more often missed the bus going home. It took half the school year, both marking periods in which Dougie failed three of his four major subjects, before someone took notice of Dougie's special needs.

Why this Jekyll and Hyde behavior, his parents asked? This compliant, easygoing youngster who had done so well in school through grade 5 seemed to have lost his momentum in grade 6. Only after the school recommended that the parents consider retention in grade 6 did Dougie's parents come to life and call for a team conference.

Educators believe that there are some youngsters who experience a great deal of difficulty in relating to too many teachers at once. The variation in demands, coordinating assignments, remembering a school schedule organized in a six-day cycle, and relating to so many people was simply too much for Dougie. There was no one coordinating the assignments for him and he wasn't ready to do it for himself.

The primary grades are a sheltered nurturing environment for most youngsters. They learn to live in one place, one desk, one classroom, relate largely to one teacher; and their time is scheduled for them in a group. Then suddenly the ground rules change. They are living out of a locker, the combination of which they often can't remember. That locker is invariably at the opposite end of the building from all their classes. They are responsible for their possessions, books, gym clothes, schedule, homework assignments, and survival. The one thing that the Dougies do is survive, however, often at the expense of all of the other demands. Kids like this aggravate parents, trouble teachers, confound administrators; and the kids are the losers unless someone intervenes to bring order out of chaos.

Too Little—Too Late

Was Dougie helped? Yes. But he was helped too late to rescue the grade-6 year. He was retained in grade 6 for a second year and experienced enormous feelings of anger and inadequacy at being unable to move on to grade 7 with his friends. During his second time around in grade 6, his teachers sent extra assignment sheets home, Dougie was given an assignment book, and each teacher checked that the daily assignment had been written on the proper page. Teachers called home before due dates for papers to let his parents know and sent home test-review sheets. Dougie was given a locker nearer to his classes, with a key lock rather than a combination; he had an extra set of sneakers and gym clothes in the locker. He was encouraged to keep a work schedule, and his teachers broke down long-term assignments into several short-term due dates to prevent him from leaving everything to the last minute as he had done previously. Dougie's guidance counselor kept tabs on his workload by communicating with his teachers on a biweekly basis. If necessary, he intervened to lighten the load.

Kids like Dougie really don't want to fail. Failure and retention is a humiliation within their peer group. When a child can't meet demands, it usually means that he or she is unready or that the demands are unreasonable for him/her. Early departmentalization in school presupposes a youngster's readiness to handle a high degree of responsibility, organization, and independence. Many kids aren't ready for all of that at the age of eleven or twelve. Many adults aren't ready, either. One high school teacher told us that he keeps a small written copy of his daily program on a label glued inside his shirt cuff. He puts a new label on each day, since his program changes each day of the week. Without his label he says he'd be lost. He is not alone in his problem; Dougie's mother admitted to her own organizational troubles. She said that she had to keep a large index card taped to the sun visor of her car because her schedule was so complicated with job, car pooling, dental and medical visits that she found herself in the wrong place at the right time repeatedly. Responsible adults organize their lives because they have learned the price of disorganization. Forgetfulness and irresponsibility cost dollars, jobs, and contracts. That is one of the economic realities of life. Kids have to be taught to handle these problems step by step if they are to become winners.

Questions to Ask about Your Child's Performance

If you have any questions about your child's poor performance that seem to be more than questions of proper placement or programming, as a parent you should request an educational evaluation. Intelligence testing measures aptitude in school-related tasks; however, it does not measure other basic competencies and survival skills. (Check Chapter 9 for further information about specific types of testing that might be available to you.) The sooner appropriate testing is done, preferably by grade 6, the sooner a school can determine the best placement for your child and the most appropriate program modifications. The optimum time to test a child is between ages five and eight.

If you request testing or program planning for your child, you must go armed with specific questions. If we seem to repeat this point, it is because we have often seen parents frustrated in their attempt to get proper programming for their child.

The availability of testing services varies from school district to school district. Most districts have on staff a person qualified to administer individual intelligence and achievement testing. However, that person may or may not be a certified psychologist, guidance counselor, learning resource teacher, or special tester (psychometrist). The caseload of such specialists varies, so that it may take as little as two weeks or as long as nine months to have your child evalauted and then use the results in implementing an educational program.

Many parents turn to the services of specialists outside the school for testing services. They feel that they are getting a more objective viewpoint and that they have the choice of specialist. They may also be frustrated by the length of time between the referral itself and the planning of a program for their child, so they shortcut this time by going to a private specialist to have the testing completed as quickly as possible. The cost of such testing can vary from region to region from a nominal fee of $10 to $25 to as much as $300 or $400. The parent can determine the cost in advance by asking whether or not the agency or testing service employs a sliding scale based on income or charges the same fee for everyone.

A parent seeking help through a private agency might ask the following additional questions:

1. How long will it take to get an appointment to have my child tested?
2. How long will it take to have the *written* results of testing?
3. Will the written report be sent to me?
4. Will the report include specific educational and placement recommendations?
5. Will someone from the agency be able to go to school to help explain and implement the report on behalf of my child?
6. What is the certification of the person who will test my child? (psychologist, educational specialist, medical doctor, etc.)
7. What kind of testing will the agency utilize and what will it be testing for?

8. Will I be charged for a visit to the agency after the testing to talk about the report and have data explained? If so, how much will I be charged?

After testing is completed and the parents go to a school conference, they often find it difficult to speak frankly. A number of factors come into play, most important of which is their own attitude toward previous school experiences. It is as though the parents were back in school again, the child's principal *their* principal, their child's teacher *their* teacher. We have witnessed this phenomenon many times in our work with parents and teachers, and experienced it ourselves.

Paula Bernstein, writer and parent, has surveyed the parent-teacher relationship. She reports that parents often leave conferences "confused, angry, frustrated, and close to tears," because of the way they are handled or mishandled.[1] "Teachers have never been taught to work with adults," says Sadie Hoffman, a parent education specialist and director of the Nassau County, New York, Mental Health Association. "They are used to working with children and therefore don't understand the techniques of counseling. Parents and teachers sometimes withhold information because they don't trust each other," she adds.

We often transfer our own feelings about our early experiences with authority figures to our children's experiences. Trust in our child's teachers is borne of earlier trust in our own teachers; and mistrust is developed in much the same way. Moreover, when a child is having difficulty in school, it is easier to blame someone else for that difficulty. The parent is likely to blame the teacher, and the teacher is equally likely to blame the parent.

Generally, parents tend to wait too long before they insist on action from the school. Like their children, many parents believe that the "problem will go away." Dougie's mother and father were guilty of that mistake. It took nearly three-quarters of the school year before they realized that Dougie was simply not going to make it. "People tend to coast all too long on their children's problems, hoping, presumably, that they will go away," says Louise Bates Ames, a noted author and researcher with the Gesell Institute. Unfortunately, problems don't go away. Children experiencing difficulty need help. Problems need solutions, and as the old adage suggests: "If [parents] are not part of the solution, [parents] are part of the problem."

Classroom Task Analysis

When a child seems to be getting little or nothing out of class, it might be helpful for the parent to attempt an informal classroom task analysis. This way parents can get a better idea of what is going on in class, and how good or bad a child's placement is. *Some questions parents might ask are:*

1. What kind of subject matter is being taught?
2. Are there special skills required of the child in this particular area? For example, advanced math requires a good foundation in earlier math skills. The study of foreign languages requires good visual sequential memory skills and fairly good auditory skills, so that the student can recognize and reproduce sounds.
3. What is the format of the class? Does the teacher use lectures only, reading and workbook, tapes, movies, fieldtrips?
4. How is the subject presented: listen and learn (auditory), look and learn (visual), try and learn (experiential), or any combination of the three major methods?
5. Is the class informal or formal in structure?
6. What kind of testing methods does the teacher use most often: paragraphs and essays, true/false questions, multiple choice, verbal exposition?
7. Are there a lot of timed tests in class?
8. Is there a lot of reading (difficult reading, easy reading)?
9. Is there a lot of writing?

If your child's skills are not strong in similar areas, he or she may have a terrible time from the first day in an inappropriate class setting. The boy who can't handle a lot of written work will hate a class in which he gets an excessive amount of that kind of work. The girl who is a slow or poor reader will avoid performing in the class that accentuates reading. Put a poor speller, with difficulty in auditory and verbal skills, in a foreign language class (except Latin), and she may be a setup for failure. And give a youngster with poor math skills algebra, advanced algebra or trigonometry because the curriculum calls for it, and you can kiss his love for math goodbye. We set our kids up for failure when we do not take their strengths and weaknesses into consideration in designing school programs.

Preparing for School Conferences

Proper preparation for a school conference begins with an educational evaluation. Write to the school guidance counselor or psychologist for the names of the tests being utilized. Ask what each test measures. All group tests are reading tests, because the child must read instructions and answer questions that he or she had to read to himself. If they are designed to test reading, they are appropriate. However, if they are designed to determine how much information a child has learned in a specific subject area, then they may give misleading results.

We will be discussing testing in more detail in Chapter 9. There are other sources of testing materials that you can refer to. Parents have a right to examine a child's records in the company of a school official who is qualified and trained in testing and evaluation. Exercise this right. To assure proper placement for your child, you will want to be aware of the kind of information that makes up his/her permanent educational record. Prior to the passage of the so-called Buckley Amendment requiring full disclosure of educational records, there was little or no control over the kind of information that might find its way into a youngster's permanent record. Often such records included a compilation of subjective comments from teachers or counselors that might have little or no basis in fact or medical record.

The U.S. Department of Education newsletter "Closer Look" in its fall 1977 issue entitled "Know Your Rights . . ." suggests that parents should know their rights and use them.

Parents have the right to due process if they disagree with the educational system's handling of their child:

1. Parents must receive a written notice before the school system recommends any action that results in change in a child's school program.
2. Parents have the power to give or withhold permission for special testing to be administered to their child.
3. Parents have the right to see all school records relating to evaluation and placement of their child. They can ask that any records that appear misleading be removed from the file.
4. An impartial hearing is available to any parent who wishes to disagree with the school's evaluation or placement of the child.
5. If the disagreement remains unresolved, the parents can go to the State Department of Education for a further hearing, and finally they have recourse to the courts.
6. The parents have a right to legal counsel and the support of any advocate knowledgeable in educational and legal regulations.

Sixth-grader Lou Bowman's parents were shocked to find a series of daily observation sheets written by a teacher's aide, detailing the behaviors and events in Lou's life at school during a four-week period. When they questioned the appropriateness of this kind of personal observational material compiled by a nontrained, part-time teacher's aide, the material was quickly removed from the file. Despite the intent or accuracy of such observational material, it is, at best, the personal opinion of one adult. It is not free of bias, nor is it the kind of information that gives us constructive diagnostic material. Even though the principal obviously was annoyed at finding such information in a file, it would not have been removed had the parents not insisted. Kids suffer from glib comments made about them in the teachers' room.

"Boy oh boy, is that Lou Bowman a terror!"

"You should have had Bobbie's brother, Red, in class; you wouldn't have had a moment's peace."

"All the kids in that family are alike, just dumb."

"I don't envy you that crew of kids—you've got the dumb class."

If unwritten comments cause damage, then a printed word becomes an indelible record of a child's success or failure. The passage of the Buckley Amendment in 1975 gave parents the right to search their child's school records for misleading information. Withholding of any records from this search is a violation of federal statute. The law has resulted in growing hesitation on the part of school authorities to insert such comments into a record. Great care is now being taken to include only clinical evaluations, standardized testing, and reports. There are benefits gained from this; but since it inhibits the placement of certain anecdotal materials in the record, something is lost as well.

Little Murders of Education

When a child complains about the unfairness with which he or she is treated in class, or is constantly feeling put down and at odds with the teacher, as parents we tend to believe that he or she is in the wrong and the teacher is probably right. However, sometimes your child is correct in an appraisal and is being subjected to unfair treatment. Of course, many complaints about the teacher are just a form of healthy exercise engaged in by most healthy, red-blooded kids. It is difficult for a parent to make an accurate judgment about the situation. The best way to handle this is to let the teacher know openly and frankly how your child feels, and to ask her why she thinks your child might have that impression. Good teachers usually respond to these situations by modifying their approach to a child, and are glad to have a child's reactions and feelings called to their attention. But kids have always experienced frustration and failure at the hands of authoritarian educational systems intolerant of individual differences.

"I remember that I was never able to get along at school," Thomas Alva Edison is quoted as saying. "I was always at the foot of the class. I used to feel that the teacher did not sympathize with me and that my father thought I was stupid." A total of twenty-six of the 400 famous people cited in *Cradles of Eminence* by Victor and Mildred G. Goertzel, were described as backward or dull in school.[2] This entertaining and revealing study of the early lives, family background, and education of hundreds of the world's best-known personalities gives us insight into certain elements of creativity. Among those mentioned, in addition to Thomas Edison, were Winston Churchill, Serge Rachmaninoff, and Albert Einstein.

Unfortunately, there are also teachers who are less than competent in their approach to kids. They are in the minority, but they do exist, and your child may lose a whole year of progress if placed in such a situation. Every school district has its unpleasant tale of the "teacher who was strong-arming kids," or the teacher who could not handle his work due to illness, alcoholism, or personal problems. In an article in the September 1978 issue of *U.S. News and World Report,* principals were quoted as saying that "when they took steps to declare a teacher incompetent, they ran up against a cumbersome, arduous, expensive legal process which is so time-consuming that sometimes it was easier not to press charges."[3]

These administrators were talking about teachers within their schools who were unable to teach the subject matter or to make organized lesson plans.

Is the Education System Failing Our Kids?

Very little real school time is spent *actually* teaching subject matter. According to former Secretary of Health, Education and Welfare Joseph E. Califano, "If in our better institutions as little as 18 percent of the time in school is actually spent on scholastic work, it is little wonder that learning levels fall beneath our expectations." Dr. John Santikle, Assistant Superintendent of Schools in Dallas, Texas, places the blame on all of us—"the permissive society, television, lack of teacher certification, lower institutional standards, and public education itself."[4] Within the teaching profession, as well as in administration and parent organizations, there is a growing demand for an upgrading of the profession itself. Meanwhile your child may be the victim. While parents are demanding that specific standards of teacher competency be set by their school boards, they must also go to bat for the child who may be neglected by the current cumbersome system. *If it is national policy that every child should have a high school education, then it must also be national policy that each child should have something to show for his/ her attendance at school for twelve years.* Kids need a set of basic competencies to help them become winners in our complicated society today.

Checklist of Proper Placement

Parents need to do homework as well as their children. In this case, homework for parents means sitting down and drawing up a list of questions to prepare for a meeting about class or program placement for their child. Among the questions might be any or all of the following:

1. What specific areas of strength does my child show in school (your class)?
2. What specific areas of weakness does my child show in school (your class)?
3. What do you judge to be his/her IQ? What tests did you use to arrive at that score? Were they group or one-to-one tests, timed or untimed?
4. Is there a more appropriate class available for my child at the same grade level? (A structured class usually is better for an unstructured child; an activity-oriented class with a lot of independent work is usually better for a child who is bored with routine workbook seat work. Male teachers seem less disturbed by hyperactive, acting-out boys.)
5. What remedial classes are available for my child?
6. How much time would he/she get in these remedial classes? What would he/she miss in home classes? (Try not to take a child out of an elective subject that he enjoys, like art, music, or physical education, to give him remediation even if he needs it.)
7. Do you feel that my child has problems that require special testing? If so, what kind of testing would you suggest?
8. When can this testing be done? (Some schools have a waiting period of as long as six months or a year before testing can be done. Check to see whether your state has a maximum time requirement in education law that prevents a school from delaying testing, writing an Individual Education Plan, and completing proper class placement.)
9. Would specific modifications within the classroom assist my child? (Special reading materials, use of a tape recorder, oral testing, untimed testing, special testing in the resource room.)
10. What kind of special class placement is available? (Mary, who failed French three times, might have done better in a special conversational class. Sally, who failed ninth-grade algebra three

times, might have done well in a one-year business math class or a math review survey course at the ninth-year level. Dougie, who repeated the sixth grade, might have been able to move on with his friends if he had been placed in an ungraded program. The program was designed for youngsters who were able to do some work at each of three grade levels and would best be served by staying with the same team of teachers for three years.)

11.   When will there be a reevaluation of my child's progress?

In the cases mentioned in parentheses, the parents did not know that alternative classes were available that might meet their children's needs, nor did they ask. Mary, Sally, and Dougie might all have been spared the feelings of a loser if there had been earlier intervention before they experienced failure. Unfortunately, parents count on the schools to initiate such recommendations. After all, we say, "They're the teachers, they should know!" Well, the reality of this is that they know, but they are often overburdened with caseloads that far exceed their maximum efficiency. In these times of school-budget cutbacks, the caseloads of counselors, psychologists, remedial staff, and learning resource teachers are moving well above the recommended maximum.

The learning resource teacher is a newcomer on the education scene; the job description varies from district to district and school to school. Generally, the learning resource teacher handles a special classroom called a resource room. This ungraded classroom is designed to provide special supportive services to small groups of youngsters in reading, math, and other specific subject areas. These teachers specialize in modifying materials, tutorial work, and teaching study skills to improve students' learning and help them keep up in regular classes. But the "they" (specialists and teachers) you are counting on are simply overworked. It is "your" child—you must take the initiative. You are the taxpayer, and the school personnel works for you!

Alternative Materials and Methods to Aid Your Child

Not only do parents often have to be the initiators of action when their child's performance shows evidence of inappropriate placement; they also are often the first to recognize the fact that their child cannot handle the kinds of materials being used in class. Although teacher attitude is the most important prerequisite to success, the materials used in class are certainly a close second in importance.

The youngster who is constantly described as careless in spelling may be one who had difficulty in recalling sequential symbols and needs specific teaching techniques and tools. Eleven-year-old Ted would respell most words phonetically. No matter how hard he studied the weekly spelling list, his mother quizzing him patiently on each word, by the time Friday morning's test rolled around, he had forgotten the words. Any pattern that was nonphonetic (i.e., words not spelled the way they sound) would produce the predictable misspellings commonly seen by most teachers. For Ted, the five years of training in a traditional approach to spelling were five years of torture and failure. He was chided for carelessness so often he began to describe himself as "sloppy and stupid." But Ted might have responded quite differently to another approach that gave more attention to the predictable patterns existing within the English language. The Orton-Gillingham approach is based on structuring related sound patterns, teaching the six basic syllable patterns that are fundamental to approximately 80 percent of the language, and mastering the use of roots, prefixes, and suffixes. When given this kind of training, most youngsters who are having difficulties with the sight memory approach to unrelated words have far greater success. In Ted's case, he began to apply rules to the spelling of new words and to increase his functional writing vocabulary as well.

However, the five years of frustration had taken its toll, and Ted was avoiding most written work by the time he reached the end of fifth grade. This was a case of a perfectly normal youngster experiencing an institutionally caused learning problem. The materials and techniques were inappropriate for him, creating problems, negative feelings, and balky behavior. Uncommon? Alas, no! Too many winners are turned into losers through the use of rusty teaching tools.

Materials and methods may make all the difference in a child's attitude toward reading. If a youngster is having difficulties in learning the shapes and forms of the letters, he may be taught through the sight word approach for years with no measurable improvement. But given a few months in a program emphasizing the tracing of letters using his whole arm extended, as is utilized in the Slingerland approach, he may be able to master these skills in short order.

Sometimes the motivation of a winner at reading may come with a "bibliotherapy" approach. By bibliotherapy, we mean the use of carefully selected stories or books to help a child handle his or her problems. Carefully selected reading can be a role model as well as a therapy. In order to become motivated, youngsters need to read about people who have "made it" despite apparent obstacles or even handicaps. Hero worship is a strong role modeler of attitudes and behavior. Many schools have discovered that there are fine collections of short stories available at low- to middle-grade instructional levels that are powerful motivators for young people. Companies like the Globe Book Company, Noble and Noble, and Merrill put out series that are based on the lives of contemporary winners in sports, drama, music, movies, and even politics. Such names as Willis Reed, Carly Simon, Henry Winkler, and Charles Bronson dot the pages like shooting stars. Kids like to read about winners and can gain confidence and direction through such reading.

Having spent years attempting to learn the basic multiplication tables by rote (i.e., 1 through 10), a youngster can give up on himself, his ability in math, and even school in general. Yet given some instruction in a simple technique of finger multiplication, this same youngster can master the problem, having a small finger calculator at his disposal whenever he needs it. Even more important, this calculator needs no batteries!

Finger Math. Finger math (not chizzenbop) is designed for youngsters who have difficulty in memorizing the multiplication facts above the 5 times table, that is, sixes through tens. It should only be taught after a reasonable amount of time has been spent trying to memorize the multiplication facts unsuccessfully. Then, at a certain point, it becomes necessary to give a youngster alternatives to handle his memory problem. Finger math should only be used after a youngster fully understands the multiplication process: that is, that multiplication is a series of repeated additions.

Step 1: Have the youngster hold up both hands (see Figure 1).

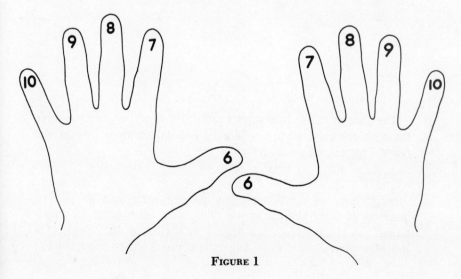

FIGURE 1

Tell him that we are going to give each finger a number, that the value will always be the same, and that the values do not change from finger to finger. On each hand, the thumb is assigned number 6, the pointer finger assigned number 7, the middle finger is assigned number 8, the fourth finger assigned number 9, and the pinky finger is assigned the number 10.

Step 2: Now that each of the ten fingers has a number assigned to it, we can use these fingers to multiply. If we want to multiply 7 × 7, we must hold up two fingers on each hand (because they have been assigned the numbers 6 and 7, and we must use all numbers up to and including those we want to multiply). Now, tell the child that each finger that is being multiplied is held up. If we are multiplying 7 × 7, then the 6 and 7 fingers, one on each hand, are held up (see Figure 2).

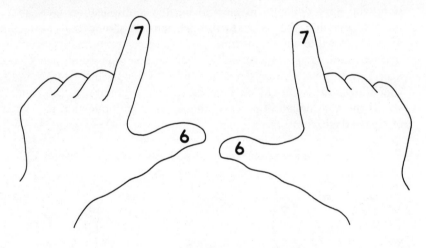

FIGURE 2

Each finger that is held up is equal to 10 in value when we solve the problem. Since we are holding up two fingers on each hand, the 6 and 7 fingers, we do the following:

$$10 + 10 + 10 + 10 = 40 \quad \text{or } 4 \times 10 = 40$$

Step 3: Each of the fingers that has not been held up is now counted. If I am holding up two fingers on each hand (6 and 7 finger), then there are three fingers left down on each hand. (Do it.) Multiply the number of fingers that are down on the left hand

(3 fingers) by the number of fingers that are down on the right hand (3 fingers), that is, multiply $3 \times 3 = 9$.

Thus, our fingers held up equal
$$10 + 10 + 10 + 10 = 40$$
and our fingers held down equal
$$3 \times 3 = \underline{+9}$$
$$49$$

Step 4: This should be repeated with all the math facts before it can be learned automatically. It is important that the child memorize the math facts for tables 1 through 5 before attempting this technique with multiplication tables 6 through 10. It is also important that the teacher commit the entire explanation to memory before trying to explain it to the child, or he will become confused.

Other New Materials. If writing papers is enormously frustrating, a secondary-level student will often find the use of a tape recorder helpful. He can break down his work into simplified substeps, using his stronger verbal skills to discuss the topic, and his more slowly developing writing skills to copy his own words at a slower, stop-and-go speed.[5]

New materials abound in the educational field, and the slick 8×10 glossy covers don't always connote quality within. However, retooling and refueling teachers with new ideas and techniques through workshops and study programs may mean a new lease on life for your child. Ask questions about the kinds of materials your child brings home. If they look too difficult, let the teacher know that your child can't do the work without your constant help, and explain that you think your child needs something more appropriate. Your nelp is important, but if it is a daily crutch, something is very wrong with the level of work being given.

Motivation—"You've Gotta Wanna"

The most common reason for failure in school is lack of motivation. Kids who are improperly placed will often exhibit a strong lack of motivation. It is a *cri de coeur,* and their boredom, passivity, or anger convey the message: "Get me out of here now!" Kids show poor motivation for many reasons. We often assume that they just don't want to perform, but the reasons are usually far more complex.

A child can be motivated . . . but cannot stick with a task to completion. Lou Bowman wanted to read his social studies assignment; however, after three or four attempts at reading material that was too difficult for him, he gave up. He was unable to handle the twenty pages, recall the facts, answer the questions, and schedule the assigned work.

A child can be motivated . . . but cannot perform on level. Freddie Yarrow wanted to do his math work but was experiencing great difficulty because he could not memorize the math facts. His feelings about himself had deteriorated to the point at which he was scapegoating other kids through teasing.

A child can be motivated . . . but cannot initiate the task and get started. Terry Brown would avoid writing assignments like the plague. Once his mother settled him down, gave him a chance to talk about his ideas, and suggested a starting sentence, he was able to complete the job. She had to "prime the pump" to get him moving. Without that kind of support, Terry gave up and appeared indifferent or unwilling to work.

A child can be motivated . . . but cannot perform any work. A child with extremely poor reading skills may want to read the textbook, but be unable to do so. He may want to write, but be unable to set the words down on paper with readable handwriting and decipherable spelling.

Finally, a child can be totally unmotivated . . . he or she just does not want to perform any work at all. This is the child who is the anti-achiever and who feels that school is impractical and irrelevant. He or she just wants to be freed from "serving time."

Next time you hear the words "unmotivated in class," explore the reasons for this lack of motivation in your child. Placing your child in a straitjacket curriculum may be the same as giving a cooking major at the Cordon Bleu a course in nuclear physics!

Turning Kids On to Reading

In search of new ways to make programs more relevant and interesting for youngsters, many schools have instituted alternative reading comprehension programs. One such program is being utilized in the Highlands School, White Plains, New York.[6] Thomas Eaton, the teacher, has his youngsters viewing popular contemporary movies like *Star Wars,* followed by dynamic verbal discussions and the incorporation of language skills. Eaton feels that this type of programming rapidly involves the student who is experiencing reading problems. Each student must master an accompanying paperback that includes twelve pages of written work and comprehension exercises. His students enjoy the challenges of the program, its variety of activities and approaches to learning. Each youngster is also asked to organize and prepare an oral presentation for the class. Kids who have experienced failure in traditional programs seem to "turn on" to innovations.

Other programs emphasize training in thinking skills that can be employed in problem solving of all types. In a seventh-grade class at Chicago's May Elementary School, reading is a thinking task. The main goal of the reading process in this particular classroom is to teach youngsters how to infer information from what they read—no easy task! Walter Thompson, reading specialist at the school, emphasizes that "Most teachers and kids equate reading with sounding-out words. However, reading is really a thinking process. We have to begin teaching it as such." If a youngster is reading in order to learn, he must be thinking, reasoning, synthesizing, and analyzing material constantly. To use what he reads, he must understand it, compare it to other things he already knows, accept it as useful, or reject it.

Teaching Kids to Think While They Read

Basic to the learning of language is the sounding-out process; however, once that is mastered, comprehension, vocabulary, and inference must all be emphasized.[7] Parents can help in this process by asking for opinions and inferential judgments from their kids. Questions applicable to any kind of material include:

1. Now that you've read the chapter from your book (novel), what do you think will happen next?
2. Has the chapter given you any specific clues to suggest what will happen next; if so, what clues?
3. Does the story fit in with any other stories you have read? How?
4. Is the outcome of the story logical or illogical in your opinion?
5. Did the characters seem real to you?
6. What personality traits did the characters have that you liked? That you disliked? Why?

Kids haven't really understood a book until they have made some judgments about it. The end product of reading must be thinking.

The Hows and Whys of Remediation

Getting the right teacher, using the right materials, and being taken through the steps in a continuous progress mastery program may mean the difference between having your child become a winner or loser at reading. But remedial classes, too, may need a new lease on life, and the traditional approaches simply may not work for your child. If he or she has had remedial reading again and again, perhaps the reward shouldn't be more remedial reading! Perhaps your child needs a whole new approach that stresses motivation, relevance, and the application of reading to life. Where does a parent find such a program? The activist asks questions of the school specialists, administrators, and school board. He gets involved in finding out how reading is taught at his school and how it might be enhanced or broadened. If your child has spent two or more years in a reading program without measurable improvement in regular class performance, there are a lot of questions you should be asking. The first question is, Why?

Most parents feel more comfortable about their child's placement when the school has arranged for remedial help. However, remediation for remediation's sake can be a kind of busy work. Worksheets are not necessarily more effective in a class of six students than they are in a class of twenty-five. One youngster, having been placed in a remedial writing class, complained: "I'm having trouble writing . . . like reports, you know, and all they have me do is write more reports! Nobody shows me what I do that's right or wrong."

Despite the fact that parents and teachers often agree the remedial class is the appropriate place for a child, the child may not concur. Kids frequently object to remedial classes because of the stigma they feel is attached. Labeling the class may be one problem; segregating it from others may be another. If such stigma exists, it is important for the parent to recognize the validity of the child's concern. Your child needs help in understanding why he or she should go to that class, and why other children tease those who need special help.

The child who feels comfortable about himself will be better able to handle being singled out for special help. However, changing a child's attitude takes time and a lot of "talking." Their concerns are genuine and often based on a good deal of embarrassment. Eleven-year-old Freddie Yarrow used to walk by the school learning resource room on his way to math each day and peer in just far enough to be seen by children and teacher and yell: "This is where the dummies go!" The resource teacher had spoken to him about his behavior on a number of occasions, but decided not to give him center stage by making too much of an issue about it. The youngsters who were in the resource room discussed the problem and decided that their response to Freddie would only feed his appetite for attention.

The teacher decided that helping the kids to handle Freddie was more important than getting Freddie into trouble. Miss Gaines discussed it with the class. "Why do you suppose Freddie needs to do that kind of thing?" she asked.

"Because he wants attention," said Jeannie.

" 'Cause he's a dummy himself," said Barry.

"What do you really mean by that, Barry? Maybe 'dummy' isn't the right word," said Miss Gaines.

" 'Cause he's having trouble in school himself."

"Kids always tease us when they need help themselves," added Jeannie.

"How can we help him?" asked Miss Gaines.

"By inviting him in to see what goes on here," suggested Barry.

The following day, the kids were armed and ready when Freddie passed. As he thrust his head inside the door, five of them called out: "Come on in, Freddie, we've been waiting to see you!" Embarrassed, he walked away in silence. More than a week went by before Freddie came back. This time he slipped inside the room for a look around but said nothing to anyone. As he left, Jeannie offered him an apple from the basket on the desk; he took it, muttering, "It probably has a worm in it anyway."

Jeannie said nothing but went back to Miss Gaines's desk, giggling after Freddie left. "Try not to laugh, Jeannie. He really is asking for help in his own way," said Miss Gaines.

Later that year, when Freddie's math work hit an all-time low, he was referred to the resource room for help. Freddie said nothing during his first few days there, but gradually began to relax and even interact with the other youngsters. One day after all the others had left for lunch, Freddie hung back, stepped up to the desk, then said to Miss Gaines: "Gee, the dummy room sure has changed this year!"

Changing attitudes is a slow, painstaking process. Changing behavior is even slower. According to Nancy Friday, in *My Mother, My Self,* "Changes in behavior usually lag at least a generation behind changes in attitude." For Freddy and youngsters like him, both attitude and behavior needed modification. Kids will scapegoat other kids when their own ego strength needs bolstering. As they become more secure and confident, there is less need to take out their frustrations on others. There is no magic powder to obliterate the stigma youngsters feel when they are having difficulties. However, there are some obvious ways that schools can avoid calling unnecessary attention to a youngster who must be singled out. Many schools have found these techniques helpful:

1. Avoid negative labeling of any special class.
2. Try to include a few youngsters who are performing well in groups attending any resource class.
3. Make attendance in a special class appear to be a privilege of sorts. One high school in Westchester County, New York, gave

its special class a room with adjoining space that became a lounge. A couch, TV set, small tape recorder, phonograph, and even a coffeepot were installed by the kids. A bookshelf, floor rug, and cushions were donated by a parent. The kids had the nicest lounge in school and they could bring their friends in from time to time.

4. A school psychologist we know devised an award system for all kids to allow them to visit the resource room. One period of the day was designated visiting time, when no kids were scheduled for specific help. Children in all classes would vie for the awards through their work and behavior, and each class was allowed to award two gold rings per week. The holders of the gold ring were invited to the resource room.

5. Finding that many youngsters are motivated to learn through experiential learning programs, one junior high school social studies teacher included monthly fieldtrips for her students with special needs. The class, which had formerly been called the "dummies class" by the kids, now became the "in" place. Other seventh-graders complained that their classes weren't nearly as much fun.

Some educational observers feel that it is not fair to all children to reward youngsters who are experiencing difficulties with payoffs as incentives to learn. Yet the special attention that such youngsters are receiving is really the sort of sound educational theory that all children need and deserve. Programs designed to provide alternate methods of teaching youngsters who don't learn through traditional modes have stimulated a general reexamination of what good education is all about.

The major thrust of recent educational policy to assist children with special needs has been toward individualized educational planning. This movement appears to be generating an interest in modifying the educational programs of all children. Now that an individual educational program must be designed to meet the needs of youngsters diagnosed as having learning difficulties or other handicapping conditions, it may be only a matter of time before such plans are established for all children.

A Ford Foundation Report entitled "Exceptional Teaching for Exceptional Learning" recommends a nongraded approach to education, allowing each child to make continuous progress moving from level to level in each subject at his or her own pace. The curriculum that locks all teachers and students into a fixed regime may well be on its way out for all kids.

Competency—In School and in Life

A competency skill is the knowledge of how to perform a task basic to survival in our complicated society. Among these skills are the following:

1. Basic math computation, such as addition, subtraction, multiplication, and division.
2. Handling money, making change, and being able to perform basic consumer operations.
3. Basic reading skills above a sixth-grade level, so that the young adult can read a daily newspaper, a want ad, or a job application adequately.
4. Basic directional skills to be able to find one's way on the local mass transit system or drive a car.
5. Basic writing skills adequate to fill out a job application or write a simple letter.

Competence in life is not always learned in the classroom; frequently, it needs to be developed in an alternate program that broadens the concept of education. The kids who are early winners seem to be those who have developed skills during their middle and high school years. In California, a blue-ribbon state commission recommended a new educational criterion of "demonstrated competence rather than time spent in the classroom." Their aim was to "broaden the learning opportunities for teenagers beyond the dull, rigid and often ineffectual confines of tradition." According to State Superintendent of Public Instruction Wilson Riles, "Schools are still in the last century and are insensitive to the various learning styles of youngsters."[8]

It is important to keep the concept of the "whole child" in mind at all times. Kids are not computers that automatically receive, process, and regurgitate homogenized information. They need social, aesthetic, and competency skills as well. Sometimes parents and schools get so hung up on academic success in the early years that they forget life skills and social relationships. The bright but socially awkward kid is not going to feel much like a winner when his peers avoid him; the less successful student who has developed social maturity and can get positive feedback from the outside world will run ahead in the game of living. Yet we must never forget that we have all grown up in the shadow of Harvard and Wellesley, and this traditional educational focus, which measures academic achievement in terms of admission to top colleges, pervades all levels of education.

Certainly, the "whole child" concept and other developments indicate changes in our attitude toward education; however, the lag in time from attitude change to behavior change may be too long to help your child. It may be necessary for you to find such programs yourself rather than wait for the school to get around to it. (This may even mean choosing a private school as the best place for your child. In Chapter 6 we talk about the various kinds of schools available to provide your child with a broader education.)

Schools that Punish

Traditionally, schools have maintained the need for strong punitive handling of misbehaving children. Left over from our seventeenth-century Puritan background, schools are "the only American institution authorized to resort to Corporal Punishment, a penalty long outlawed in prisons and armed forces."[9] Only two states, New Jersey and Massachusetts, have abolished corporal punishment in the schools; two others have placed restrictions on it, leaving forty-six states with permission to engage in this archaic form of obedience training. Thirty states actually allow classroom teachers to hit students if they deem it appropriate, while the other sixteen permit such actions by authorized personnel only (this usually means administrators).

When determining your child's rights, you should be aware that as recently as 1977, the Supreme Court stated that the Eighth Amendment offered no protection to children. In turning your child over to a school for education, you may get more than what you bargained for in the area of obedience training. The American Psychological Association, profoundly disturbed at the possible damage to a child's ego and personality inherent in this kind of treatment, has taken action to reverse this policy. It has filed a brief before the Supreme Court citing a recent study carried out in Portland, Oregon, indicating that an increase in the use of corporal punishment in a particular school correlates with an increase in acts of vandalism against that school.[10] Treat kids with violence and they will respond with violence; treat them with respect and they will learn respect. Harsh treatment of kids may beget quiet classrooms, but it does not necessarily result in good education.

We know of one teacher who claims that he became a left-hander for years in grade school because his right hand was so often beaten across the knuckles with the teacher's ruler. Paddled kids end up paddling other kids. Check your school program carefully and find out how normal acting-out behavior is handled. Let your opinion about your school district's policy on corporal punishment be heard *before* your kid gets paddled.

Another method of treating recalcitrant behavior in the secondary schools is a process called internal suspension. Usually this system keeps a misbehaving youngster incommunicado, in an office, forced to sit and do nothing for the day. The average, active, slightly "hyper" male student, when forced to be immobile, is on his way to further trouble. The most unnatural thing for a normal teenager to do is *nothing*. Many schools seeking more constructive methods of handling have dropped this system. One we know of has substituted an internal suspension room, the so-called "womb room," where a combination of adjustment counseling and homework assistance is the order of the day. The school has found that these helping havens have lowered the rate of recidivism. Kids develop a relationship with the person in charge, and the new form of support system has paid off in numerous ways. If you can get such a program established at your school, do so. If you can't, be very aware of the kind of negative reinforcement your child is getting in school. Punishment is not a substitute for education, but better education is certainly a substitute for punishment!

Schools that Educate Winners

In looking for the best school placement for your child, there are a number of intangible qualities that make some schools excel while others fail.

When schools treat kids as people, not as objects to be directed and disciplined without regard for personal growth, they produce winners. An interview between school personnel, parent, and child will give a parent a good idea of the school administrator's attitude toward kids. If the administrator or teacher directs his conversation, questions, and comments at the child, he is probably in the business of educating children; if he ignores the child and directs himself to the parent, that could suggest his lack of respect for the child.

A school's willingness to break with tradition to meet kids' individual needs indicates a constructive approach. On the other hand, suggests Betty Lou Kratoville, author and former school principal, a comment like, "Well, if we do it for your child, we will have to do it for everyone," means the system comes first.

However, since no two schools and no two teachers are exactly alike, the parent has to find out which values individual teachers stress, and what individual teachers set as their goals. Recent studies confirm that class size affects not only the quality of education in that class but also the teacher's attitude. In an analysis of over 300 classes of more than 900,000 students during the past fifty years, two researchers at the University of Colorado concluded that decrease in class size to an average of twenty students from the average class size of thirty students lead to a gain in achievement that is "substantial."[11] In addition, there is a gain in humanness in the classroom. In larger classes, teachers often feel overwhelmed and helpless. However, in the smaller classes they reported an immediate change to a more relaxed atmosphere, fewer discipline problems, better interaction with students, and overall improvement. Teachers felt better about themselves and the job they were doing and kids enjoyed the classes more.

Argument as to why kids are graduating from schools without the basic skills of reading, writing, and arithmetic continues. But being addicted to the habit of finding complex analyses to solve simple questions, we will probably go on with policies that seem penny-wise and pound-foolish.

If you want your kid to feel successful in school and become a winner, try to analyze the class teacher's attitude toward kids, handling of discipline, philosophy of education, and class size.

Our eighteen-year-old son, Alan, summed up his feelings about the way one learns to be a winner in a traditional school setting by saying: "Feeling like a winner in school is not just a question of getting the highest grades. Sure it's great to get good marks, but that isn't the important thing in learning. What really counts is getting the most out of a course. My parents never 'bugged' me about grades, as long as I continued to learn. It was more important for me to understand and incorporate new things I learned than to regurgitate the teacher's own words. Winning at school is knowing that what you have learned is important to you, and feeling a sense of self-respect and confidence."

CHAPTER

6

---◆---

Finding the Right Private School
When Public Schools Get Your
"F" for Failure

By rights, you should be able to get your public schools to provide the kind of schooling your child needs to be confident, happy, and constantly developing at peak potential—in short, to be a winner. You learned in the last chapter about the whole arsenal of tactics with which to fight for those rights.

But battles for your child's right to the kind of public education the youngster needs may still prove to be stalemated. That happened finally with Tommy Irwin of McHenry, Illinois, when he was in fifth grade. So exasperated were his parents by years of mishandling in public school that they filed suit against the school district for $1 million.

Teachers labeled Tommy a "behavior problem" from the time he entered first grade. Mainly, he didn't obey, and raced through his schoolwork fast and sloppily. Then, Tommy's third-grade teacher really alarmed the Irwins by telling them he had a learning disability. They were astounded. The little boy seemed very bright to them. For instance, Tommy had spoken in complete sentences starting at age two, and had won chess games against his grandfather at age four.

Testing by a psychologist in private practice relieved their fears, but increased their anger. Tommy's intelligence test results came out at the extraordinarily high level of 169 IQ. Tommy was judged by the psychologist to be among the "gifted"—a child well up in about the top 3 percent of the population in native intellectual capacity, so far as can be determined. He was also found to have no learning disabilities, but to have instead the extraordinary learning capabilities typical of rare, gifted children.

The boy was nonetheless at first refused admission to the school's twelve-week program for the gifted because of past restless behavior. And the program had little effect when he did go through it because the district had no teacher trained or otherwise skilled in working with gifted children.

In yet another move, the increasingly vexed parents got permission for Tommy as a fifth-grader to take a Spanish course at the local high school. But after the school board revoked the permission to avoid setting a precedent, the Irwins at last blew up and sued.

The Alternative of Private School

An increasing number of parents today similarly find that they eventually have no choice but to give their public schools a big, resounding "F" for the failure to be at all effective in helping to realize their child's birthright to be a winner. Fortunately, parents have an alternative: private school.

More and more today, parents turn to the alternative of private school. They turn particularly to the country's 800 or so private, non-church schools that exist expressly to serve nonreligious educational needs that are not met by public schools.

The decisions of parents and students not satisfied by public schools caused total enrollments of these 800 schools to rise by 25 percent, to some 100,000 young people, through the 1970s. At the outset of the eighties, applications to these schools continued to climb at rates varying between 10 and 60 percent a year in many parts of the country.

So that you may see what help is available, whatever your child's difficulty, this chapter presents a broad panorama of alternatives to fit a variety of needs. The advantages of private schooling for admission to top colleges are discussed in the event that this may be a consideration for you. The sections that follow tell you how to find complete and current details about private schools, select and visit promising ones, then cope successfully with getting your child admitted and with meeting their substantial costs.

First Possible "F": No Way for Your Child to Grow Soundly in Public School

"No way—there's just no way my child is going to develop well and happily in our public school." That's the kind of conclusion reached perhaps most often by parents finally forced to consider private schools. And it's likely to be your prime reason for giving an "F" to your public school for its failure.

This is the situation in which you'd find yourself after making all the efforts outlined in the previous chapter—but to no avail. A federal law enacted in 1978 now requires all public schools to design and implement special programs of education for the nation's more than three million pupils who are judged to have unusual difficulty in coping with school—those officially found to be "handicapped." The resulting "Individualized Education Programs" (IEPs) for each child are expected to change public schooling dramatically.

But even this mandate, backed by $804 million in additional federal aid to the schools for 1979–80, does not universally result in the right help needed by children with learning difficulties. Checking by federal officials has found that some school systems in Arizona and North Dakota, for example, are mapping out IEPs without having parents join in as required by law; that was also found to be true of some public schools in Illinois, Kentucky, and Alaska.

Many public schools throughout the country do a remarkably good job for children with all varieties of learning problems. But a number of school districts fail to meet this responsibility to some small or large degree, often due to no fault of their own in these inflationary times. Providing the extra teaching time and services called for in IEPs proves expensive. Quite a few school officials have said that the added federal aid still does not enable them to meet their costs in properly educating handicapped children.

You could find your child inadequately served in public school if the child qualifies as handicapped—that is, if your child is found to have such difficulties as learning disabilities, hyperactivity, speech impediments, perceptual problems with hearing or vision, or seriously poor coordination in writing. Your child's IEP may simply not prove to be enough.

But public school could also prove ineffectual for your child if the child is markedly unusual in ways not judged to be "handicaps" (which are extremely hard to diagnose at best, and at worst can act as labels that inflict much damage on the child). Perhaps most ironically, public schooling can prove grossly ineffective for gifted children, as we saw in the case of Tommy Irwin. This can also happen, and does, with children who are slow to develop but not ascertainably "handicapped" in any way. It happens with children who are extremely energetic and high-spirited, and who increasingly antagonize repressive schools that brand them as severe behavior problems.

For any reasons such as these, then, you might well conclude that there's just no way in which your child can grow soundly in public school. If so, the time has come to turn to private school alternatives.

Second Possible "F": Disastrous Social Climate in Public School

It would be bad enough if public school proved merely ineffective in helping your child grow soundly as a winner. But it can be worse— much worse. For many thousands of parents a year who feel forced to resort to private schools, public school has become nothing less than a disaster.

Reaching that conclusion was especially hard for Carol Washington, but she felt she just had to for the sake of her eight-year-old, Davy. Carol and Ben, her husband, were too strapped financially even to think of moving from the house that they'd inherited from Ben's folks in a changing neighborhood. Besides, they deeply believed in the innate goodness of all kinds of people, rich and poor. Carol especially thought of their local grade school as a wonderful place, where children with all kinds of fascinating, different backgrounds could meet and learn from each other.

Then, one day about two weeks after curly-haired Davy had started second grade, he came home crying. On the four-block walk home, he'd been knocked down by "some big boys" and the 15 cents he'd earned drying dishes the night before had been stolen. After comforting her little boy, Carol phoned both the principal and the police. They sympathized with her anger, saying that it was only an isolated incident and that they'd take every precaution to keep it from ever happening again.

Over the next seven months, however, Davy was robbed five more times. One of the sixth-grade boys was stabbed from behind in a washroom at school, though not seriously, and a third-grade girl was pushed down the stairs. Finally, Davy came home on a sunny May afternoon with his clothes grimy and torn, his left eye swollen shut, and his nose and lower lip gushing blood. He'd had no money and had been beaten.

Furious and sick at heart, Carol talked long and gravely with Ben that night. Carol herself took Davy to and from school every day for the rest of the year. The next fall, their boy started private school.

Like the Washingtons, you may find that your public schools have become a nightmare for your child even though your boy or girl likes the teachers and is well taught there. The social climate could prove a disaster. Uncontrolled violence in and around the school is often likely to be the cause. In many public schools today, not only pupils but teachers live in fear of physical attacks. Shocking as it may sound, one in every twenty teachers nationwide is physically assaulted by pupils every year, and 17 percent of all teachers are almost always afraid they may be attacked in their schools.

Violence is highest in areas with troubled social conditions, usually cities. For instance, a safety handbook for teachers in New York City urges them never to be alone in school and to go home as soon as they finish with their last class: "If no one else is present, leave immediately for a room with people in it. While serious sex crimes are rare, when they do happen they occur in classrooms, faculty rooms and workrooms when the teacher is alone."

A survey by the Chicago Teachers Union found that the common psychological effects of such a social climate on teachers included mental fatigue, anxiety, depression, and low self-esteem. Difficulties like these are exactly the opposite of what is needed by a child you want to feel like a winner. Yet children immersed in the same disastrous social climate cannot help but be afflicted much like their teachers.

Unfortunately, violence is only one of many evils that can prey on your child in a public school poisoned by a disastrous social climate. Others that are all too damnably familiar include drugs, alcohol, insolence and foul speech, immorality, and criminality. It is heartbreaking that conditions of American life turn so many children into muggers, addicts, alcoholics, prostitutes, and murderers. Still, you cannot afford to have your child injured or corrupted by other children headed tragically for such doom.

Once your child starts getting hurt by a social climate, you have no choice but to give the public school an "F" for failing to meet his or her needs. It may be no fault of the school if it is completely overwhelmed by the social problems of large numbers of children. But your course of action is still clear: You'll have to get your child out of that school, fast. Move to another school district, or, if you can't, find a private school.

Third Possible "F": Only Mediocre Aims in Public School

Many parents today finally give their public schools a resounding "F" for failure to meet their children's needs more out of disappointment than catastrophe. These are often the parents who would have been delighted with the public schools when they were flourishing a decade or so ago. But inflation and "Proposition 13" fever to hold taxes down have taken a heavy toll of special course offerings, programs, and activities in public schools. Fiscal troubles have even led to long school closings in some districts through teachers' strikes or budget shortages.

Moreover, such parents tend to be the ones who, more than most, really want their children to feel like winners. They badly want school to be something special for their child. Even without closings, they can't bear to see their child continue to go to a school with only mediocre aims. One father took all four of his children out of the public schools of Annapolis, Maryland—a suburban town of 30,000 that is also the state capital. The main reason he gave was that "The system clamps down on all originality and creativity."

As a particular result of such disappointment, one headmaster sees applications to his private school rising rapidly, even though the suburban area from which his increased applications are pouring in is known for its generally superior public schools and unusually high freedom from crime and troubled social conditions. Applications have boomed at his and other suburban private schools, he says, mainly because "the parents are just unhappy with the public schools."

Surveys bear out his contention. One made recently among the suburban residents of a large metropolitan area found that 11 percent of the suburbanites gave their public schools a vote of "no confidence" when asked if they thought their children would get "a good education in the public schools."

There's some fair chance, then, that you may be deeply dissatisfied by your child's public school, even if the child is getting along well enough with it. Rest assured you have much company today if you decide that well enough is simply not good enough for a child with all that potential going untapped, and opt instead for a really challenging and exciting private school.

Fourth Possible "F": If Your Child Is Suspended or Expelled

"Suspended . . ."

"Expelled!"

Nameless terror clutches the heart of any halfway conscientious child at the mention of these threats. Even with school years far behind you, they can still summon up the dread of some ultimate punishment with crushing, hideous disgrace for you and, worst of all, your mom and dad.

Yet, for all the fear surrounding it, suspension is a surprisingly common weapon used by public schools against children. Schools serving poverty-level, minority-group families suspend pupils most heavily, as one probably would expect. But you might be amazed at *how* heavily. In one recent school year, no less than 40 percent of all high school students in Rochester, New York, were suspended; so were 60 percent of the pupils in one school in Buffalo, New York! And suspension rates like these are not at all unusual for public high schools in cities across the country.

But public schools in middle-class and even wealthy communities also suspend substantial numbers of children—and do so under much the same circumstances as schools serving less affluent families. The children suspended often are, ironically, the very pupils who most need to be helped by their schools. Such suspension could well be called the school's ultimate confession of its failure to meet its responsibilities.

Isolated cases of suspension, of course, might come out of the blue in response to your child's impulsive action or prank, as with the sixth-grader, Billy, whose suspension after climbing the schoolyard fence was described in Chapter 4. Unforeseeable suspensions of children who otherwise have no problems with their public schools are rare. Should this happen to your child, it alone would probably not be sufficient reason for you to consider having the child go to a private school.

Far more typically, the hammer-blow of suspension by a public school is preceded by failure of the school for years to meet the learning needs of the child. That blow most often falls after a long-descending spiral representing an all-too-familiar pattern. One recent study says of almost all children who suffer the blow of suspension: "From the earliest years, they have known both the sting and frustration of repeated academic failure, and the humiliation of being unable to keep up with their classes. Disruptive behavior, selective and total truancy—all ways of avoiding serious academic effort—lead to worse and worse performance and usually provoke disciplinary retaliation in the form of suspension. . . ."[1]

How this could happen to your child, however well off you may be, is illustrated by the case of Hal Palmer.

Hal lives in an estate section of a well-to-do suburb, and through his elementary school years never did as well in school as the other children in the family. He became more and more pained with his schoolwork the further he went in his very pressured and academic junior high school. He began getting failing marks that made him feel ashamed and angered. Increasingly, he made friends with students who felt as he did —other rebellious boys, the school's troublemakers. He cut classes, spoke back to teachers, and got warnings from the school. He and two friends were arrested when caught wrecking roadside mailboxes and were given suspended sentences. Then, more school cuts and outbursts brought Hal's suspension from high school.

It was only for three days, but his parents saw it as the end. It was essentially the same as expulsion because, by that time, hostility had risen to a very high level on the part of both Hal and the school. Schools rarely take the further step of expulsion these days in order to avoid legal complications. But many public schools expel, in effect, by one or more suspensions which, as in Hal's case, make it personally and socially impossible for the youngster to return. Such actions by schools are in large part responsible for the national dropout rate of fifteen out of every 100 young people.

At that point, Hal's parents did the only thing they felt they could. They found a private school that, for the first time, really provided the education Hal needed. It also got him away from his bad companions, for it was a boarding school a half-day's drive to the north. Hal liked and did well at the school, and had no difficulty in getting his high school diploma there.

Should your child be suspended, it is dismally probable that your experience will unfold much as it did with Hal and his parents. You might even act early if you see your child heading clearly toward suspension, because the rising frustration and shame of the youngster that almost always precede suspension can badly undercut that winning attitude you want in your child. But whether you act before or after suspension, you can be sure of finding a private school where your child can make real progress in learning, development, and friends—in short, function as a winner.

The Wide Range of Alternatives in Private Schools

Once you have decided that your public school has failed hopelessly to provide what your child needs, you can take new heart and new hope. Private schools have developed in all parts of the country precisely to furnish the many kinds of education and school community that public schools cannot or do not deliver. From the very wide range of alternatives opened to you by private schools, you should be able to find at least several both feasible for your situation and very good for your child.

Suppose, for instance, your child is gifted like Tommy Irwin, whose rare abilities led only to conflicts and boredom in public school. Scores of private schools throughout the country have very strong academic programs and pupils of very high abilities. Any one of these schools would welcome a gifted child, and should have teachers thoroughly delighted and able to help your child to develop to full potential. (Later in this chapter it is explained how you can locate such schools.)

As another possibility, you may have finally decided to seek a private school because public school is not carrying out an effective IEP to help your child overcome some handicap, such as a learning disability. Many private schools offer programs and services designed specifically to help pupils overcome handicaps or difficulties. These schools often characterize their work as serving students who are "underachievers" with "make-up, review, and remedial" studies. For instance, the Gables

Academies operate seven schools in Georgia, Florida, Alabama, and Louisiana for "children with learning difficulties" in the first through the twelfth grades. The Denver Academy in Colorado specializes in helping boys and girls from the ages of six through twenty who have "learning disabilities" and "motivational problems."

If a disastrous social climate in public school is your prime reason for turning to private schooling, your choice is especially wide. You could select from great numbers of day schools or boarding schools where most of the children are well behaved and carefully guided. You might prefer to choose a day school in this case in order to save money and to enjoy having the child continue to live at home.

You would have a similarly wide choice if it were only mediocre aims in public school that led you to seek better education elsewhere. Probably the most common purpose among America's private schools is to offer education programs of particularly high quality and breadth.

Finally, you would also have many choices of fine private schools if your child had been or were soon to be suspended from public school. In a situation like this, you would look for private schools that help students with overcoming learning difficulties, with developing good habits and self-discipline, or with catching up on studies in which they have fallen behind. The heads of private schools with such programs usually see no problem in admitting a child who has been suspended, once they understand that inadequate teaching and handling in public school were the basic causes of the suspension.

In the next few sections, let's look in more detail at the major kinds of private schools among which you can choose in order to satisfy the particular needs of your child.

Private Schools to Help Children with Learning Disabilities

In recent years, many private schools have designed special programs to help children with learning disabilities. If your child has one or more of the common types of learning disabilities (as explained in detail in the next chapter), you should be able to find effective programs among either day schools or boarding schools, schools with traditional scholastic approaches or schools with an "open education" or "progressive education" philosophy.

Should you have a learning-disabled child, the important quality of an effective school is not its general type but the extent to which the specific program of the school meets the specific needs of your child. You should evaluate each possible school with the particular needs and educational skills of your child in mind. It's also essential to consult with a psychologist, guidance counselor, or learning consultant who is knowledgeable about learning disabilities and effective programs to relieve them.

Here are some actual examples of good schools for children with learning difficulties to give you a concrete idea of what they are like. *Pine Ridge School,* in Williston, Vermont, on the slopes of the Green Mountains near Lake Champlain and the city of Burlington, is a boarding and day school for boys and girls from thirteen to twenty years old. Its educational program is devoted entirely to children of average or higher intelligence who have specific learning disabilities. Classes are small and each student receives daily one-to-one instruction in language skills. Activities are an integral part of studies and include informal sports, camping, hiking, skiing, crafts, arts, photography, and school yearbook and newspaper. While Pine Ridge is an accredited high school, it seeks to enable each student to return to regular classrooms as soon as possible.

In the vicinity of Springfield, Massachusetts, *Eagle Hill School* (in Hardwick), a coed boarding school for people from eight to eighteen years old, also offers a program designed entirely for children who have learning disabilities. The students pursue individualized study programs and have perceptual and motor training daily. Its aim is to work with children until they can return to normal schooling. Eagle Hill occupies a 150-acre estate with woods, orchards, and lawns; there is a branch campus in Greenwich, Connecticut, a New York City suburb.

North of Boston in picturesque Prides Crossing, Massachusetts, is the *Landmark School.* It is a boarding and day school for boys and girls from ages eight to eighteen, and offers instruction covering the work of grades 2 through 12 on an "ungraded" basis. A unit of the Learning Disabilities Foundation, Inc., it provides an excellent program for children with such difficulties. Pupils are accepted for one or two years' intensive remediation aimed at their return to regular schools.

Among numerous other private schools in the New York metropolitan area with programs for helping to surmount learning disabilities, *Windward School* in White Plains, New York, is a coed day school with twenty teachers for an enrollment of about fifty pupils of ages five to fourteen. Windward exclusively serves children of average or better intelligence who have mild learning disabilities. Each of its small classes includes children representing a span of ages and conventional grade levels. The program is noncompetitive and features much tutoring as well as gym every day, art, music, library, and woodworking. Its goal is to prepare students academically to go back to regular schools.

On West 74th Street in Manhattan, the *Baldwin School* of New York City is a coed day school for children aged twelve to eighteen. Its classes are small and it takes an individual approach to learning. Work that can help children with certain kinds of learning disabilities is offered in Baldwin's extensive remedial program and its tutorial division. It has a full range of extracurricular activities and athletics, and is affiliated with two other Baldwin schools in Puerto Rico.

Outside Philadelphia, the *Kildonan School* in Solebury, Pennsylvania, is operated primarily for students plagued by the kind of learning disability generally known as "dyslexia" (often evidenced by extreme difficulties in reading and writing). Kildonan provides intensive remedial work in language and mathematics skills tailored individually to the students' needs. It is a school for boys from nine to sixteen years old, and may be attended on either a boarding or day basis.

Also near Philadelphia, the *Vanguard* schools serve young people of ages six to eighteen on a nonboarding, coed basis, with an especially strong program for children who have reading or speech difficulties. They seek to enable them to reenter regular schooling after two or three years. Vanguard includes Lower and Middle schools on a 50-acre campus in Paoli, Pennsylvania. Vanguard High School is in nearby Haverford, Pennsylvania. Another Vanguard School for both boarding and day students aged six to eighteen is located in Lake Wales, Florida. In addition, there is a Vanguard School for day students in Coconut Grove, Florida.

Although the majority of private schools are located in the East, there are several good schools in other parts of the country.

In the Midwest, examples of schools in the Chicago area offering special learning-disabilities programs include the *Grove School* in Lake Forest, Illinois, and the *Tikuah Institute* for Childhood Learning Disabilities on Chicago's Near North Side. Grove is a coed school for young people from three to twenty-one, and has both boarding and day students. Tikuah, a day school, serves boys and girls from four to eighteen.

In the West, *Oak Creek Ranch School* in Arizona illustrates a kind of private school that is helpful for some children with learning disabilities. A coed boarding school for children eight to eighteen, Oak Creek serves mainly slow learners and underachievers who have not succeeded in conventional schools. Basic learning skills are stressed in instruction, and camping, riding, skiing, and other outdoor activities play an important part in the curriculum and school life.

In Los Angeles, California, the *Marianne Frostig Center of Educational Therapy* is a coed day school, offering children of ages four to fifteen help through a team approach to diagnose learning disabilities and plan an appropriate program. The usual length of a stay for its special training is two years. Students attending public junior high schools can get supplementary help at the Center. It also gives a six-week summer session of intensive academic instruction.

Still other private schools concentrating on work with children who have learning disabilities are affiliated with colleges and universities. Among schools like this in the West, the *Fernald School* of the University of California at Los Angeles offers an ungraded day school program covering the work of first through twelfth grades. It enrolls some seventy young people.

If you have a child with learning disabilities such as those described in the next chapter, just knowing that there are private schools of the kind highlighted here may well bring you much relief. How to find such schools in your vicinity would be a natural next question. The experts on learning disabilities with whom you would be consulting (as explained in the next chapter) should be able to tell you not only about such schools but also about the many other varieties of effective help available for your child. Your best source in print for the names of schools in the United States and Canada is the current edition of the *Directory of Educational Facilities for the Learning Disabled* (available from Academic Therapy Publications, 1539 Fourth St., San Rafael, Calif. 94901; or Association for Children with Learning Disabilities, 4156 Library Road, Pittsburgh, Pa. 15234).

Private Schools to Suit Not Only Your Child's Needs but Many Preferences, Too

If your child needs private schooling for reasons other than help with learning disabilities—reasons such as sound growth, a decent social climate, or more than mediocre aims—you have a very wide variety of private schools from which to choose.

Day schools are the ones you might think of first, because your child could continue to live at home and commute to school; also, you wouldn't have to pay boarding costs that run some $1,500 to $2,000 a year. Day student tuition costs for the more sought-after, nonchurch private schools range from about $1,200 or $1,500 to some $3,800 or more a year; annual tuition at a school usually increases by some hundreds of dollars in the upper years.

Some private day schools are in good-to-fashionable neighborhoods of large cities, and have academic quality and reputations easily as high as any of the highly regarded boarding schools. For instance, a girls' school on New York City's upper east side, *Brearley,* usually places more than half of its graduating class of about forty in the top rank of colleges—Harvard-Radcliffe, Yale, Stanford, Bryn Mawr, and Vassar. *Trinity,* another New York Ctiy school for boys through age twelve and coed for students thirteen to eighteen, has been educating children from prominent families for more centuries than most colleges. It dates from 1709.

Country day schools represent a variety with extensive grounds and sports programs paralleling those features of admired boarding schools. They are often located in outlying areas or suburbs of larger cities. One, for example, is the *Chadwick School*. Chadwick is at Rolling Hills, on the Palos Verdes peninsula some 25 miles south of Los Angeles.

Boarding schools are ones at which your child would be educated and developed under the school's influence except during school holidays. A boarding school could be important if the child needs to get away from bad companions (as in the case of Hal) or should change or develop good habits, not only in study but also in such areas as playing and relating to other people. Boarding school programs are designed to help young people in all areas of their lives.

Boarding schools tend to be located in small towns in rural areas far from large cities. Quite a few of them are in suburbs, though, and enroll substantial proportions of young people on a day basis. Even those in rural areas will usually allow families living nearby to have their children attend as day students.

(Further information on private schools and how to obtain full details about them appears in Appendix 1 on Private Schools at the end of the book.)

How to Investigate Private Schools

Let's assume you have now gotten the names of a few private schools that look promising. Here is how you might go about analyzing and selecting among them.

First, a "Checklist for Selecting a Good Private School for Your Child" is given below to serve as a guide in your evaluation of each school. Make whatever notes you want for each item in the checklist, ranging from a simple "yes-no" or "good-poor" to longer phrases or paragraphs. Base your notes on what you learn from literature about the school, your visits to it, and conversations or conferences you have about it.

Checklist for Selecting a Good Private School for Your Child

Essentials:

   Does it have the special programs or features required for the child—including coed, or for boys or girls?

Does it have an otherwise good educational program for the child?

Is it likely (or sure) to admit the child?

Can it be afforded?

Has it state or further accreditation and recognition?

Is it attractive to the child?

Rate the following features either "poor," "medium," "good," or "excellent":

General character and reputation

Physical plant—buildings, equipment, grounds, library, student facilities

Access to off-campus community facilities or facilities of another school

Activities and sports program

Quality and character of administrators

Quality, character, and number of teachers

Teacher/student ratio, size of classes, teacher turnover, student turnover

General character of students and their backgrounds; ethnic diversity of student body

Effective handling of any discipline problems with drugs, alcohol, sex; suspensions, expulsions

How graduates fare

Reactions of students and parents to the school

The Importance of Early Evaluation

Unless you are facing some emergency or crisis situation in your child's schooling, you should try to start finding out about and evaluating private schools at least ten months before your child plans to enter. It would naturally be best for the child to enter at the start of the school year in September; ten months earlier would accordingly be the preceding March back to November. However, for schools of the "St. Grottlesex" status, you would have to start two to three years earlier.

You may be able to find a fairly good private school for your child if a mid-year or immediate admission at some other point during the school year is imperative. Some schools with programs designed to help troubled youngsters will admit them at irregular times under genuinely compelling circumstances. In a case like this, though, your range of choice would tend to be sharply limited.

Even for a planned fall entrance, you should start early in general, because increasing numbers of parents are turning to private schools today. Openings in classes of the more sought-after schools can largely be filled as much as eight or nine months before September. Moreover, starting early gives you more time for searching, evaluation, and planning.

Begin your evaluation by writing or phoning each promising school of which you have learned, to request a set of its current literature for interested parents. After you have examined and considered the literature and perhaps discussed the school with individuals, you should make an appointment to visit it if at all possible. Your child should visit with you, and the visit would include plans for an admissions interview of your child.

The Essential Factors

Special Programs or Features Required for the Child. The primary factor in the private school you are considering will be the special programs or other features that led you to turn to private schools in the first place. These may be a good program for gifted youngsters like your child, or the specific program needed to help your child with a learning disability. They would probably include a wholesome social climate, or academic aims far higher than mediocre. Consider whether the school is coed or for one sex only—this may be important for your child.

An Otherwise Good Educational Program for the Child. Beyond the program or feature that represents your reason for seeking a private school, you will want to make sure that the overall educational program provides two crucial elements. One is a sound coverage of the basic knowledge and skills important for all well-educated children. The second is an attractive range of additional offerings, perhaps in such areas as the arts, sciences, foreign languages, social studies, sports, outdoor life, and work experience.

Likely (or Sure) to Admit the Child. It would only waste your time (and money) to go too far in evaluating a school before finding out whether your child has a realistic chance of being admitted. Some general idea of the capabilities and other qualities important for admission to the school should be conveyed in the current literature it sends or gives you. Beyond that, at an early point in considering it, you should ask the school's head or admissions officer to tell you approximately what chances of admission your child seems to have. The person you ask may be able to answer from general information you give, or may need an early copy of your child's official school record and possibly other information. The answer you get should be a fairly reliable guide for further actions of yours, whether to look more deeply into the school or to investigate others instead.

Can Be Afforded. Tuition charges at the nonchurch private schools discussed here amount to $1,000 a year or more for day students, and $6,000 a year or more for boarding students, as noted before. You will want to consider costs carefully early in your search, and perhaps seek less expensive alternatives. The school's literature may indicate the availability of some scholarships; the Porter Sargent *Handbook* also reports on scholarships at individual schools. On the secondary level, some schools have opportunities for work or "self-help" income. Such financial aid at most private schools is quite limited; however, you might inquire about aid at a school difficult to afford but in which you and your child are strongly interested.

Has State or Further Accreditation and Recognition. Any private school must be licensed by the state in which it is located in order to operate, but state licensing or chartering is worth confirming if you happen to be considering a school just getting started. One form of endorsement of quality beyond state approval is accreditation of an elementary or secondary school by associations of private or independent schools in several states and one region (among them, the Southwest region and the states of Connecticut, Florida, New York, and Pennsylvania). Another quality endorsement of secondary schools beyond state approval is "regional accreditation" by the same organizations that similarly accredit colleges. These organizations are:

· Middle States Association of Colleges and Secondary Schools
· North Central Association of Colleges and Secondary Schools
· New England Association of Schools and Colleges
· Northwest Association of Schools and Colleges
· Southern Association of Colleges and Schools
· Western Association of Schools and Colleges

Schools holding the distinction of any of these forms of accreditation are sure to note it in their literature.

Membership by the school in other associations in the field tends to reflect professional and informed operation of the school, and does not involve accreditation. Among such groups are the National Association of Independent Schools (NAIS); state, city, or other independent school associations; and the Educational Records Bureau (ERB), which schools join to provide extensive services for the testing and preparation of records on the abilities of their students.

Such memberships and accreditations may give you further assurance of a school's quality; however, a school could still prove effective for your child without them.

Attractiveness to the Child. Naturally, as you look into private schools, you will want to involve your child in the process from the first steps on, at levels appropriate to his or her understanding. The child may well be enthusiastic about private school if he or she has been miserable in public school. At any age, friends at the private school would be very important to the youngster. You may accordingly want to go out of your way to reassure the child about friends there. You and the people at a promising school would probably be able to generate your child's enthusiasm; but in any event, any feasible private school would have to be one that looks generally attractive to your child. You'd want it that way. And if public school has made the child feel like a loser, being able to look forward to a terrific new school could help bring the confidence, optimism, and zest that mark a winner.

Other Desirable Factors

In addition to those elements that are essential in any sound private school for your child, you will want to evaluate a number of other factors desirable in such a school. The basic factors were identified on your checklist (p. 131). You may well want to add other desirable factors of your own, depending on the interests of yourself and your child.

Such factors could be evaluated by examining school literature and directory entries, talking to informed persons, asking a lot of questions, and observing carefully on one or more visits to the school. The school will surely give you an opportunity to see it in regular operation, and to meet and talk with students, teachers, and other parents.

Managing Admission, Cost, and Financial Aid

In the course of your inquiries and assessments of a promising school, you will probably have learned about details of applying for admission and possibly financial aid, and payment of charges. Handle the admissions process in a direct, natural way. It will involve filling out the application form before a deadline, and having your child's previous school send a transcript of courses, marks and other information. Health records will probably be required, and one or more medical examination may be requested.

The school will very likely want to interview your child. Encourage the youngster to be relaxed, considerate, and spontaneous in the interview. Admissions tests may well be required, such as the SSAT (Secondary School Admission Tests). If so, the tests will be very much like the printed multiple-choice tests the child has probably already taken a number of times. Again, urge him or her to be relaxed and confident in taking any such tests. (The suggestions given in Chapter 9 on tests may also prove helpful.)

If you are also applying for financial aid, you may have to fill out special forms. The information needed would probably include summary data on family finances, which would be kept strictly confidential.

Saving or allocating money in advance in order to have funds for first-term bills and other expenses is probably the most economical way of managing your finances for private school. If you can't save very much ahead, start early to work out credit at the lowest rate you can find from a source such as a bank or credit union. Last-minute credit for private school costs can prove expensive. Also, plan if possible to arrange for enough money to meet costs without any financial aid for which you may have applied. Then, if you should be awarded the aid, you can hold the excess on hand for future costs.

As you see, private school can mean much extra effort and care on your part. But going to such trouble can be richly rewarding if it's really the best or only way to see your child develop as a winner.

7

---◆---

Learning Disability: The Hidden Handicap You Can Overcome

What Is a Learning Disability?

"Today in our urbanized, highly competitive, aspiring culture, to have any handicap is to be disadvantaged . . . not to measure up to social expectations because of any degree of illiteracy is to be consigned to a pedestrian existence for life."[1]

"Your child has a learning disability," says the school psychologist. This announcement may bring a sense of fear and guilt to a parent, many believing it to be a euphemism for retardation or brain damage.

How can a parent be certain when even the experts disagree about the definition of a learning disability? The lack of scientific precision in the field of testing and diagnosis has contributed to perpetuating that confusion. In 1969 the National Institute for Neurological Diseases (NINDS) issued a report entitled "Disorders of Central Processing in Children—A Review of Research," officially recognizing a symptom pattern that we now call "learning disability."[2] Since then, state governments have further supported the idea that such handicapping conditions exist by creating legislation aimed at helping youngsters who seem to suffer from learning disabilities.

Presently, children receive assistance of variable quality, depending upon the existence of support services within their community. For approximately 12 to 20 percent of our school-age population, becoming a "loser" is the name of the game unless massive doses of support and remediation are built into the regular school program. No child with a diagnosable learning disability can make it through the system without some kind of support, either at home, at school, or in a private school or specialized tutoring sessions.

Handicapping conditions range from dyslexia, dyscalculia, reading disorders, language development disorders, and disgraphia, to simple speech disorders. Of course, handicapped children exhibit many kinds of difficulties varying from simple to complex, from mild to severe.

Historically, the earliest recognition of specific language disorders dates back over 100 years to the Scandinavian countries, where these children were mainstreamed or channeled into the most appropriate apprenticeship training for their particular goals and academic limitations.

Currently, we recognize that a simple maturational lag in the sensory processing system or a minimal neurological dysfunction can cause learning problems. The functions demanded in reading, writing, spelling, and mathematical computation seem to be the most vulnerable to these disorders, which can occur despite otherwise normal intelligence. Disabling conditions are defined as "disorders in one or more of the basic psychological processes involved in understanding or in using language, spoken or written, which disorder may manifest itself in imperfect ability to listen, think, speak, read, write, spell, or do mathematical calculations. . . ." These disorders are caused by "perceptual handicaps, brain injury, minimal brain dysfunction, dyslexia, and developmental aphasia. Such terms do not include children who have learning problems . . . primarily the result of visual, hearing, or motor handicaps, or mental retardation, or emotional disturbance, or of environmental disadvantages."[3]

Because the educator's diagnostic tools are less precise than the physical scientist's, a wide range of conditions shelters under the umbrella term "learning disabilities." Often there is confusion and disagreement as to funding for assistance under federal and state legislation.

There are those of us who simplify this whole problem of diagnosis by saying, "If a child can't learn the way we teach him, we had better teach him the way he learns."[4] This philosophy places the responsibility upon a school system to adjust and alter its traditional methods and curriculum to meet the needs of youngsters who do not seem to learn the way others do.

Jargon and technical terminology in any area act as a barrier to communication between layman and professional. There is nothing more frustrating for parents than being told their child has a problem and not having that problem translated into meaningful language. Many parents ask the schools: "Tell me what kind of problem my child is experiencing, and how I can help him to deal with his problem."

Checklist of Learning-Disability Symptoms
Observable by Parent or Teacher:

The following checklist notes the symptoms that any parent or teacher can identify as suggestive of some kind of learning problem.

Go through the checklist reading each item. Decide whether your child exhibits this specific behavior. Mark your response, yes or no, on a separate piece of paper. Total the responses; then decide whether or not they suggest that your child may have a problem in one or more areas of learning.

Reading

Does your child—
   read mechanically, without expression?
   read unevenly, ignoring punctuation?
   read past mistakes without attempting to correct errors despite awkward meaning?
   guess at words after recognizing only a few letters, e.g.,
      smile for small
      there for three
   read very slowly, sounding out single words constantly?
   seem to have difficulty blending sounds together when reading words?
   seem to have difficulty understanding the meaning of what he reads despite the ability to sound out words correctly?
   seem to understand the meaning of material when it is read to him better than what he reads himself?
   seem unwilling to read without constant prodding and reminder?
(If you have 4 or more "yeses," you should check with your child's teacher about a possible reading problem.)

Writing

Does your child—
   have difficulty organizing his ideas into meaningful written paragraphs?
   have difficulty when trying to write a complete sentence?
   have difficulty with all punctuation?

reverse letters in a word or transpose them when writing them,
e.g., gril for girl
was for saw?
respell words phonetically when writing them, e.g.,
enuf for enough
throo for through?
cross out work frequently, leaving pages looking messy and
poorly composed?
exhibit extremely poor or illegible handwriting that seems to
show little improvement after frequent rewriting?
have difficulty writing within lines?
write erratically, his work deteriorating when he works too fast
or when he has a long assignment to write?
have difficulty keeping math in columns, numbers on lines?
avoid written work whenever possible?
(5 or more "yeses" suggest that your child may have a developmental
writing problem; consult the teacher.)

Speaking

Does your child—
articulate words incorrectly so that his speech is not clearly understandable?
omit some of the final sounds in words, e.g., runnin for running?
seem to repeat incorrectly words he hears, e.g.,
emeny for enemy
aminal for animal?
speak so quickly that he seems to swallow parts of words, run
them together, and is difficult to understand?
seem to talk in circles, never quite getting to the point?
interrupt or distract himself when speaking, change subjects frequently, and appear fragmented and disorganized?
have difficulty in finding words when speaking?
(3 or more "yeses" may suggest a problem in speech and language.)

Listening Skills

Does your child—
seem inattentive?
seem to forget instructions at home and in class?
seem to have trouble understanding spoken language at times?
seem easily distractible?
(2 or more "yeses" suggest a problem in auditory attention span; consult your school specialist or the teacher.)

Mathematics

Does your child—
   have difficulty remembering math facts, e.g.,
      addition   (if learned)
      subtraction   (if learned)
      multiplication   (if learned)
      division   (if learned)?
   have difficulty with carrying in addition?
   have difficulty with borrowing in subtraction?
   misunderstand language problems in math?
   have trouble learning how to tell time, seem always unaware of
      time passing, often late?
   have difficulty understanding concepts of space, especially mea-
      surement?
   have difficulty with the signal words in math, e.g., in addition to,
      more than, how many are left, etc.?
   have difficulty with calculating the value of coins?
   have difficulty working with fractions (if taught)?
   have difficulty working with decimals (if taught)?
   have difficulty working with percentages (if taught)?
(5 or more "yeses" may suggest a learning problem in math.)

Attitude

Does your child—
   seem to feel negative about school and himself?
   handle his frustration by acting-out behavior?
   tend to be a loner or seek playmates among younger children
      rather than those his own age?
   often appear lethargic, apathetic, bored, without energy or en-
      thusiasm?
   have a shorter attention span, more distractible behavior than
      his peers?
   shy away from competitive activities such as sports or social in-
      volvement for fear of failure?
   seem unable to follow through and complete assignments?
   perform far better in one subject than in another, e.g., good in
      math, poor in reading?
   avoid going to special help classes at school, or insist he doesn't
      have a problem?
(4 or more "yeses" may suggest that your child has a negative attitude
toward school.)

Children develop attitudinal or motivational problems when they experience repeated frustration and failure. And they often manufacture a set of techniques to save face. School adjustment counselors, psychologists, or learning specialists can help you to manage the problem at home. However, no matter how much you try to improve a child's attitude toward his schoolwork, he needs academic assistance and specific remediation to solve his learning problems.

If you have responded "yes" to more than the given number of questions in any category, your child may have a specific problem in that learning area. Following through at school is essential. Your child may be experiencing a learning lag that will certainly produce some difficulties; children who experience persistent school difficulties develop feelings of inadequacy, which in turn make them feel like a loser. If you want to raise a winner, school success is a primary prerequisite.

One word of caution: your observations on the preceding checklist constitute an informal screening. They do *not* represent a suitable substitute for professional testing. If you have any doubts or questions, consult your child's teacher, the school learning specialist, or an administrator about your concerns.

Patterns of Behavior that Suggest a Problem

Discerning the symptoms of a learning disability is not an easy task. However, certain patterns of behavior do suggest difficulties. Things are not always what they seem at first glance. Children learn how to mask their problems early through various kinds of acting out and withdrawal behaviors. It often is necessary to look beneath surface behavior to determine the real basis for a child's actions.

Suppose you were the parent and your eleven-year-old son, Ted, mentioned in Chapter 5, avoids all writing tasks for school. He continues to make simple errors long after you and the teachers feel they are appropriate. Often his report cards list "careless performance," "sloppy handwriting," or other negative comments. This kind of problem seems to have been a constant throughout your child's five-year school career.

The teacher tells you that he also avoids written work in class, handing in one or two sentences when other youngsters his age write full paragraphs. The teachers have had him doing extra corrective practice in spelling for years, but he continues to make what seem to be simple careless errors in the most common lookalike words, such as their-there, throw-through, and so on. When you look at his papers, you can see constant transpositions of letters in sequence, such as gril for girl, or thier for their.

The so-called carelessness that your son exhibits may be a difficulty in acquiring sighting (visual) to writing (motor) skills, and a spelling problem, with characteristic patterns of phonetic respelled words and letter sequencing problems (visual-sequential memory). His avoidance of writing may not be a problem of effort and attitude but one of specific learning disability with fear of taking a risk, because he knows that his work will be criticized for carelessness, poor spelling, and bad hand-writing. With appropriate diagnosis, remediation, and modifications in classroom demands, he may be willing to chance errors.

The older the child, the more complex the problem, the more overlay will be observed in acting-out behavior—and the more difficult the solution. However, just because your child is eleven, thirteen, or even eighteen years old does not mean he is "over the hill," as one school administrator we know so callously observed. Young people *can be helped to succeed at any age.* They, too, can become winners even if they have a learning disability.

What to Look for in Your Child's Behavior

The following checklist of symptom patterns is designed to give you some idea of the specific behavior a parent may see at home, the behavior reported at school, and the underlying causes of such behaviors. These behaviors are often seen as emotional factors; however, they are frequently the result of specific learning problems.

At Home

If your child—
  hates to write letters, compositions or papers of any type
  procrastinates when it comes to doing a written assignment
  avoids all written work requiring putting his own ideas down in
    his own words
  overreacts when his written work reflects poor performance

At School

If your child—
  tries to avoid written work by forgetting assignments, not com-
    pleting work, etc.
  has good oral expression but poor written expression
  does written work that the teacher describes as careless, sloppy,
    poorly organized, and unreadable
he may be experiencing a lag in visual to motor integration skills and a

delay in language reorganizational skills. This means he has trouble copying and writing things on paper, especially putting ideas into his own words.

You may be able to help your child by acting as secretary for him and putting some of his ideas down on paper. Some parents find that they can help by encouraging the child to use a tape recorder to verbalize ideas and then write them from the tape.

At Home

If your child—
- talks baby talk, has difficulty in saying multisyllabic words with syllables correctly sequenced; for example, says aminal for animal or emeny for enemy
- appears not to be listening, confuses words and instructions, and becomes generally confused with complex language
- has trouble following radio broadcasts or seems to lose track of long conversations

At School

If your child—
- appears inattentive, may act out because of difficulty in keeping his attention focused
- does very poorly in lecture classes or classroom discussions
- appears to have poor articulation skills, sloppy pronunciation
- speaks quickly, runs words together
- does poorly in spelling nonphonetic words

he may be experiencing difficulty in auditory sequencing and auditory recall.

It would be helpful if all verbal instructions were given in simple, clearly enunciated language. Have the child repeat instructions to you or demonstrate his understanding. Whenever possible give him a list to follow, like a pilot's checklist. Make sure that all homework assignments are written down and checked as completed. Whenever he is learning something complicated that can be pictured, diagrammed, or demonstrated, use visual material to help him in remembering.

At Home

If your child—
- does his homework assignments and studies for tests but gets poor marks
- seems confused about how he could improve his marks or the reasons for his poor grades

At School

If your child—
   does reading assignments but does not seem to understand the
      work when he gets to class
   has poor test scores despite an effort to do the work
he may be having difficulties in comprehending the reading material that
is being used in class.

He may need modified material on the same topic at a lower instructional level. If none is available, try to arrange to get a tape made of
the textbooks or, if necessary, tape the material yourself. Your child can
listen to the tape as he reads, and the simultaneous input of reading and
listening will improve his comprehension.

At Home

If your child—
   appears alert, intuitive, and interested in what is going on at
      home and in school, yet has poor achievement scores

At School

If your child—
   shows great discrepancy in performance between aptitude (in-
      telligence) and achievement, and seems not to be trying
he may have a good speaking vocabulary and good understanding of
spoken language, good intelligence, and a specific learning disability
that is interfering with achievement.

You can help your child by getting him the evaluation and remedial
help he needs. At home you can encourage learning through experience,
trips, demonstrations, and so on. Try to build the child's confidence
through his strengths and deemphasize the weaknesses.

At Home

If your child—
   seems to read adequately, but does not like to read
   will engage in any other activity to avoid reading

At School

If your child—
   just meets reading requirements but avoids any extra work
   often does not complete longer reading assignments
   cuts corners when doing a book report by reading the beginning,
      the end and a few paragraphs in the middle of the book

he probably has never learned to enjoy reading because he struggled so hard learning to read he was not able to read to learn or read for pleasure.

Read and discuss unusual, interesting articles with him. Give him books of cartoons, short stories, and magazines to encourage reading shorter materials for pleasure. If there is some special interest that "turns your child on," such as sports or rock music, try to find material in that area that will stimulate his interest. Try to see movies that have been turned into books or adapted from books, and encourage his reading of the book after seeing the movie. Most important, don't badger, threaten, or bribe him to read. Then let nature take its course.

At Home

If your child—
    will read what interests him but very slowly
    has difficulty keeping up with reading work at school

At School

If your child—
    seems to have difficulty in tests involving the answering of long
        complicated questions, but can do well on matching tests,
        true/false exams, or simply worded multiple-choice exams
he may be an extremely slow reader.

When highly motivated, he reads. However, schoolwork may be more difficult and less interesting to him. You can help him by composing some questions to answer when he reads an assignment so that he will know what to look for while reading. Sometimes it is helpful to show a slow reader how to make good use of the table of contents, chapter summaries, and index for shortcuts. Try to arrange for your child to be given extra time to complete long reading assignments, or tests requiring reading. The success he feels at school will be the key to future success in reading.

At Home and School

If your child—
    seems to take little or no initiative in school work
    has no academic goals despite good potential to learn
    has a negative attitude about school, himself in relation to school
he may have had so much previous frustration in learning situations that he no longer feels the value of the experience.

Try to find a better class or school situation if all else has failed. (See

Chapters 5 and 6.) Sometimes a year or two in the right private school can turn a child around from previous feelings about academic experience. If this is not possible, try to find alternative programs within your school system designed to motivate youngsters. Many schools have mini-schools and alternative work-study programs designed for youngsters who are not appropriately placed in the regular program.

Sometimes a strong personal interest can motivate a youngster and turn him or her on to learning once more. Such sports as skiing, bike-hostel trips, cross-country travel, Outward Bound programs, sailing programs, canoe trips, and so on, often give kids a new lease on life. This interest and the new enthusiasm it brings can feed success in peripheral areas. Sometimes a vocation will follow from one of these strong interests.

Case Study of a Hyperkinetic Child

Seven-year-old Mark was a delightful youngster, fair-haired, blue-eyed, with a pixie-like facial expression. Mark would wrinkle up that freckled pug nose and look at you with wide-eyed innocence as you mopped up the debris from his latest disaster. He was truly a bundle of joy and frustration to his parents and teachers. How could a youngster look so innocent and get into so much trouble all the time?

Mark was the first up in the morning and the last to go to sleep at night. He ate the least and ran the most in the whole Johnson family. By the time his parents brought him for diagnostic testing, Mark's mother seemed so nervous that she was verging on exhaustion.

Mark's short attention span, low tolerance of frustration, impulsive behavior, and irritability were very trying. "He's driving me crazy," said petite, vivacious Mrs. Johnson. "I get no rest, little sleep, and a lot of aggravation. He knows neither day or night; there are nights when the only reason Joe and I don't just let Mark put us to sleep is that we're afraid he might dream up some stunt while we're asleep and none of us would wake up in the morning!"

This wiry, well-coordinated seven-year-old was into everything within reach in our office. Distracting him from the touching, holding, or dismantling of toys was a full-time operation.

Youngsters like Mark are so driven to activity that they wear out the others around them. They are so short on attention span that they can wear out any teacher who tries to get them to complete just a fraction of the routine classroom assignments. They are impulsive, reacting to any stimuli in the surrounding environment, and distracting to themselves and their classmates because of their interruptions and attention-getting behavior.

"Mark is the world's greatest mess-maker," said his mother. "But in my rare moments of solitude, as I think about his behavior, I am convinced that he is a normally bright child and that something is interfering with his behavior."

Mark was referred for neurological and psychological testing, which suggested that he is a child of better than average intelligence on the Wechsler Intelligence Scale and that he exhibited symptoms of hyperkinetic behavior.

The Wechsler Intelligence Scale for Children (Revised Test) is a widely used individual test involving a number of subtests to gain a broad estimate of the general intelligence of a youngster. The testing consists of twelve subtests, divided into two subgroups categorized as skills of verbal proficiency and skills of performance. The subtests can be categorized in many ways to gain insights into the learning styles, strengths, and weaknesses of a youngster.

Children like Mark often are assisted through some kind of medical management. In Mark's case, a small amount of medication made him more teachable. It is paradoxical that the administration of stimulant drugs—such as dexedrine, methylphenidate, or Ritalin—are of such benefit in treating hyperkinetic children. Mark's sleep pattern improved and his family was able to spend a few hours of rest in the evening as Mark's highs and lows evened out.

Hyperkinetic behavior is characteristic only of approximately 2 percent of our school-age population, and these youngsters often respond well to a combination of medical management, diet supervision, or allergy treatment. Despite the lack of agreement among medical and psychiatric specialists, some of these youngsters show marked improvement in behavior control when they are placed on diets that eliminate food additives, salicylates, or refined sugars.

A youngster who is constantly in motion will not learn well in school. He will become a problem to himself and to the others around him; in turn, this will set up negative vibrations that may make him feel like a loser. Although his parents may be patient and accepting, the rest of the world will react to him with annoyance. He will come to feel like "Bad Mark" rather than "Good Mark," and he will not understand the reason why he feels this.

The child who experiences adult displeasure on an ongoing basis will blame himself. Many youngsters with school failure experiences learn to hate school. As we noted before, sociologist Christopher Jencks has suggested that the pattern of achievement or nonachievement is basically set by the sixth grade. To raise a winner, we must help youngsters feel like winners as early in their life as possible.

Specific Language Disability—Dyslexia

It has been said that a condition called primary dyslexia, or specific language disability, affects the learning of approximately 5 to 7 percent of school-age children. Dyslexia is thought to be a minimal form of neurological dysfunction that interferes with certain information processing within the brain. Although researchers are not in agreement as to whether or not dyslexia is related to cortical development or inner ear function, all agree on the kind of learning behaviors exhibited by the dyslexic youngster.

Such a youngster is usually male and has male relatives (such as father, uncle, cousin) who have had similar symptoms. One such youngster, Jerry, age eleven, was the third of his family to experience dyslexic symptoms. He had experienced some degree of hyperactivity in earlier years, but with medical management and diet control had calmed down considerably and was exhibiting less impulsive behavior, longer span of attention, and less distractible behavior. He was still exhibiting cerebral mixed dominance, that is, a mixed right and left performance in performing such tasks as writing, throwing, and kicking.

Jerry experienced a great deal of difficulty in handling any task that involved directionally related learning. His mother said he still didn't know his right from his left and showed continued difficulties with letter forms such as b and d, p and q. His spelling was poor, and when he read, he often transposed letters within words, reading was for saw, or won for now.

Youngsters who have dyslexic symptoms appear to have difficulties in handling learning dependent upon directional orientation or proper sequencing. Children exhibiting mixed cerebral dominance and left-handedness appear to have more of these problems. It is believed to be largely a result of rotation of visual images in messages passing between the left and right hemispheres of the brain. These children respond well to training that helps them focus upon learning through directional clues to compensate for their confusion.

When working on mathematics, Jerry would often start adding three columns of numbers from the left rather than the right, resulting in a wrong answer:

$\longrightarrow$		$\longleftarrow$
569	rather than	569
784		784
+593		+593
7418		1946

Directional-Related Learning Skills

Some youngsters experience ongoing difficulties in directional-related learning skills. These children often exhibit confusion in any kind of learning that is dependent upon right and left orientation. When they are very young, they often have difficulty in identifying right and left body parts. Later, this problem is demonstrated through confusion in following directions, sequencing steps in problem solving, or letter form rotation. The following is a list of some of the skills demanded in the classroom that might be affected by such problems. It is important to note that not every child will exhibit all the problems mentioned. However, there is a tendency to see them in groupings, and most youngsters with such a disability will have difficulty in more than half of these directionally associated learning skills. Since mastery of these tasks is a benchmark measure of success in school, they are extremely important.

Among the directional learning skills that may be delayed in youngsters experiencing primary dyslexia are the following:

1. Identification of right and left body parts.
2. Following directions involving right and left orientation.
3. Establishing body direction in space.
4. Identifying right and left parts on another person facing the child.
5. Identification of letter forms (e.g., b–d, p–q, m–w, n–u) that are rotations or inversions.
6. Identification and recall of number forms (e.g., 6–9).
7. Sequencing of letters after sighting them on a flashcard.
8. Sequencing of numbers after sighting them on a flashcard.
9. Recalling and writing a sequence of letters (spelling) after it is dictated.
10. Recalling and writing a sequence of numbers after it is dictated (e.g., teacher says, "279," child writes, "297").
11. Orienting oneself on a map (e.g., moves west instead of east).
12. Solving problems that involve a series of steps in a specific sequence.
13. Recalling information given in a series (e.g., following a group of instructions).
14. Comprehending three-dimensional problems described verbally (e.g., geometric theorems).
15. Solving three-dimensional problems without concrete objects to demonstrate or work on.
16. Understanding time-rate-distance problems in math.

17. Dealing with unknowns (revisualizing), moving placeholders in the early grades,

    e.g., $4 + 2 = \square$
    $4 + \square = 6$
    $\square + 2 = 6$

18. Understanding positive and negative numbers.
19. Understanding position on time lines in social studies.
20. Memorizing the correct spelling of a foreign language that is not phonetic.

All directional concepts should be taught to these youngsters through concrete tools, demonstration, experience, and emphasis of certain general rules.

The following suggestions are designed to help parents set certain guidelines when working on school-related activities with their children at home:

1. When working at home with your child in learning tasks, keep work periods short (20 minutes), regular (after dinner), and predictable (nightly with few exceptions).
2. Keep tasks simple, but insist upon completion.
3. If your child balks, be firm but gentle; try not to get angry or impatient. Don't allow the child to gain control of the situation through tantrums. If he does, don't overreact. After the tantrum or scene is over, go back to the tasks.
4. Keep the language of instructions simple (few words); demonstrate tasks rather than using too many words.
5. Be patient, allow your child to think through your instructions, but when you think he has had enough time and is ready to respond but may have trouble initiating the response, give him an alarm button command: "Ready! Go!"
6. It may be necessary to get the child physically into the task by moving his body into the operation, placing his hand on the paper, turning him toward the work, two hands on shoulders. This is also necessary when ending tasks; you may have to take the pencil off the paper, take it from the child, take him by the hand, and move him on to the next job.
7. Avoid threats (unless you plan to carry them out and they are reasonable). Avoid promises you can't keep. Avoid giving too many choices or give only two alternatives (when you feel the child is ready to make choices).
8. Use a quiet, authoritative tone of voice; give commands; try not

to formulate commands that sound like questions or your child will respond to your ambivalence by balking at the task.

9. Be sure your child looks at you when listening to instructions, repeats them aloud to you after they are given, and keeps his eyes involved in performing the task.

10. Try to anticipate the things that make your child resistant, such as children playing outside in hearing distance, a TV set on in the next room, hunger, fatigue, etc. These are not the times to work with him unless you can avoid the other stimuli competing for his attention.

11. Avoid uninteresting drill work. Repetition of a skill three or four times per session is enough. Boring drill will turn off your child.

12. Be consistent. If you insist upon something today, be sure to insist upon it tomorrow. If you change the ground rules, he will balk the next time you try to impose the same regulations.

13. Use an egg timer or cooking timer during work sessions to motivate performance within a time limit. Be realistic, though. Children who are overpressured will refuse to try. Encourage the child to beat his previous time for each task. Let him set the timer and turn it off.

14. Try to use the word "No" infrequently. If you use it too often, it will be meaningless to the child. When you do use it, stick by your decision, don't renege on it.

15. Try to teach your child to relax, breathe deeply, think about some interesting image. Some relaxing things to try are having the child sit down and think of a red balloon just over his head. Have him close his eyes and try to imagine the balloon floating in different directions. This is a great relaxation device prior to working.

16. Try to think about all the positive skills that your child has developed, not just the things he can't do. We tend to become so aware of learning "disabilities" that we often forget the learning "abilities." This will help you to enjoy your child more, relax and appreciate him.

17. Don't let your child be caught in conflicting demands from two parents. If you disagree, don't do it in front of him. Children learn to survive by playing one parent against the other in a situation like this and the parents are left fighting while the child leaves in confusion and guilt.

18. Love him, enjoy him, laugh with him, and play with him. It will help you to see your child as a person rather than a problem.

How You Can Help Your Child—At Home

There are many simple methods that can be utilized to assist a child to learn directional skills. One father coded his seven-year-old son's bicycle hand grips in red and green (green for right hand and red for left). He attached similarly colored streamers for additional emphasis. Another parent, whose youngster had difficulty handling the compass directions on a map, was taught to utilize a simple homemade direction finder. We suggested that his father cut out a rectangle of clear plastic overlay (using a page from a photo album). On this he drew the points of the compass, using an indelible magic marker. We suggested he fasten an arrow made of colored paper to the center of the rectangle so that it could be turned on the fastener to point in any direction on the rectangle. As the youngster looked for northwest on the map, he would point his direction finder between north and west and move along the map.

Simple techniques such as this help youngsters gain a better awareness of directional learning. The lack of these skills can be a handicapping condition for a child, contributing further to feelings of inadequacy and failure.

When we give parents suggestions for home-teaching techniques to assist youngsters to win at school, we often begin by setting up general guidelines. We have found that youngsters exhibiting difficulties in learning seem to need a structure for work done at home.

Learning-disabled youngsters often have difficulty filtering out excessive stimuli. When they do homework in the midst of family traffic, telephone and television noises, they cannot concentrate. Often relocating the homework place can do a child a world of good and lengthen his or her span of attention by decreasing distractions.

Frequently, learning-disabled youngsters overlook the visual clues that a more efficient learner marshalls up for recall and word identification. Color often enhances memory for words, patterns, and factual information. Write specific letter groups in color—this will help a youngster focus his attention on that letter group. Do this when teaching the groups or patterns in word families. Suppose your child is having difficulty learning the *ate* pattern in words like grate, mate, slate, plate. If you write the words in column, with the *ate* emphasized in red magic marker, the child's attention will focus on the specific part of the word he or she should notice. Use this approach in writing numbers, math facts, word patterns, factual information, letters within words that are difficult to spell, and any other information that needs emphasis. Poor memory leads to errors, and the child who makes many errors in class will feel less like a winner than his peers.

Research psychologists have emphasized that learning is predictably better when achieved through more than one channel. For example, a carpenter can tell you with words alone how to use a screwdriver, but the explanation would be difficult to follow. If he said, "Now, watch what I do. I take this in my right hand and making the tip of the screwdriver fit into the indentation on the head of the screw, I turn the handle in a clockwise direction," the observer would have to remember the words, revisualize what was done, and understand what "a clockwise direction" means. The best kind of learning would occur if use of the screwdriver were explained, demonstrated, and tried, all at the same time.

Hearing information is of limited value; hearing and seeing of more value; and hearing, seeing, and doing of the greatest value. Wherever a teaching operation can be turned into action, youngsters will learn best.

Informal teaching is best performed by parents. It is extremely difficult, if not impossible, to get a youngster to sit down at home to an experience that seems to be a repeat of school. Games teach many things. Youngsters learn visual perception, sequencing math, and lengthening span of attention through card games. Games with words—Bingo, Concentration, Spill and Spell, Numbers, and Triominoes—are all good teaching tools. It is important that the game be chosen carefully, for without the motivation to win, the child will lose interest, and if the game is too difficult, winning will be impossible. Games that teach have a secondary value as well; they help parent and child to relate in a different way, and just have fun together.

Youngsters who experience difficulty in learning seem better able to learn skills if you teach them in a sequential, step-by-step fashion. The less complicated parents can make any task, the easier it will be to learn. Something as simple as learning to set the table, or follow a recipe, must be simplified to its component parts. Something as difficult as the care and feeding of a cat can also be broken down in this fashion. The series of steps must be listed and repeated frequently to become a habit.

Most important in the parent's battery of tricks, however, is "success." If success is built into any instructional operation, the child will be willing to try more difficult tasks. But if "failure" becomes the name of the game, kids will balk, procrastinate, and avoid trying again. Often we have seen kids encouraged to learn something new, only to feel stupid and inadequate at the end of the experience. The child becomes angry at himself, says something that angers the parent, and a quarrel or temper tantrum follows; or the parent may expect too much from the child and the frustration leads to the same negative experience. Failure leads to failure, while success leads to success—which leads to winners.

Don't Be a "Guilty" Parent

An overpowering emotion that can interfere with constructive problem solving is the feeling of guilt. The experts tell us that a certain amount of guilt is normal and appropriate to responsible adulthood. However, profound feelings of guilt can be destructive, and usually are based on distorted perceptions of one's personal responsibility for one's child.

Parents seem to move through a series of predictable stages when they find that they have a youngster with problems. One mother of three learning-disabled youngsters told us that her initial feelings, upon confronting the problem, were those of shock and denial. She simply refused to believe that there was a problem. She said she had blamed the school, picked up, and moved to a town with the "best" program of readiness education. As the boys' educational problems persisted, she felt an enormous sense of isolation at having to face the problem alone. Her husband, a traveling executive for a major oil firm, could listen sympathetically for a few moments, but basically the round of frustrating school meetings was her sole responsibility.

She was unaware of the local parent action groups that were affiliated with the Association for Children with Learning Disabilties or the Orton Society.[5] "I felt as if I were facing these problems alone and I was often angry at my husband for not being available to help me."

The group support that comes from meeting and communicating with other parents who have experienced the same problems was denied her. She felt that school districts have a responsibility to tell parents about the associations and newsletters that are available to parents to broaden their understanding of their children's problems. "I never would have known about the Connecticut Association for Learning Disabled Children if another mother hadn't met me in the supermarket on a rather bad day and helped me to find a source of help," she added. "Not only that," she said, "but she gave me a source of local specialists she had obtained through the New York Orton Society. I never knew that there were so many professionals working to help parents and teachers understand more about learning disabilities until I went to one of their conferences. You know," she continued, "I really blamed myself for my kids' problems. I thought I was a rotten mother until I found out that many families have more than one child who experiences the problem and that it is very common in boys."[6]

Once the parents understand the causes of learning disabilities, they can handle the child's needs more realistically. Parents are the most important source of support for a youngster with problems, yet through neglect they are often the last to understand that problem.

State and local associations for children with learning disabilities have monthly newsletters to acquaint parents and teachers with educational developments, the law, children's rights, and other important issues.[7]

Schools should provide an important service for parents by holding workshops and meetings on educational topics, providing a reading library on learning disabilities, and sources of further information for parents. Parent education can make or break the most important link in the educational chain for the child with learning disabilities.

Identifying a Learning Disability

When a youngster has experienced ongoing difficulty during early school years, he often develops such a great fear of failure that he is no longer willing to try. The benefit of early identification and remediation cannot be emphasized enough. So much of what passes for poor adjustment, emotional disorders, and acting-out behavior in later school years is a result of earlier failure.

Nine-year-old Harry was referred to us for a severe reading problem. When tested, he was found to have learning difficulties in the following developmental areas:

Gross motor coordination: Harry was awkward and bumped into furniture wherever he went. His parents called him "klutzy and careless."

Fine motor coordination: When Harry handled anything involving fine motor movements, e.g., screwdriver or pliers, he had great difficulty.

Digital dexterity: Harry was clumsy with writing tools. He had extremely poor handwriting.

Visual memory for a sequence of symbols: Harry had difficulty recalling words dependent upon letter configuration.

Visual memory to writing: Harry had difficulty recalling spelling or sight words through the traditional writing mode of learning.

Auditory memory to writing: Harry had difficulty making a consistent correlation between sounds and symbols in sequence.

Harry is a bright, average youngster, with a better than average ability in expressive and receptive (listening) vocabulary and math concepts. Yet he was scoring at a grade 1 level in reading and could not be scored at all in spelling skills. He was truly a youngster with a diagnosable learning disability.

Boy-Girl Bias—Fact or Fancy

Learning disabilities appear to occur four times more frequently in boys than in girls. This estimate is complicated by the fact that boys mature later than girls in certain areas of development. Unfortunately, the expectations characteristic of early grade classrooms in a traditional school setting involve largely the skills that girls develop earlier than boys.

It has been suggested that expectations during the early school years appear to be a form of "conspiracy" against boys. In the early school years, children concentrate on reading and writing skills that largely favor girls. As a result, boys fill remedial reading classes, don't learn to spell, and are classified as dyslexic or learning-disabled four times as often as girls.[8] It has been estimated that hyperactivity is nine times more prevalent among boys than among girls, and that 8 to 10 percent of the school population is presently under medication. This leads one to question whether or not the behavior of many so-called hyperkinetic boys has been properly diagnosed or is just mislabeled because of boys' greater nuisance value at an early age to teachers, administrators, and parents.

Much of what passes for learning disability may in fact be caused by systems that are not cognizant of the basic biological differences among boys and girls. At present it seems that our schools misuse some of the abilities of boys, by encouraging sedentary activities rather than gross motor learning activities, and written testing rather than performance testing. Moreover, they fail to develop some of the girls' skills in later years as well. Girls are neither encouraged nor properly taught to enter fields such as advanced mathematics or physical sciences, despite their aptitudes.

Parents should be wary about glib recommendations made by educators that pertain to the medical management of youngsters' behavior and activity levels. They should be equally skeptical of suggestions made by guidance or vocational counselors unless underwritten by test data.

Always go to meetings prepared to ask questions. Carry an appropriate list of questions with you and insist upon a response to your inquiries.

Checklist of Questions about Services for the Learning-Disabled Child

1. What kind of services are available for my child in the classroom, special resource room, reading or math learning center, or in counseling?

2. How often will my child get help (once a day, once a week)?
3. What kind of training have the teachers and teacher aides who will work with my child had?
4. Will my child be out of his regular class to get help? If so, how long will he spend out of class and what subjects will he miss?
5. What is the physical setup of the special remedial or resource class? (We have seen resource rooms in school basements next to the furnace room, coat closets without even a coat of paint, or former storerooms that are cold and drafty.)
6. What testing procedures will you use before placing my child in a special program? (We have also seen children being placed in classes for mentally handicapped, emotionally disturbed, or neurologically impaired children without parents being appraised of diagnostic techniques or specific findings.)
7. Has an Individual Educational Plan been set up for my child? If so, ask for a copy. If not, why not?
8. How often will my child be reevaluated?
9. How often will I get reports on my child's progress?
10. Will my child's work in the regular classroom be modified? If so, how? If not, why not?
11. If my child will be in a special class, or remedial class, what kind of problems do the other children exhibit? Are their problems the same as my child's or different?
12. Is this placement the "least restrictive environment" for my child?
13. When will the next conference for reevaluating progress be scheduled?
14. If I do not agree with your plan for my child and wish to get a private evaluation or consulting opinion, will the school district pay for that evaluation?
15. What are my legal rights of appeal if I do not agree with your educational plan for my child?

Obtaining an Individual Educational Plan for Your Child

Schools, like the individuals who run them, often develop complacent habits that become ingrained because "We've always done it that way." Just because all so-called disruptive youngsters previously have been placed on Ritalin does not mean it is equally appropriate for your child. Just because poor readers are referred to vocational classes doesn't mean it is the right place for your child.

After your child has had some testing, a meeting should be scheduled to explain findings and an educational plan worked out. Often reports and individual educational plans include the use of jargon and complicated language. We have listed a few of the most common terms and tried to describe these phrases in practical language for the understanding of parents and nonprofessionals.

Let us suppose that your child's report includes the following:

Diagnosis	What It Means in Practical Terms	Suggestions
1. Short span of attention	He has trouble concentrating, moves about a good deal, is often out of seat.	He needs many opportunities to engage in active play and learning through movement.
2. Distractible	He has trouble finishing school tasks, staying with a job in noisy, busy surroundings.	Give little rewards for job completion. Make sure homework is done in a quiet place.
3. Inappropriate behavior	The child appears to say and do things that seem immature and seem out of place.	Explain how certain kinds of comments affect others, in a quiet, calm voice. Ask child how he/she would feel if someone said or did that to him.
4. Visual to motor problem	The child often exhibits poor handwriting, or has trouble in sports, hitting or catching the ball.	Use finger paints at home, coloring within lines, drawing by numbers, any games that encourage aim and eye-hand coordination.
5. Visual perception	The child does not always understand what he sees. He may mix up letters such as b–p–d, u–n, m–w; or he may say "was" for "saw," "spot" for "stop." He may appear to be guessing at words.	Don't criticize the child for these errors. Try to show him/her ways of remembering the difference between similar letters and words by color, form, or tracing.

Diagnosis	What It Means in Practical Terms	Suggestions
6. Auditory perception	The child has difficulty in thinking of a sound whenever he/she sees a certain letter. He/she appears to be guessing at words, rather than sounding them out.	Practice rhyming games. Make letter book. Cut pictures from magazines for sounds. Focus upon initial, median, and final sounds in spelling.
7. Auditory memory	Child appears to be forgetful. Instructions need simplification and repetition. Child forgets information, needs constant reminders about chores, time schedules, homework.	Write things down when saying them. Have child repeat all instructions at least once. Give instructions one step at a time or demonstrate step by step. "Prime the pump" by starting child off at chore, assignment.
8. Visual memory	Child may be forgetful of what he sees. Misplaces things constantly, loses way in halls, easily confused. May be a very poor speller, have poor comprehension at reading.	Always explain things when showing them; thus the child hears while watching. Spelling is best taught through linguistics, word families; avoid memorization of sight words through visual channel. Have the child try simultaneous oral spelling while writing his words. Encourage revisualization skills. Encourage visual memory and concentration games.
9. Difficulty in math concepts	Child has problems when reading a math problem and deciding what to do. Difficulty with such operations as measure-	Illustrate or demonstrate all new problems. Use rulers, number lines, paper plates, etc., as concrete demonstrations of concepts.

Diagnosis	What It Means in Practical Terms	Suggestions
	ment, division, fractions, decimals, and percentages.	Use concrete operational teaching methods, such as finger math for multiplication, times tables, calculators. Use plastic or paper fractions, number rods, money, poker chips.
10. Difficulty in computational math	Child has trouble recalling addition, subtraction, multiplication, or division facts. Child may have difficulty putting numbers in columns.	Use motor math, finger math, techniques using all senses for learning facts, and turn lined paper sideways or use graph paper for all math.

Many parents are concerned with the reasons why their children are experiencing so much difficulty in learning. However, it is important not to exaggerate a problem out of perspective and wear a child's problem as an emblem of distress. Parents can become so preoccupied with the problem that they lose sight of the child's strengths and focus only on the weaknesses.

What Causes Learning Problems?

It is often quite difficult to determine exactly what has caused a child's problems. It takes medical, psychological, and educational testing, and even then experts can disagree. It is generally believed that most learning problems are a result of the following:

A. Developmental lags
B. Physiological causes
    (1) Neurological dysfunction
    (2) Biochemical dysfunction
C. Environmental deprivation
D. Poor adjustment
E. Inappropriate teaching methods

When dealing with causation, it is important to investigate the cause only so far as it helps us decide on treatment. When it is determined that a child is experiencing maturational lags he should be in a combined program that helps teach the missing skills and takes the pressure off him until the "missing stitches" of maturation can be taken up and woven back into the fabric of his learning.

When the causes appear to be physiological in nature, a medical team must decide on the best course of action in setting up a program of medical management, dietary control, and educational support. Any one therapy without the other may prove to be a hit-or-miss affair. A child whose distractibility, activity, and attention span make learning impossible needs assistance in filtering out the interfering stimuli. No amount of teaching or tutoring will bring change in the learning pattern of such a child if his biochemistry interferes.

The child exhibiting neurological dysfunction and accompanying problems of disordered thinking may need special class placement, or a resource room program, or referral to a special school to bring about the desired therapy. Such youngsters also need medical management and the same kind of teaching approaches mentioned above.

When neurologists refer to a youngster exhibiting a minimal problem, they usually speak of "soft signs." Most youngsters diagnosed as having neurologically based learning disabilities are in this category. Among the so-called soft signs are such symptoms as delayed or incomplete establishment of dominance, and inability to establish preference in the choice of eye, hand, or foot. There may be slight differences in reflex response on the right or left sides of the body, or even fine and gross motor difficulties. Early hyperactivity, poor impulse control, distractibility, and moody behavior are often evident. Early identification and remediation is the most important solution. Unfortunately, when identified late, such problems often masquerade as emotional disturbance or personality disorder.

To Learn in School a Child Must Be Ready, Willing, and Able

Another type of a learning problem can be caused by environmental deprivation, which usually is responsive to compensatory intervention early on through Headstart, or later through Title 1 Services. These services, provided to the schools under federally funded Title 1 programs, are normally designed to assist economically disadvantaged youngsters in any district, where the parents may not be able to provide some of the educational nurture and readiness activities basic to learning.

The earlier these programs are begun, the better is the result. The Levenstein mother-child program mentioned before, and others going into the home, have met with great success. Parents must involve themselves to whatever degree they can in assisting their children. However, they cannot give appropriate help without professional direction supplied by the school. Many Title 1 programs include additional programs or workshops for parents and teachers to help them gain insight into their children's problems and how to alleviate them.

The Vulnerable Child

When a child exhibits poor adjustment he usually is a candidate for counseling. Such counseling is best undertaken with other members of his family, if that seems appropriate. Sometimes parents and children get fixed into certain patterns of stimulus and response, like our young "plunger" in Chapter 2. When a trained observer clearly identifies a family reaction pattern that is harming a child, practicing new kinds of communication can often cause a marked behavioral change in the whole family. Kids become conditioned to react in certain ways to survive stress. If the stress is removed and the behavior identified, and the family group is willing to practice new ways of relating to each other, much improvement can result.

Educationally Caused Learning Disabilities

Often children seem to absorb information largely through one channel of learning, despite efforts to teach them in a variety of ways. Kids may learn best through seeing words on a printed page, or hearing words spoken or read to them, or by having something demonstrated concretely and then doing it.

When an educational system utilizes methods that don't encourage learning through the child's strongest mode, the child is deprived of his or her right to learn with ease. Frequently, this results in failure and frustration for kids. Such failure and frustration can turn your child into a loser.

As one twenty-three-year-old dropout told us on his return to our office for educational help to raise himself above a fifth-grade reading level: "My learning problems may make me learning-disabled, but society has made me handicapped." Whether or not a child has a handicap becomes largely a question of attitude.

Triumphing over Disabilities

Many of the lives of famous people have been punctuated by obstacles that did not become life-long handicaps—they were overcome or compensated for. One such story is that of Louis Braille, a visually impaired individual who refused to allow his blindness to become a handicap. Braille experienced the loss of his eyesight at the age of three. Adapting a system invented by Charles Barbier, using raised dots and dashes to send messages at night from the French battlefield, he invented the Braille system presently used as the primary method of teaching reading to the blind. Having been deprived of one sensory input system, visual learning, Braille used another system, that of tactile learning, to compensate.

Nor was Braille an exception; many learning-disabled people have done useful things with their lives. Among them are President Woodrow Wilson and Vice President Nelson Rockefeller, dyslexics who learned to read late in their school careers; British Prime Minister Winston Churchill, a hyperactive youngster who was noted for his fearless, out-of-bounds activities during his growing-up years; and Albert Einstein, world-renowned physicist and mathematician, who was considered slow by his teachers, due to late development of language skills. Even Thomas Alva Edison was considered eccentric or "addled" by his teachers.

Given the incentive to take the initiative, function independently, express himself freely, and gain the self-confidence to take a risk and make a decision, the learning-disabled person can not only master his handicap but broaden his experience through it. Home is a learning place—and a place in which the "winners of the future" can be nurtured.

Appendix 2 contains further information about educational facilities for older children with learning difficulties.

CHAPTER

8

◆

Your "Burden of Great Potential"—The Gifted Child

"Capacities clamor to be, and cease their clamor only when they are well used," said Abraham Maslow, a well-known psychologist, in describing the relentless drive of talent and creativity in those who are gifted. Gifted children generally are viewed by educators as youngsters who have very high orders of talents and capabilities—capabilities on which the children rank up in the top 5 percent or 3 percent of the population.

If you should have a gifted or near-gifted child, you'll see many signs of that "clamor" cited by Dr. Maslow. You will also want to have the child make the most of those rare gifts, through efforts of yours in the home and of the child's teachers and schools. This chapter tells how you and the schools can meet such a challenge.

Gifted Kids: A Challenge and a Frustration

It is a formidable challenge. Like all kids, gifted children must be given a chance to act like children and to master the three Rs; but they need much much more. They need to be taught through a curriculum so enriched that they do not become bogged down in busy work or boredom.

165

Unfortunately, gifted youngsters do not always endear themselves to those with whom they must live and work in their earlier years.

. . . Which parent among us is patient enough to enjoy having a teenager who disagrees with everything he says?

. . . Which ten-year-old enjoys having a precocious younger sibling who can add, subtract, multiply, and learn everything faster than he can?

. . . Which class of schoolchildren will be receptive to the "little professor" among them who tries to beat everyone to the draw, answers every question, barges in with his comments, knows it all, and is lacking in social awareness?

. . . Which teacher looks lovingly at the twelve year old who does not hesitate to correct her errors in front of the class and causes embarrassment for her?

. . . Which administrator is enthusiastic about disciplining youngsters who have little respect for established tradition or pat answers, and are unpredictable, enterprising, and challenging?

These kids often defy our patience and fortitude. They are difficult to identify, hard to understand, and unpredictable to manage; and they are gifted!

Behavioral Characteristics of Gifted Children

Phrases like "dogged persistence," "a high tolerance for frustration," and "shy, withdrawn, and lonely," were used to describe such historic *Wunderkinder* as Wilbur and Orville Wright, Henry Ford, and Albert Einstein. Other outstanding personalities were even described as "addled" and "dull and stupid."

The life of Winston Churchill exemplifies that of the gifted hyperactive youngster. Young Winston's outrageous exploits were usually without consideration of safety or consequences. Each day at Blenheim, a servant was assigned to shadow Winston to avoid catastrophe. The servants drew lots in the kitchen every morning to decide who would fall victim to this dubious honor.

What is it like to live with a gifted child? Often the child's gift masquerades as an enigmatic sort of behavior, and no two children are exactly alike. Any two gifted children may be alike in some ways and different in others.

Gifted Behavior Defined

Since outward behavior often obscures the gifted personality from immediate recognition, how are we to identify this "diamond" from the rough-cut stone?

"Gifted and talented children are those . . . who, by virtue of outstanding abilities, are capable of high performance. These are children who require differentiated programs and/or services beyond those normally provided by the regular school program in order to realize their contribution to self and society."[1]

These children usually demonstrate achievement scores in the top 3 percent on standardized testing and superior potential in any of the areas described below.

Gifted Performance is suggested by:

High IQ

. . . General intellectual ability as shown in an IQ measure of approximately 130 points or higher. Group intelligence testing, however, is far less accurate than scores received on an individual IQ test. (See section on testing, Chapter 9, for further information.)

A Special Aptitude

. . . Indication of a special academic aptitude, a particular skill that has been mastered at least two years above grade placement. A youngster with a superior math skill, extremely high reading aptitude, or science skills that measure far above expectations may be a gifted youngster despite poor performance in another academic area.

Creative and Inventive Thinking

. . . Youngsters who exhibit highly creative or productive thinking. The child may be project-oriented, constantly rebuilding machines, clocks, radios, or other mechanical and electronic gear. He/she may be a gifted youngster despite poor academic achievement.

Demonstrated Leadership

. . . The youngster who exhibits leadership qualities among his/her peers may be a gifted youngster. These children seem to gather their friends about them like the proverbial honey pot. They are always coming up with innovations, challenging projects, and unsettling ideas.

Strong Talent in Performing Arts

. . . Youngsters who excel in the visual or performing arts express a gift to be nurtured. Each budding painter, photographer, musician, or actor expresses creativity in a different way. Each has a unique view of the world and a message to be heard.

No gifted child exhibits all of these qualities; however, any one or more of them certainly places a child in the category of the gifted.

Standardized testing, as it is presently designed, does not examine perseverance, creativity, motivation, or the ability to make appropriate value judgments. Moreover, although many generations of our children have been tested repeatedly on various kinds of aptitude and intelligence tests, we still do not have any accurate scientific definition of what is actually being measured in these tests.

The testing measures school-related performance, the ability to handle the testing situation, and reading level; but this leaves the measure of social perception, judgment, and other performance skills unknown.

Some characteristics of children make specific individuals extremely poor candidates for good performance on testing despite their extremely high aptitudes. Hyperactive youngsters, those with reading problems, or youngsters with specific areas of poor learning skills may show evidence of poor aptitude or achievement on standardized testing and still be gifted and talented. The fact that a youngster is in the range of the gifted does not preclude the possibility of his having a learning-disability problem, poor concentration, or a specific skill lag. Unfortunately, poor methods of identification, and subsequent educational neglect or ignorance concerning the capabilities of the gifted, deprive these youngsters of their educational birthright. The poor education of the gifted is one of the "little murders" of our system. Once more it is up to the parents to bring their child's talents and needs to the attention of the schools.

How Some Gifted Kids Go Unrecognized

Jason, a fourteen-year-old exhibiting great musical and performing talent, was the star of every school performance. An articulate youngster of superior aptitude, he was an underachiever in the regular school program. He might have gone unnoticed had it not been for the keen insight of an eighth-grade teacher who recommended his placement in an alternative mini-school for such youngsters. Certainly, Jason's marks were no measure of his potential, for he barely scraped by with C's and C—'s from year to year. But the new placement was the road to academic success. The small teacher/student ratio approach to learning and individualization paid off, and his marks began to reflect the kind of achievement this youngster deserved.

Josh had an extremely high aptitude in math, yet classroom exam scores never showed the extent of his superior ability. Simple memory problems kept him from memorizing multiplication and division facts, and he was almost denied admission to ninth-grade algebra because of this one flaw. With special arrangements he was made a conditional student in algebra, going on to advanced calculus under the same system. When Josh took the College Entrance Exams (untimed), he spent a few minutes drawing up a 10 by 10 multiplication table, notifying a proctor that he was doing so. He had a math aptitude score that was second highest in his school when compared with the other youngsters taking that test.

From time to time, "teen tycoons" may turn up in a variety of endeavors that are not the traditionally noted areas of gifted performance or creativity. Young entrepreneurs "make it" through the system as winners because they take good ideas and have the "chutzpah" to take a risk and make it work. Brad Pelo, third eldest child in a family of ten, said: "I made up my mind [at sixteen] that I was never going to be the normal middle-class American person."[2] He took the skills in the use of audio-visual equipment learned in an eighth-grade class and turned them into a corporate service for builders and construction companies, earning him an average of $3,000 to $5,000 a month.

Two brothers, Daniel and Michael Barr, were recently denied permission to set up a securities investment partnership during their summer vacations because they were both under eighteen and could not be legally bound by any contract they entered into. When they appealed the decision, the maturity shown by the two young men was commended by the judge, who said that they showed a "sophistication and knowledge rarely possessed by their parents at a comparable age." Such are the gifts of teenage tycoons. They show remarkable ability to build, create, take risks, and make decisions at an age when their peers are throwing a baseball or a Frisbee around.

When interviewed, these teen tycoons seem optimistic about the future of the American economic system, and their own futures as well. They see opportunities as challenges to be met, not problems to be avoided. They enjoy hard work and have a gift for making positive judgments about themselves. They take responsibility for themselves and their lives early. Such kids are winners in the very broadest sense. They have the creative gift to make something where nothing existed before. Though not considered gifted in the traditional academic mode of success, they find other avenues to explore.

Andy was an eleven-year-old who appeared quiet, withdrawn, and lonely. Attending a well-known private school, he showed little or no interest in sports, social activities, or academics, but just plugged along in his own quiet way. Worried by his shyness and social immaturity, his parents sought psychological counseling for him to help him deal with his "problems." Andy's interests were in the area of mechanical operations, and the only real friend he had made at school was the maintenance engineer who kept the furnaces, air conditioning, and general equipment in good order. Andy would spend lunch hour, recess, and afterschool time following the patient Mr. Barrows around the school grounds in search of projects. When the teaching team conference was held on Andy, his academic reports were poor, and comments of "lazy," "disinterested," "withdrawn," and "apathetic" were heard. Omitted from the report were the words of Mr. Barrows. He might have said: "This young fella has a fine understanding of the way things work and does all kind of repair jobs for me."

It wasn't until the afternoon the air compressor broke down and the students couldn't have physical education classes in the indoor inflated gym balloon that Andy's unheralded talents became obvious. Andy spent the lunch hour with Mr. Barrows at the machine, fiddling with dials and hoses. Finally, after a lot of trial and error, Andy made a suggestion that led Mr. Barrows to the solution of the problem. He reported it to the headmaster and quiet, "lazy" Andy was the hero of the day!

The new recognition had a strange effect upon his position in school. The teachers began to look for things to give Andy to do that involved mechanical problem solving. Even the adjectives they used in their reports were modified to meet his new image.

Gifted Kids—Often the Victims of a Negative Self-Fulfilling Prophecy

With Andy, expectations played an enormous role in affecting the success-failure equation and tipping the balance to success. Once Andy's strengths were recognized, his teachers bent over backward to meet his needs and emphasize his successes. What if the air compressor had not broken down? How long would Andy have gone unnoticed? Like Tommy Irwin, mentioned in Chapter 6, the school testing had not discerned Andy's excellence.

In a study made about fifteen years ago, psychologists Robert Rosenthal and Lenore Jacobson found that teachers' expectations of kids are affected by what the teachers are told about the youngsters' aptitudes. Having been given information about their students that suggested that some were (high aptitude) "winners" and some were (low aptitude) "losers," the teachers were given free rein for the school year. At the end of the year, testing confirmed the fact that the so-called winners had made marked gains in contrast to the identified "losers." Actually, the students had been randomly designated winners and losers. This suggests that teachers help kids become what they expect them to become— winners or losers.

We have seen that teacher attitude is the single most important variable in predicting the way youngsters will feel about their performance in school. The success-failure ratio is a direct result of the child's attitude concerning him- or herself in the early years. Although other factors such as basic aptitude, economic status, home enrichment, parental attitude, and materials used are extremely important, the attitude of the teacher seems to be the most significant factor in a child's early progress.

Teachers who set goals, make realistic demands, and insist upon standards gain kids' respect and help them feel that they are good enough to meet these expectations. This is especially helpful to gifted youngsters. Left to their own devices, they may excel and find constructive outlets for their creative energy—or they may fail.

When youngsters are surrounded by other creative and challenging peers, they often sharpen their skills and respond well to the interplay of minds. This may mean that gifted youngsters need to be placed in school programs designed to meet their needs.

Many school systems have introduced programs for the gifted. Most of the impetus for setting up these programs came from concerned parents and enlightened administrators. The child who is recognized as slightly different may need to be educated differently. We have worked with many youngsters who were gifted but had not been recognized as such by their school. Often, they exhibited "deviant behavior," which suggested they were not the compliant, easy-to-manage youngsters that teachers may prefer. These youngsters were frequently restless in class, bored at traditional workbook demands, impulsive, demanding a good deal of attention, and generally "a pain in the neck" to the teacher. A few of them simply withdrew from the classroom scene by burying their noses in a book.

Davy, at age eight, was a nonreader with a severe speech impediment. He was generally immature, restless, distractible, and difficult to manage in class. After three years of tutorial work for specific language disability problems, this gifted youngster was reading two years above grade level and could handle most other demands of the classroom except for handwriting and spelling. The homework and worksheets of the sixth grade bored him, so he rushed through them impatiently to get back to the latest engrossing book borrowed from his father's library. Davy was criticized by the teachers for having his nose buried in a book, the wrong book, even though the level of the material was far beyond the work level of the class. He saw the humor in this paradoxical situation, saying: "In second grade the teacher used to tell me that I wasn't able to read because I never read; now in sixth grade the teacher complains because I read too much. I can't win!"

Entering a special mini-school for unique learners in grade seven, Davy rose to leadership like the cream in milk; he was the class president in the seventh grade, and winner of the science award at the end of the eighth grade.

Davy's former teachers were amazed at his "improved attitude," growth, and maturity. They were surprised at his improved grades. Though his measured IQ on an individual Wechsler (Wisc) proved to be over 140, on the previous school aptitude tests, Davy had barely measured in the range of normal (90–110). There was a good deal of backpatting and chest thumping in Davy's high school when he went on to win a Westinghouse Science Talent award a few years later. His early grade teachers were still surprised—they never dreamed he was so gifted. Davy was a victim of the built-in bias so often held by those who work with children. If the expert has not recognized the youngster's talent, he or she acts amazed when that youngster succeeds.

As the study we mentioned before suggests, when educators become bound by their own preconceived notions concerning a child's aptitude, that child may fall victim to a negative self-fulfilling prophecy. The child accepts the expectations of others as accurate and so thinks less of himself. Children often apply the expectations of others to themselves. They may work to achieve what they have been taught to expect. They may wish to "win" but work to "lose," because others expect them to lose. These limiting expectations impose restrictive boundaries to their lives and their performance.

"The fortunate person is the one who has learned that what s/he wants and what s/he expects are one and the same thing. That person will actively pursue success in school and job. That person will seek out positive payoffs."[3] The person who does not seek positive payoffs may narrow his or her achievement options and limit the chances to feel like a winner.

Gifted youngsters come in a variety of shapes, sizes, and colors. No one ethnic or racial group has a monopoly on producing creative minds. Gifted youngsters also exhibit a variety of behaviors, and some are not those that fit the stereotyped pattern expected of winners.

Some gifted children are shy and withdrawn, preferring to be alone rather than indulge in the behaviors and activities of their peer group. Many of these children don't care for group athletic games, the boy-girl social world considered "in," or the usual status activities of teenagers.

Other gifted youngsters show confidence and outgoing behavior early, and may demonstrate enormous drive and leadership from their very first day in school. Psychologists tell us that class members can select the future winners and losers from their group by the end of the first month in the first grade. Surprisingly enough, their predictions of success/failure are extremely accurate. The confident, outgoing youngster who shines from the center of his first-grade world is probably a gifted child, with advanced social and verbal skills, to whom the others turn for leadership and who they choose to select as a winner.

But not every gifted youngster will show high achievement from the earliest day in school. Davy, a superior youngster, had speech and reading problems due to a developmental problem. Josh exhibited problems in handling tasks demanding rote memory, despite superior skills in mathematics reasoning. Jason was an underachieving youngster, who only "turned on" to school when he was placed in an alternate environment that gave him more latitude than the traditional program to create through the performing arts. Despite similar difficulties, all of these youngsters are gifted in different ways.

The Signs of a Gifted Child

Parents are often the first observers to identify their gifted child. They need the appropriate information and tools to make such observations, however, and the know-how to encourage the talents exhibited by their children.

Precocity is often shown in the early development of speech. Gifted youngsters frequently develop a full sentence vocabulary quite early, and they are quick to incorporate difficult multisyllabic words into their vocabulary. Some precocious children actually "coin" words they haven't heard before or are capable of sophisticated and original punning at a very early age. The articulate, highly verbal toddler amuses and amazes those around him with his ability to design colorful descriptive phrases. One precocious four-year-old described the shoreline as "the place that the water comes up to." Another astute six-year-old, on being given a full-scale individual Wechsler Intelligence Test, was asked "whether it was better to give money to an organized charity or to a person begging on the street." He replied: "To an organized charity because you can deduct it on your income tax!"

Many children who are advanced in the development of speech will become extremely curious about the printed word and, barring any early perceptual deficiency (see Chapter 7 on learning difficulties), will start to teach themselves to read. Educators often discourage parents from teaching their youngsters reading before they attend school. The classic argument against preschoolers reading is that these children might become bored in the typical first-grade program. However, if early success is the keynote underlying teacher and child expectations, early reading skills represent "money in the bank" for some youngsters. They can excel early, advance rapidly, and develop a strong sense of positive feedback that will stand them in good stead during their remaining years in school.

Many gifted children show a marked interest in how things work, asking a multitude of questions wherever and whenever they are exposed to a new problem. How tragic when parents feel so battered by such questions that they either ignore the child or tell him to "shut up and stop asking so many questions." A golden opportunity to explore is lost forever. Furthermore, once ignored or put down, kids may feel that their questions are unimportant and that they themselves are insignificant as people. If they are too often hurt and humiliated, they may never ask again. The youngster who keeps asking for information needs answers, and parents are often the closest and most available source for help and enlightenment.

The child who is able to focus his or her attention, concentrate, and stay with a task for long periods of time may be a gifted youngster. The ability to complete tasks and not give up in frustration is often a sign of a superior youngster. However, one who is medically hyperkinetic may not show this ability to focus attention in the early years, but only develop it later. A world-famous medical researcher of our acquaintance claims he did not overcome his hyperkinetic behavior until the third year of high school. Without a required stint in the Army, he feels, he probably would not have matured enough to handle medical school!

A high level of creativity and a sophisticated sense of humor are often seen in the gifted child. Of course, to a parent, the situations this humor causes are not always considered "humorous." One father we know suspected the scientific talent of his son when one morning while brushing his teeth, his entire mouth turned royal blue in color! After a shocking few moments confronting the mirror, he knocked vigorously at nine-year-old Billy's bedroom door. A sleepy, pajama-clad towhead crept out into the hall. Glimpsing his father's face, he said: "Oh, Dad, I forgot to tell you about my experiments with the blue vegetable dye." Billy had been experimenting and inadvertently left the newly dyed toothpaste in the bathroom for the family to use—Father was the first to take the "Blue Dye Crest Test"! We'd like to be able to tell you that Billy went on to win the Nobel Prize for Chemistry and all was forgiven. However, that wouldn't quite be the truth. Nonetheless, Billy is a pre-med in college these days and the blue has finally worn off his father's teeth.

Such troublesome acts often lead us to conclude that a child is mischievous or difficult to manage, when actually they are the products of an inquiring but undisciplined mind. Parents need to be on guard against the error of making a snap judgment about their children. To be comfortable in parenthood, one needs to develop the sixth sense: a sense of humor.

Youngsters who are able to perform tasks involving advanced reasoning and are quick at concept formation are often gifted. Kids like these can function as a sharp thorn in the side of a math or science teacher. They are extremely inquisitive, asking more than the usual number of questions of those around them. The youngster who defined a plumbline as a "line with a top at the bottom" was exhibiting his ability to conceptualize three-dimensionally. While his father was doing the necessary mathematical computation to find the exact center of a square cut from flooring in order to drop a center pole for a circular staircase, this nine-year-old took two pieces of scrapwood, crossed them in the center, and located the midpoint quite easily. Many youngsters have the gift of three-dimensional conceptualization. They can demonstrate the meaning of words through practical, understandable illustrations long before another individual could explain them verbally.

Gifted children learn to process information very early in their lives. Their power of information assimilation often surprises us. Given this talent, they often exhibit the ability to solve problems at an extremely difficult level; this ability and their initiative often set them apart from other youngsters of their own age. Yet they are still children and need all of the tender loving care (and chicken soup) required by all children.

They also often demand more patience of us—and that patience may be sorely tested. Billy's father may have been quoted as saying some unquotable things after he took Billy's "Blue Dye Crest Test"; however, he kept his cool, or so he tells us now!

The energy level and degree of imagination that these youngsters demonstrate can tax us to our limits. Terry, a budding nine-year-old chemist, while experimenting with powder taken from firecrackers nearly sent her seven-year-old brother Bud skyrocketing into space. She was simply unaware of the danger and had been left unsupervised. Fortunately, that experience was not destructive, and Terry was thereafter limited to experimenting while her parents supervised. She was also told to check with them before attempting to mix unknown chemicals. Just because a child shows superior intelligence or aptitude in a specific area does not mean that she has a superior awareness of potential danger. There is no predictable correlation between maturity, intelligence, and common sense!

When a child performs well academically, it is relatively easy to evaluate that child as "gifted." High achievement is the most obvious performance criterion and the easiest to recognize. Generally, schools use a performance level of two or more years above the chronological age expectation (or grade expectation) as a criterion of superior performance. Thus, the superior math student, the exceptional reader, the child who excels in science may be such a student.

What to Do if a Gifted Child's Talents Are Unrecognized

Unfortunately, many gifted youngsters do not show superiority in academic subjects for a variety of reasons, some already discussed in this chapter. The child who experiences a perceptual or speech problem, like Davy, may elude early identification. The "math whiz" may be kept from advanced math classes because of a simple memory problem, like Josh. Even Jason, the articulate musical young man, hid his light under a bushel of plain boredom. If your child is like one of these, his superior qualities may be lost if he or she is placed in the wrong school situation, gets negative feedback, or is generally misunderstood.

Parents must bear the responsibility of getting special attention and class placement for their child, either within the public school setting or in an appropriate private school. A simple modification of the curriculum to include more advanced reading, math, or special project activities may not be enough. With gifted youngsters, the quality of teaching and the depth to which a subject is taught are all-important. Two reference studies that will prove helpful to parents and teachers alike are *Teaching Clever Children,* by N. R. Tempest[4] and *Teaching the Gifted and Talented* by Marsha M. Correll.[5] Both studies suggest that gifted children must have special help and direction. This, in turn, means that the teacher must have special training and resources at his or her disposal. "Minds, like parachutes, do not work unless fully opened," according to a New England folk saying. The gifted mind is a national resource that needs nurture of a highly specific kind.

The federal government's Office of the Gifted and Talented estimates that *only 4 percent* of the nation's 2.5 million gifted youngsters are getting appropriate education. This tragic waste of potential is confirmed by a top-level official in the New York State Department of Education, who says that "few teachers are trained in gifted education and most of the programs leave much to be desired." One school administrator was quoted as telling a bright youngster that he was "no better than anyone else, just luckier." This same youngster at the age of sixteen was the youngest freshman admitted by an Ivy League college.

The paucity of programs is shocking, especially when we think that these are the minds that might be capable of ferreting out the mystery of cancer, solving the problem of radioactive waste, painting a masterpiece, or engineering the car that can get 60 miles to the gallon!

When bored or excessively restrained, the gifted child may do anything from throwing spitballs, acting out in class, or becoming the class clown, to daydreaming and withdrawing. Many bright children are victimized by the system, by teachers who put them in a "holding pattern on the runway," so that they don't get too far ahead. Dr. Julian C. Stanley, director of the Study of Mathematically Precocious Youth at Johns Hopkins University, Baltimore, suggests that many of these youngsters may make their teachers uncomfortable. Therefore, the teachers hold them down as an alternative to letting the child outshine the teacher in class. Such youngsters may be considered class misfits rather than class leaders.

Parents who feel the need of further information after contacting their child's teacher or school administrator can get in touch with groups such as the Concerned Citizens for the Education of the Gifted and Talented, located in New York City; other similar groups can give assistance in other localities. Furthermore, help can be given in locating some of the fine private schools throughout the country that have superior programs for gifted youngsters. Such help is available through the American Association for Gifted Children (15 Gramercy Park, New York, N.Y. 10003; see also Chapter 6 for other information on schools for the gifted).

Meeting the Needs of the Gifted Child

The gifted youngster thrives in an environment that encourages exploration and creativity. Four prominent innovators responded to questions put to them on how to create creativity.[6] Buckminster Fuller, multi-talented citizen-of-the-world, said, "I call it the miracle of the obvious. The great secret for increasing creativity is reducing an idea to practice. Do it!" By "doing it," the child is making a practical reality from an abstract fleeting idea. It isn't enough to dream the dream or talk the project to death; it is necessary to make the idea into a concrete operational tool. How many of us know adults who have a plethora of fanciful ideas but little or nothing concrete to show for their dreams? They are always waiting for their "bonus," "raise," "the final house," "when the kids are in school," "next year's vacation," or "someday when their ship comes in."

"The ability to take risks" helps create creativity, said Dr. Frank Barron, professor of psychology at the University of California. Like Albert Einstein's celebrated "leap into the unknown," the creative mind must move from what is known and accepted to what is unknown and often unaccepted. In Chapter 1, we mentioned that "losers wait while winners initiate." The youngster who is unafraid of taking a chance with a new idea will have an open mind, allowing the fresh ideas to clear away the cobwebs and debris of "We've always done it that way." Stale minds, like stale rooms, need to be opened and aired.

Dr. Silvano Arieti, a well-known professor of psychiatry at New York Medical College, challenges traditional school programs and ideologies by suggesting that creativity is enhanced when schools encourage solitude, daydreaming, inactivity, and freethinking. Who among us has not been chided for "doing nothing in our free time," or "daydreaming" when there was work to be completed? When did you ever hear of "think time" before an exam? It's always beat the clock, write as much as you can. Teachers worry about the child who is alone at recess, and parents worry about the child who is inactive on a Saturday afternoon. Inactivity makes us nervous. We must always be doing something; therefore, so must our children. But too many students are just "busy with busy," says Ann Antipas, a high school English teacher from Pleasantville, New York. Too little time is given for thinking, dreaming, and creating ideas.

Dr. Rollo May, noted author and psychiatrist, suggests that we must "completely overhaul our educational system." The schools must reward youngsters who exhibit original and nonconforming ideas. Presently, the youngsters who win the brownie points and gold stars are the conforming thinkers, trouble-free and obedient. Teachers don't like the unexpected; they are more comfortable with the predictable. Youngsters who are creative are unpredictable and ask surprising questions. "This irritates teachers who dislike surprises," says Dr. May.

Gifted youngsters learn from problem-solving experiences. However, they also need the stimulus of freewheeling imaginative thinking, storytelling and the performing arts, and creative artistry.

How to Make Home a Learning Place for Gifted Kids

Home as well as school must be a learning place for the gifted youngster. Parents can create an environment that encourages kids to explore and create without being destructive or hard to manage. Many types of commercial games are available to stimulate youngsters in thinking and learning. Depending on their ages and interests, puzzles, word games, and math games can teach without "teaching," as can traditional games such as bridge and chess.

Hobbies that include peripheral learning and encourage concentration as well are found in coin collecting, stamp collecting, model building, rock collecting, and photography. Growing one's own herb or vegetable garden either indoors or out offers a wealth of scientific data—and practical results. When school does not meet their needs, youngsters will often turn to these hobbies for the personal satisfaction and positive feedback that they need. These are hobbies that offer a lifetime of pleasure, as well as a wealth of learning.

Music lessons and work in the performing arts are often highly satisfying outlets for the gifted child. The ability to express oneself through music, dance, or drama is a great builder of poise and confidence.

However, it is quite easy to fall into the middle-class "lessons, we take lessons" trap. One youngster was overheard bouncing a small rubber superball and chanting: "Lessons, I take lessons, I take lots and lots of lessons." He was bright and talented, but was overscheduled to the point of drowning. Parents can go too far, unintentionally burying a kid's initiative by overprogramming his or her life. Remember what Dr. Arieti said about schools encouraging solitude, daydreaming, inactivity, and free thinking; these skills can be stimulated equally well in the home.

Gifted youngsters often need direction in learning to handle the world around them. Just as we stressed the need to monitor and supervise bright youngsters as much as those who do not exhibit gifted behavior, it is equally important to train them in tolerance, acceptance, and patience with others who may not be as alert or quick-thinking in their responses. "The burden of great potential" is a gift and a responsibility. Having such a gift is a privilege, to be nurtured and developed, but also to be shared with others through a creative vocation. The bright youngster with quick responses can be quite impatient and unforgiving with others who do not demonstrate either his/her powers of concentration or problem-solving abilities. This child's impatience with others will only set him or her apart from peers as a kind of pariah. He or she needs to be constantly reminded that others who do not share such gifts need help when they cannot handle the kind of tasks that are so easy for him or her. *The Gifted and the Talented: Developing Elementary and Secondary School Programs*[7] is a book that should prove useful to anyone, parent or teacher, who is working with these youngsters on an ongoing basis.

One Example of an Innovative Program for the Gifted

One Long Island, New York, school district recently instituted an innovative program. Under the direction of the district superintendent, Dr. Ira Singer, youngsters are considered for the program on referral by parent or teacher if they fulfill the requirements as set:

. . . The child must exhibit a score of at least 128 on an individual intelligence test (e.g., the Wechsler Intelligence Test—Revised).
. . . The child must exhibit high levels of creativity as shown on individual projects and scoring on a Creativity Achievement Test.
. . . The teacher is asked for an evaluation of the performance and attitude of the child.
. . . The child is then interviewed and personally evaluated by the administrator for special services.

According to Dr. Singer, approximately 12 percent of the youngsters in grades 3 through 6 were identified and placed in the program. These selected students are mainstreamed for four and a half days out of the five-day school week. On the remaining half day, they are placed in a special program in the company of their gifted peers. A specially trained teacher, the head of psychological services, Dr. Robert Pierangello, and the director of special services, Dr. Charlotte Podalsky, supervise and conduct a highly specialized program.

In this program, which is partially supported by state and federal funds, gifted youngsters are exposed to areas of learning specifically designed to meet their individual needs and talents. Dr. Singer plans to extend the program into "Career Education for the Gifted." Under this plan, if a student is interested in pursuing some career training in the performing arts, for example, a fully equipped television production studio will be available with the necessary hardware to produce hour-long documentaries or other programs. Students will be encouraged to handle everything necessary in the production, including scriptwriting, directing, acting, costume and set designing, and musical accompaniment. Local professionals in the New York City area will be invited to direct and teach kids the basics in the skills of their particular trade. Not only will these students be given exposure to working professionals; they will also experience working with them, and then initiating their own projects. Since programs are projected for educational areas—mathematics, foreign language, English, science, and social studies—other students will be invited to act as consultants in the production of the various programs, helping in the chosen field. The documentaries produced will then be made available to all classes and schools as supplementary teaching tools. One unique aspect of this program is that it will attempt to gain the actual participation of retired senior citizens in the community.

Public school districts are becoming increasingly aware of the need to devote special training and resources to the education of the gifted and talented. More and more innovative programs are being developed throughout the country. Unfortunately, the rate of growth in this educational area is slow; and, as we mentioned before, only a small percentage of these youngsters are being served adequately at the present time.

One of the most popular programs that has spread throughout the schools is the use of learning resource centers. Often located in school or town libraries, these centers usually have unusual materials, audio-visual equipment, even record libraries, cassettes, and television. In New Jersey, special Saturday classes specifically designed to meet the needs of gifted youngsters are offered in over fifty schools and libraries as a supplementary enrichment program for youngsters who can benefit best from the program.

Many states (Illinois is a notable leader in this endeavor) have resorted to regional consortia of school districts that cooperate to provide and share costs for these services. Kids who are normally placed in heterogeneous classes with youngsters at all ability levels are offered the opportunity to get together with their talented counterparts throughout the area for such programs. Specialists in the education of the gifted and talented see positive value in youngsters working within two kinds of settings: the heterogeneous one (comparable to the real world of work and play), and a more homogeneous one, in which they meet only other extraordinary kids. Such kids need the challenge of working with others of equal intellect, but they also need the acceptance, tolerance, and broadening learned through working and living with children of lesser attributes. This mainstreaming concept is similar to that current in the education of the learning-disabled and handicapped, as well. Since we live in a world in which all kinds of people with various strengths and weaknesses must live, we must learn to relate to all, rather than be educated in a cocoon, wrapped in cotton batting to protect us from the outside world.

To Be or Not to Be Advanced?

Educational administrators and psychologists do not agree on the subject of advancing gifted youngsters a year or two ahead of their chronological age group. It is generally agreed, however, that in order to benefit from advancement to a higher grade, a child must be both academically and socially mature; otherwise, we find a bright child placed in a socially inappropriate situation. Many professionals believe that gifted youngsters should be kept in social situations with their peers to avoid the social isolation that can occur when they are removed from a comfortable setting among their friends. Gifted youngsters are often relatively unsophisticated and unready to be placed with youngsters a year or two older than they are. Social ostracism is as harmful for the gifted child as it is for any child. To feel different may imply unacceptability. To feel lonely may be even more destructive for a child.

Frequently, schools advance youngsters according to their ability without consideration of age, especially where there are no programs available for the gifted and talented. Freeman Dyson, mathematician, physicist, and architect of the quantum electrodynamics theory, was the product of such a system, as described by Kenneth Brower in his book *The Starship and the Canoe.*[8] Brower tells us that Freeman was usually three years ahead of his contemporaries in school. His older classmates did not seem to resent him; however, he suffered many a beating at the hands of a gang of his peers, who resented and rejected him. Educators have become increasingly aware of the fact that the super-bright youngster may simply be a "fish out of water" when placed with more mature youngsters.

If advancement is recommended, the grades usually skipped are kindergarten, sixth grade, or the senior year of high school, as these are transitional grades. At grade-12 level, advanced placement courses are often made available. Some of the better colleges and universities may provide enrichment programs or early admissions policies for fifteen- and sixteen-year-olds, as well as supplemental curriculum and social guidance if necessary.

Some schools will provide Individual Educational Plans for youngsters who are advanced in a specific subject area. Thus, a third-grader may be encouraged to do fifth-grade math, but remain with his class for all other subjects. An advanced fifth-grader may be provided with seventh- or eighth-grade reading material to enrich her reading program and excused from the routine workbook material that does not interest her. A reading program such as the well-established SRA (Science Research Associates) covers material through the twelfth grade and is designed to allow students to work on their own, at their own pace. Many bright kids can complete high school-level work by the seventh grade. There are other such "programmed" curricula available in other disciplines.

The Gifted Student in the Real World

The adult working world is not always pleased at having a gifted young adult in its midst. Talented, nonconforming personalities who exhibit unusual creative, imaginative thinking often make the rest of us feel uncomfortable. They may be mistrusted, disliked, and considered peculiar for their idiosyncratic habits. Thomas Edison was considered strange by those around him; Einstein was notoriously absentminded. Walt Disney was fired by one of his first employers, a newspaper editor, "because he had *no new ideas.*" Paul Cézanne was rejected by the Beaux Arts School in Paris when he applied for admission. Eugene O'Neill, William Faulkner, and F. Scott Fitzgerald all experienced "failure at college." Mozart was told he could "never be a composer."

E. Paul Torrance of the Bureau of Educational Research at the University of Minnesota notes that "Unusual or original ideas are common targets of peer pressure to conform." The lives of the gifted and creative have been punctuated with their experiences at the hands of others—including their peers, their teachers, and even their parents—who ridiculed, misunderstood, and rejected their ideas. It was only their dogged determination and the inbred qualities of winners that kept them going. They were disciplined, persevering, and retained an internalized vision and goal that sustained them in spite of criticism and contempt.

The gifted youngster who would be a winner must be prepared to be made to feel self-conscious about his or her ideas at times. Children call each other "smarties," "teacher's pet," "freak," or "queer" when the different behavior of one of their peers makes them uncomfortable. Teachers may insult youngsters for their brightness; as one math teacher said to one youngster we know: "Just because you go to that smart kids' program doesn't make you something special in my class."

Gifted youngsters are often described in a variety of ways, some of them inappropriate or totally incorrect. Teachers have used the words "shy" and "withdrawn," when describing the loner who is intensely involved with his own ideas and projects. They have used the words "simple," "naïve," and "dumb," when describing the creative spontaneity of such youngsters and their powers of divergent thinking. They have used the words "neurotic" and "maladjusted" to label the socially inappropriate behavior they may exhibit. Much of this is the result of a lack of understanding of the traits exhibited by those who think creatively.

Parents must help their youngsters to understand that their gifts or special talents may make them appear a threat to others around them, through no fault of their own. Critical comments are made because the less gifted adult or child feels the need to engage in a power struggle to save face for himself. Gifted kids usually have the sensitivity to understand and accept the hostility of others after it has been explained to them.

Parents may tend to set unrealistic goals and expectations for their children once they have been identified as gifted. They may expect these youngsters to achieve at a superior level and be "winners" in all areas of performance. But history is filled with stories of great scientists who could not spell, doctors who could not write legibly, mathematicians and engineers who could not compose a cohesive paragraph, and artists who could not do basic math. Styles of learning as well as intelligence must be taken into consideration. All of us do not exhibit the same aptitude in all areas of endeavor. The gifted athlete may have been an extremely poor student, and the gifted student may be a klutz when it comes to athletics. The engineer may have a tin ear for musical tone, and the great musician may get lost walking around the block because he is so spacially disoriented.

How You as Parent Can Help

Gifted youngsters often need a battery of creative and imaginative extracurricular activities to keep them growing and learning. Some activities are best provided in a school program, while others can be encouraged at home. They will provide kids with additional exposure, new interests, and new self-confidence.

For example, youngsters who show an interest in art should not be limited to crayons and paper. Other art media are available in after-school recreational programs or can be provided at home. Watercolors and an easel, clay, finger paints, mosaic art, and many others are available in inexpensive kits. Most of these need a bit of supervision at first, but once established, preparation and cleanup procedures become relatively simple to follow.

Sewing is a highly creative operation; boxes of scrap materials, feathers, trimmings, old socks and pillow stuffing, with an array of fabric glue, needles, and thread will provide hours, days, and months of interesting doll-, animal-, and puppetmaking. Kids who feel comfortable taking raw materials and making something creative out of them can develop that skill and get great satisfaction out of the experience.

All kids benefit from the collection of a library of their own books. Paperbacks abound at every grade level and kids can now afford to own a small collection. Don't be surprised if your child continues to reread books; reading an old book is like renewing the acquaintance of an old friend. If your child shows an interest in writing, encourage the child to send an opinion of the books he or she reads to the authors, care of the publisher's address. Youngsters we have encouraged to do this have received a series of exciting letters directly from authors, who were impressed with their interest and encouraged them with repeated responses. Imagine what a letter from an author would do to encourage your would-be Hemingway! One sixteen-year-old, David Kaufman, had some definite opinions on articles he read in the paper, things he purchased, and so on. He began writing letters making suggestions, giving his opinion, and asking for responses. His letters were sent to political leaders, corporation presidents, et al. He has compiled a remarkable collection of his responses in a scrapbook, and some of the letters are penned with names from *Who's Who in America*. All of this grew from a suggestion from his mother, Mrs. Beryl Kaufman, and his own creativity and enthusiasm.

Kids can be encouraged to read more critically by suggesting that they write any of the following:

. . . An opinion of the book in a paragraph or two.

. . . Their own version of an advertisement for that book, highlighting what they consider significant, illustrating the ad. Send it to the publisher. One lucky youngster had his selected for use in an ad campaign.

. . . An original story based on the book, but taking it beyond the original plot.

. . . A rewrite of the ending of the story as they would have liked it. Send it to the publisher; the child will get interesting responses. One youngster who did not like the fact that the cat ate his pal the rat in an early primer series, wrote to the publisher. Six months later, another book came out in the series, in which major surgery was performed on the cat to save the rat. Imagine the effect on the youngster who was credited with the idea.

. . . Children who like to write rhymes or limericks can be encouraged to keep a collection of these.

Kids with musical aptitude find great fun in working with musical groups, setting up a band, performing for friends, parties, etc. However, they can't do this without a place to practice and understanding parents who are willing to put up with the cacophony of experimental music. Many youngsters have earned their expense money through high school and college performances with a band; but they've earned more than money. They've earned confidence, a sense of success, and a further step on the way to a vocation or avocation.

Artistic youngsters can draw comic strips complete with a dialogue and plot. One young man we know turned his cartooning hobby into a paying job with a local newspaper while he attended college at night.

Gifted kids with mechanical aptitude can learn from stripping down and rebuilding a car engine. We've seen too many kids denied the pleasure of getting their hands dirty and their parents' garage messy with such a rebuilding job because their parents felt that dirty work was not appropriate for such a bright child. In this day of planned obsolescence, imagine the pleasure of having your own live-in mechanic. If you consider auto mechanics beneath your child, think of the young doctor we know who was top in his class at college and med school, and "moonlights" as a surgeon to keep his real vocation going: rebuilding antique Mercedes-Benz automobiles!

The bright, competent youngster will feel like a winner a good deal of the time, but there will also be moments when he or she may feel like a loser. None of us can be a winner all the time; even those who excel at something will lose, feel disappointed, and have to spring "up from the ashes (like) the roses of success." Gifted youngsters have to be ready to face some failure as well as success without self-recrimination or hypersensitivity. This is often difficult for the straight A student. A grade of B, C, or F comes as a shock, but they may experience failing grades at some time. In our capacity as learning consultants to the Westchester Psychiatric Group, it is sad for us to see a steady parade of gifted kids who become depressed and oversensitive to their one academic failure despite their other successes.

Gifted youngsters who have not been helped to recognize that experiencing failure is an integral part of achieving success will often deny themselves learning experiences, fearing possible failure. Feeling confident enough with oneself to take a risk is one of the characteristics of the winner. No one can give us a gold-plated guarantee that we will succeed in everything we try, yet we must try. Fear of risk-taking may lead kids to play it safe, take courses only in subjects they are good at, or take the easy credit courses that are a sure B or A. Sadly, this is no real solution; the students who do this for an easy grade go on feeling guilty, knowing that they are selling out for the sure thing, that they are really cheating themselves.

Jerry, a bright Reed College student of twenty, said: "I can take a risk because I have confidence in what I know. A bad grade is only the subjective opinion of a teacher, and that doesn't reflect on me as a person. I'm not going to school for grades *per se,* but to learn. My own interpretation of self-worth is more important to me than reflecting what others think. If I think I'm right and others think I'm wrong, I'll reconsider my position; but if I still feel the same way, I'll fight to convince them of the strength of my argument."

Intellectual gifts are a privilege, but they are also a responsibility. Youngsters with special talents and gifts go unrecognized in the vast majority of our school programs. This is a resource that we do not have to import, manufacture, or sacrifice to OPEC pricing. However, these kids are a challenge to parents and teachers alike, who must educate them adequately, provide special programs, help them to gain the social perceptions commensurate with their abilities, and still let them grow up as kids. This is the job necessary to nurture potential winners.

If you need extra information on the "care and feeding" of your gifted child, a number of national organizations are available to give you further information and direction. Among them are:

. . . The Council for Exceptional Children, which distributes fact sheets on gifted youngsters and readings for parents as well as the names of consultants in each state. Write to the Council at ERIC Clearinghouse on Handicapped and Gifted Children, 1920 Association Drive, Reston, Virginia 29991.

. . . The National Association for Gifted Children, 217 Gregory Drive, Hot Springs, Arkansas 71901, which publishes a gifted child quarterly.

. . . *The Roeper Review,* a new quarterly journal on the gifted youngster; for information write to Roeper Review, 2190 North Woodward, Bloomfield Hills, Michigan 48013.

. . . A new magazine, *The G/C/T* (Gifted/Creative/Talented), designed for parents, teachers, and youngsters themselves, includes practical suggestions for enrichment. Write to G/C/T Publishing Co., Box 66654, Mobile, Alabama 36606.

. . . The National State Leadership Training Institute for Gifted and Talented, 316 West Second St., Los Angeles, California 90012, which will provide you with a bibliography for approximately 55¢ to cover mailing.

It is very important that you share this information with your school personnel. Don't assume that they know it just because they are teachers or administrators. You can provide them with material they may never have seen.

Making a gifted child a winner requires a concerted effort on the part of all who work and live with that child. This is the challenge. Parents

and educators must help the gifted and talented youngster to set his/
her expectations at a level commensurate with his/her talents. When
wants and expectations are the same, that child will maximize achievement and become a winner.

CHAPTER

9

---◆---

The Myth of Testing—and Vital Countermeasures

Testing in school can gravely undercut your child's developing sense of self as an optimistic, assured, open-hearted winner. Yet tests used to compare your child with others almost certainly face the child repeatedly all through the years of growing up. Nearly all schools in the country regularly give pupils tests like these every year or two precisely to see how your child compares generally.

Your child might suffer very badly from comparisons like these, based on "standardized" tests or "competency" tests. For instance, a child could be branded as a chronic "slow learner" very largely on the basis of standardized test results. This in turn could lead teachers, classmates, and administrators to view the child consistently as so dull-witted or dumb that he or she accepts their view as proof of hopeless and permanent inferiority.

Your child could be mistakenly labeled as an "underachiever" on the basis of tests, with teachers pressuring the child to do better work than is really comfortable and perhaps even marking schoolwork unfairly low to force the child to try harder.

Or, in late teenage years, your child might feel devastated by one of the newer competency tests sweeping the country. Competency tests have been rapidly adopted in recent years by an increasing number of states as a requirement for the high school diploma. Suppose that your boy or girl did have a reading perception problem that was improving through special help, but had worked three times harder than average students all through high school to meet every requirement made by the school for graduation. But then, because of the perception problem, the child fails the state-mandated competency test at the last minute and is refused permission to graduate.

You can imagine how furious and crushed the child would feel. Yet a shattering disappointment like this could easily happen. At this date, some states that require competency testing for diplomas have provided no alternative methods by which such "special education" children might earn their diplomas.

Finally, ironically enough, testing might by accident shower your child with good fortune, as you'll see. But because the consequences of testing misfortunes can be so grave, you should be armed with a basic understanding of such tests and the strong countermeasures given in this chapter. With them, you can effectively fend off onslaughts that might torpedo your child's growth as a winner. Moreover, this chapter tells how you can take many steps to help your child score higher on tests.

The Myth of Testing

Why the Myth of Testing Really Can Hurt Your Child

Testing really might hurt your child mainly because of a myth that exists in the minds of most people in schools who use standardized testing. The myth is that such testing is scientifically accurate. What they don't know, or ignore, is that the truth is exactly the opposite: any standardized test scores for your child—on such crucial qualities as intelligence, "achievement" (progress in learning school subjects), or personality development—are *scientifically inaccurate*.

Let's take, for instance, the often burning question of "IQ" or Intelligence Quotient, which is one notorious form of standardized test score. Don't feel relieved if someone in your child's school says they stopped using IQ tests a few years ago. In the face of mounting attacks on the misuse of IQs in recent years, many schools and test publishers have switched to tests that are essentially the same in content and purpose but different in name—tests of things called "mental ability(ities)," "scholastic potential," "school ability," or "aptitude." But much the same harm can be done to your child in much the same way, whatever the name of the test used to gauge how bright your child may be.

Suppose that your child's test results show an IQ of 83. On the basis of that number alone, the child's teachers and principal are likely to see the youngster as one who may have trouble in even finishing high school, who probably should not be encouraged to go to college, and who ought to be steered into some manual or clerical occupation. They might also think that any high marks the child gets are almost certainly the result of some fluke—a teacher's indulgence, or the child's working fantastically beyond potential. And they could have strong reservations against assigning the child to any special classes or enrichment experience for high-ability pupils. Their general expectations for your child would be low—which could well color their whole way of reacting to the boy or girl. Their thinking would be shaped by ingrained, traditional views of IQs (as indicated in the "IQ Significance" chart below).

IQ Significance—Traditional Views (But Don't Take It as Gospel!)

140 IQ   viewed as start of genius level, in one famed study

120 IQ   about average for four-year college graduates

110 IQ   about average for high school graduates

100 IQ   average for whole population

90 IQ   limited reading and writing skills; adequate for routine manual work

75 IQ   may have trouble passing elementary school studies; scores at about this or a lower level like 60 IQ may be officially defined as "mentally retarded" in some parts of the United States

All this could also stem from their unconscious belief in testing. Testing is indeed scientific; psychometrics, or psychological measurement, is perhaps the most highly developed area of experimental science in psychology. And your child's 83 IQ test score is a fact, an experimental observation obtained in giving the scientifically developed IQ test.

However, what your child's teachers and principal might well overlook are the crucial qualifications that make any one test score for a child scientifically inaccurate. When such essential—and fully scientific—qualifications are added, here's what that 83 IQ test score really means:

1. 2 to 1 odds that the child's theoretical "true" score lies somewhere in a range between a low of about 77 and a high of about 89 IQ.
2. 19 to 1 odds that your child's true IQ score lies in a range between about 72 to 95 IQ.

3. Smaller but no less important odds that your child's true IQ score could actually be still lower or higher—maybe as high as 120 or 130 IQ.

Ridiculous? Not at all. The manager of a large bookstore began to worry about college for his son not long after the boy started high school. The boy wasn't at all bookish and generally got only mediocre marks in school. One night the father gingerly mentioned college.

"Oh, I'm no good for college," his son casually replied. "I've got an IQ of only 100, my guidance counselor says."

Shocked, the boy's parents had him take the Stanford-Binet IQ test at a private counseling bureau, and he earned a score of 128 IQ. He later attended and did well at the University of South Florida.

One comment beyond the obvious should be made about that dreadful but alas not uncommon guidance counselor. An IQ test score around the average of 100 or even much lower should by no means rule out serious consideration of college for a child.

There is an additional vital scientific qualification to any one IQ or similar test score for a child, such as that one of 83 IQ: You can attach no validity to any interpretation of a test score unless it's based on a specific study made with children clearly demonstrated to be comparable to the individual child in question—say, your child. And even then, interpretations can be only probabilities, never certainties. These essential features of scientific inaccuracy apply not just to IQ or similar tests but to tests of all kinds. Tests at best yield only clues about individuals, not certainties.

Because the testing myth makes tests seem scientifically accurate, they can wreak havoc in your child's schooling and sense of self-worth, whenever his or her test scores happen to be lower than eventually justified—and such justifications may not arrive until many years later.

Why Tests Can Be Good for Your Child When Used Diagnostically

The diagnostic use of standardized, multiple-choice tests could help your child, possibly to a substantial extent, even though the scores of any one child on these tests are scientifically inaccurate. As the term suggests, diagnostic use of tests is carried out for the purpose of providing active help to the individual examined. It differs markedly from the frequent use of tests to judge some overall quality of a child, like general intelligence or aptitude, or ability to "read at grade level."

Let's look at the actual case of a ten-year-old girl, Debbie B., to see how a diagnostic use of tests might work for your child. In the fourth grade Debbie took a group of the subject matter "achievement tests" that are given by many schools. On a number of the tests in the group, Debbie got scores ranging in the top 25 percent, compared to the scores of representative fourth-grade pupils nationwide. She scored in the top 25 percent on each of the tests for word knowledge and word discrimination; reading; and spelling and language usage.

But she scored only average in the test on arithmetic problem solving (which involves more numerical reasoning ability than actual figuring). The reason was suggested by one remaining score of Debbie's—on the arithmetic computation test, her score fell in the bottom 10 percent.

Debbie's teacher interpreted these results diagnostically. Debbie's low score in arithmetic computation seemed to indicate strongly that the girl needed extra help in arithmetic fundamentals like adding, subtracting, multiplying, fractions, and decimals. Debbie's marks in classroom math quizzes earlier in the year and her general discomfort in class over math tended to bear this out. So the teacher gave Debbie extra help with her arithmetic, and by talking to her parents got them to spend time with her at home on arithmetic. A few months later, Debbie's marks on math homework and quizzes—and her interest in math—rose considerably.

Achievement tests like those Debbie took are very broad surveys of scholastic attainment, and usually contain only a few questions in any one small segment of learning. This feature limits the extent to which achievement tests can be used for detailed diagnostic purposes. As a result, schools interested in having their teachers take a more detailed diagnostic approach often give tests of another kind, ones in individual subjects developed specifically for learning diagnosis—for example, diagnostic reading tests or diagnostic arithmetic tests.

If your child should fall seriously and increasingly behind in some schoolwork, diagnostic testing of other kinds could prove not only constructive but essential. Your child's difficulty might well stem from a mild or severe learning disability of the kind described in Chapter 7. Testing in circumstances like these should be done individually by an expert (school psychologist or private psychologist, guidance counselor, or learning specialist). The tests used should be ones especially designed for such purposes. Among them might be the Benton Visual Retention Test, the Berry-Buktenica Developmental Test of Visual Motor Integration, or the Slingerland Screening Tests for Specific Language Disabilities.

As we explained in Chapter 7, you should welcome rather than resist having your child tested diagnostically in a case like this. Such testing is frequently the only way to discover what blocks to learning are causing the child's difficulties and consequent frustrations. Identifying these causes in turn leads to exercises, practice, and encouragement, all of which in time can relieve the difficulties and ease the strains on your child. More important, effective help will boost the child's self-confidence so that, with an effort, he or she can win out over whatever problems life brings. Confidence like that marks a winner.

How an Accidental Testing "Halo" Could Bring Real Benefits for Your Child

You saw before how, quite by accident, your child could earn a test score of only 83 IQ, even though the youngster's true IQ score could instead be as high as 120 or 130. In a case like this, your child would have gotten entirely by chance a lower score than was justified by his or her true capabilities.

However, also entirely by chance your child might earn a high IQ score of 120 or 130 although the child's true score is only about 83 IQ. If a completely accidental high score like this should be scored by your child, it would bring very real benefits. These benefits would stem from the testing "halo" your child had acquired—a halo of mental "brightness" that looms large in the way teachers perceive a child. Your child would be someone special—someone worth more attention, cultivation, and expectation.

Count yourself and your child lucky if this happens. You can judge how lucky from a fascinating experiment run recently by Robert Rosenthal and Lenore Jacobson (he was then professor of social relations at Harvard University; she was principal of the Spruce School in south San Francisco). Their experiment tried to determine whether high expectations for individual children on the part of grade school teachers could actually increase the capabilities of those children—even if the basis for such high expectations was completely false.

A typical public elementary school with some 650 pupils was used by Drs. Rosenthal and Jacobson for their experiment. Teachers in the school were not told of the actual purpose. Rather, they were told that a special test of academic "blooming" or "spurting" was being given in May, with followup tests the ensuing January and May.

This "Harvard Test of Inflected Acquisition," the teachers were also advised, would reveal which children were likely to show a spurt or blooming in the near future. The researchers said that children scoring in the top 20 percent on the test would show a more significant "inflection" or spurt during the next year than those scoring lower. They added that children and parents could not have the test explained to them because of its experimental nature.

The test was given that May and, when the school reopened the following fall, each teacher was given a list of from one to nine children in his or her class whom the test had supposedly identified as scholastic spurters. In fact, the children listed had been chosen randomly, not by test scores. There was no difference between those listed as "bloomers" and a comparable control group of fellow pupils—no difference, that is, except for the teachers' expectations.

Those higher expectations, even when falsely based, actually did act as a self-fulfilling prophecy. In their book reporting on the findings, *Pygmalion in the Classroom,*[1] the two investigators discussed the children to whom they had given artificial testing "halos": "These unusual or 'magic' children showed significantly greater gains in IQ than did the remaining children who had not been signaled out for the teachers' attention."

They added: "The change in the teachers' expectations regarding the intellectual performance of these allegedly 'special' children had led to an actual change in the intellectual performance of these randomly selected children."

From this, you can draw two useful guides for action aimed at helping your child develop as a winner.

First, go out of your way to be as effective as you can in leading your child's teachers to view the child as potentially bright. Empty bragging won't do this. More effective is noticing and reporting to teachers rather impressive things your child does, even little things. Other effective actions include being consistent in neatly dressing and grooming your child for school, and cultivating in the child (if possible) special qualities of consideration for others and good manners.

Second, maintain sympathetic but high and confident expectations for your child (as we urge throughout this book). Your own influence on the child is far stronger and more lasting than the influence of any teacher. You are the main person who can give your child the necessary "halo" of a winner.

Helping Your Child Score Well

Since standardized tests in school are a fact of life for virtually every child in the country, you may want to give your child special help in scoring high on them. The most important kind of help you can give doesn't pertain directly to tests; it concerns fostering your child's learning in scholastic areas generally.

Building Reading Ability, Crucial for High Test Scores

Your child's reading, at any age, should receive very special attention from you if you want to strengthen the child's performance on tests.

Reading and vocabulary are key, fundamental elements in almost all tests given by schools, even tests in mathematics and science.

You should help to build your child's reading ability and vocabulary in all ways possible from infancy on. Show that you enjoy and regularly spend time on reading yourself, and have enticing magazines and books around the house—from your public library, should you find it hard to buy them. In the earliest years, read storybooks to your child. With the best-loved stories that you read together dozens of times, your boy or girl will in time glow with delight knowing what the words and pictures are going to say as you turn each new page.

At older ages, try to see that your child always has available some things to read that are too interesting to resist. Good possibilities among the enormous choice of books for youngsters of every age can be suggested by children's librarians and bookstore staff. Or you might want to refer to standard works like the widely respected *Parent's Guide to Children's Reading*[2] by Nancy Larrick.

Reading aloud with a child who has begun to be able to read can be especially enjoyable and productive, with you and the child taking turns. This way you can work with the youngster on the new or bigger words by helping sound them out, syllable by syllable. It's very effective to have a dictionary for your child's age range at hand, in which to look up the bigger words. (It's good too for your child to get in the habit of using the dictionary independently.) You can also have fun by using the bigger words you discover together in everyday conversation with the child.

Over the years, talk often and casually about what your boy or girl is reading, and about what you read that's especially interesting. And above all, always keep it fun. Should you hound or harangue the child about reading, you're likely to turn the child against either doing it or sharing it with you.

In younger years a child usually takes very naturally to reading with an approach like this. How fast, how soon, and how much your child advances in home reading can vary a great deal. Never force it or make the youngster feel pressured or guilty about it.

Moreover, being close and easy with your child in early reading at home should put you in a good position to notice early signs of possible reading difficulties. Don't pay much attention to any such difficulty before the child's classmates have become beginning readers—approximately through late in the first-grade year and on around the middle of second grade. But after that, if your child doesn't read at least some words and show some progress in storybook sessions with you, you might consider having the child's basic skills tested diagnostically. An emerging learning disability could be starting to block the way for your child. (How to have such diagnostic analysis done was explained in Chapter 7, which also explained how to help the child overcome such disability.)

Of course, after your child starts school, your interest and help in other school subjects besides reading will certainly boost his or her ability to score high on tests. It's good to be interested in your child's schoolbooks and homework. Provide a regular, quiet place and a time for homework. The place can be the kitchen table or an old card table, if your home is crowded. For Lincoln, it was the fireplace hearth, you may recall.

You may want to give some special help with arithmetic. After reading ability, mathematical ability is probably the next most important basic element for getting high test scores.

Ways to Sharpen Specific Test-Taking Skills

Quite a few ways in which you might build specific test-taking skills in your child are open to you. Many of these involve your child's enjoyment of certain kinds of games, puzzles, toys, and tricks. Some develop abilities such as those tested in the multiple-choice approach. Others accustom the child to the pervasive "trickiness" of standardized tests. These tests are often tricky. For instance, professionals who make them call the wrong answers among each set of multiple-choice possibilities the "distractors." As that name suggests, distractors or wrong choices given after each test question are often deliberately designed to mislead the hasty or uninformed children taking the test.

A word of caution about your child and games like the ones we are about to suggest—and indeed any games played by your child. It's very well known among school coaches of youngsters that pitting even a promising young athlete against over-strong competition eventually kills that young athlete's interest in the sport. You should accordingly be sure that, in playing games, your child wins often enough to remain enthused. A child who plays too much against older kids in the family can come to hate games. Parents should choose games that their children can win, but should *never* "cheat" by allowing the child to win. Gifted children who consistently beat their parents at adult games, such as chess, should be encouraged to seek more challenging competition.

Games to Build Word Skills. Many games help to build skills with words and language important on tests. Here's a free and easy one. With a normally developing child of seven or eight or older, you can teach and play the old-fashioned game of "pig-Latin." Children like it because it gives them a "secret" language for talking with close friends, especially when younger kids are around. Just take the initial consonant off the start of a word, put it at the end of the word, and pronounce it followed by the hard "a" sound, "ay." For instance, in pig-Latin, "How are you?" is pronounced: "Ow-hay are ou-yay?" Pig-Latin helps develop skill in telling vowels and consonants apart, and in visualizing words and word spellings.

Here are a few examples of the many games you can buy to help build a child's abilities to handle words. These happen to be for children who have begun reading and writing. *Go Fish,* provided by the Remedial Education Center in Washington, D.C., hinges on the ability to identify the sounds of syllables and words, and to put syllables in sequences that make words. Spelling skills grow with the playing of *Scrabble for Juniors* (the game is produced in adapted form for children by the Scrabble firm, Selchow and Richtor) or *Rolling Reader,* which is played with plastic cubes (from Rolling Reader Co., Westport, Conn.).

Games also widely available in toy and stationery stores and good for fostering further language skills include *Password* and *Concentration.* One that children often find especially funny is *One Too Many* (Dexter and Westerbrook, Baldwin, N.Y.), which gives sentences made ridiculous by extra words that the players must spot and remove.

Games to Build Abilities in Math, Visual Perception, and Memory. Card games for children can improve basic skills and familiarity with numbers. Among such games are *rummy* and *baseball.* The well-known old game of *dominoes* also exercises fundamental abilities in recognizing, counting, and adding numbers.

Triominoes is a similar but more complex game (available from Pressman Manufacturing Co.). In it, the child matches triangles with numbers on them and gets practice in adding and recognizing sets of numbers to be totaled for scores.

A variety of books describing simple games with numbers and math for children can be found in libraries and bookstores. One, for example, is *Arithmetic Games,* by Enoch Dumas (Fearon Publishers, Palo Alto, Calif.). It tells how to play games with children ranging in age from about six through fourteen, and for which you can make what materials are needed easily and inexpensively.

Among games that are especially effective in developing skill in visual perception and memory are those named *Memory* and *Pairs* (both games for children of ages from five to about ten, issued by the Milton Bradley firm). They also include, for tots aged three to seven or so, the widely available *Set 1 ABC Puzzles.* Playing such very familiar games as *checkers* and *tic-tac-toe* helps develop perception in children from about six to twelve, as does playing *chess,* usually for older youngsters.

Puzzles for Imaginative Thinking. Learning to enjoy solving puzzles should generally strengthen your child's test-taking powers. Answering test questions and solving puzzles take much the same kind of keen, wary thinking. You should have no trouble finding many books of puzzles involving words, numbers, and riddles that would intrigue your child. Examples of such books for children of about eight and up are *Fun with Puzzles* by Joseph Leeming (made widely available in schools by Scholastic Book Services), and *Puzzles for Pleasure* by Isabel R. Beard (a Follett paperback). Still another is *Mazes* (Grosset and Dunlap).

Further Ways to Help Your Child Score High on Tests

Beyond cultivating your child's basic test-taking skills, you can do three more things to help the youngster get higher scores on tests.

1. *Encourage a relaxed, confident attitude toward tests.* Test anxiety tends to become a habit in some children, who in time come to fear all tests. This is most unfortunate, for anxiety of course cripples the child's capacity to show whatever abilities and knowledge he or she really does have. Almost everyone has known certain children (including some very bright ones) who simply "freeze" on tests.

You should be able to avoid having your child develop such fear by taking to heart what we've said so far in this book. The same general kind of handling by parents that makes a winner in life also develops a winner on tests.

It is most important for you to be sure your child knows that you think the kid is just great, however the test turns out. Sure, you and the youngster view the test and studying for it seriously; they're important jobs to be done. And you talk with the child about the test marks, naturally and sympathetically, to help see what they might suggest about constructive things for the child to do in the future. But the child should always have your complete acceptance, approval, and affection.

There's a chance your child might seem jittery about a test because other children are nervous. If so, tell the child that it's nonsense to be jumpy about a test. Being jumpy only gets in the way. The best approach always is to be relaxed and confident.

2. *Explain why not to be rattled by many hard questions.* Especially if your child is a conscientious student, you may want to explain an often jarring feature of multiple-choice tests when the youngster is about

twelve or older. Doing so could help relieve your child's discomfort in facing tests. Your explanation could go something like this.

"Look, Billy (or Sue), maybe once a year or so in school you take some tests that are special. The directions and questions are printed in booklets they hand out. And you don't write out your answers to them on your own paper. You mark the answers in boxes on a special sheet of paper they hand out with the booklets. Right?

"Now, I know those tests don't count directly in your marks in school, as they probably tell you. So you see they're nothing to get at all concerned about.

"What I really want to mention, though, is one thing about those special tests that might really bother you. I hope from what I say that it won't bother you any more.

"The thing that may bother you is this. Those tests almost all include lots of very hard questions that you're not even supposed to be able to answer. Yes, really. You can get a very high score on one of these tests even if you can't answer as many as a third or more of all the questions it asks. Honest.

"So don't feel a bit bad about lots of hard questions on any test like this that you can't answer. Instead, expect to see them. And work through the test like this. Go through it and answer the questions easy for you first, skipping the hard ones. Answers to easy questions count just as much as answers to hard questions on almost all of these tests. Then, go back through the test again and work some of the hard ones you had skipped, if you can figure them out with more time. And simply ignore any hard questions you can't even begin to answer. See what I mean?

"Let me finish by saying why I think you might be bothered by running into so many hard questions you can't answer on these tests. You're used to the different kinds of exams given by your teachers. Those exams ask about what's been covered in the class. Sharp, hardworking students should be able to answer just about all questions on the teacher's exam. Right?

"But, as I've said, these special tests are different. They're called 'standardized' tests, and are made to be given to a great many different kinds and ages of youngsters all over the country. They include hard questions for even the oldest and most hardworking students to work on—plus some things even they can't work out.

"Anyway, don't feel bothered at all by running into lots of hard questions you can't answer. Just ignore them and go on feeling good about yourself."

3. *Suggest special care with the directions for answering test questions.* On some other occasion, you might make one further observation.

While simple, it could go far to improve your child's test scores. It's this: Take special care to understand the directions given for answering test questions. Perhaps even read them twice, just to be sure.

This can be important because one set of directions often is followed by a whole group of questions, possibly ten or more. Mistaking the directions can thus mean getting all ten questions wrong, even when the child knows the answers to all of them. Yet children often fly right into the questions themselves as the important thing, without ever getting the directions straight. And directions can ask for just the opposite of what might be expected by the look of the questions at first glance.

Competency Tests for the High School Diploma: Fighting Through This New Threat

In the last few years at least seventeen states have introduced requirements for passing competency tests in order to receive the high school diploma. Such diploma-competency testing fever has swept whole states like Oregon, Florida, North Carolina, and New York, and many individual school districts as well. It may have spread to your child's school district by the time you read this.

Statistically, your child runs only small chances of harm from this new kind of testing. More than 99 percent of all seniors pass the tests in virtually all schools where they've been required.

However, if it should occur, your child would probably find the experience of not passing acutely painful, as suggested at the start of this chapter. The experience would also certainly bring a major crisis in your own efforts to raise your child as a winner.

How might such a crisis arise for your child? And if it should, what could you do about it?

Your risk of meeting such a crisis is perhaps largest if your child has been working to succeed in the face of a learning disability or an even more severe handicap. Children like this, and minority-group children from poverty-level homes, have been almost entirely the ones who fail on competency tests for diplomas. The tests are generally easy for children not troubled by learning problems or deprivation.

Suppose your child is in a high school where competency tests are required for graduation, and that the child seems likely to fail them. In a case like this, you have four alternatives:

1. *Try early tutoring help.* Find out about and anticipate a possible competency testing crisis early, as much as two years before graduation if at all possible. Then, don't delay in seeing if tutoring or other special help provided by the school might be sufficient to get your child

through the test. Help of this kind should be available in your child's school, for many schools have introduced such help in response to the test requirements.

2. *Ask about the possibility of alternate testing methods.* You might inquire at the school about the possibility of having your child tested with acceptable alternate methods. Alternate methods that provide fair and effective means through which students with learning disabilities or other difficulties can demonstrate their capabilities have been introduced in some competency testing systems.

3. *Transfer your child to private school in another state.* Before your child's senior year in high school, you may want to have the youngster transfer to a private school in a nearby state where competency tests are not required for the diploma. For instance, if you live in New York State, you might have the child attend a private school in Connecticut or New Jersey. The latter states each have competency tests for selected grade levels (with remedial work for those found to need it), but do not require the tests for graduation. Also, a private school offering especially good help with a learning disability (like those discussed in Chapter 6) could be one in which your child would be likely to make better progress even if there were no graduation problem.

4. *Plan on a college that does not require a diploma for admission.* Growing numbers of colleges in many parts of the country have programs for students with learning disabilities, and admit students to them without insisting on all the usual requirements—including high school diplomas. A pioneering college of this sort, for example, is Curry College in Milton, Massachusetts, a suburb of Boston. Freshmen with learning disabilities make up at least 10 percent of each entering class of 350. Some later make the college dean's list and go on to graduate study. (You can get an extensive, up-to-date list of "College/Universities that Accept Students with Learning Disabilities" on request from the Association for Children with Learning Disabilities, 4156 Library Rd., Pittsburgh, Pa. 15234.)

Knowing of this possibility, you could have your child complete all coursework in high school without worrying over the competency test requirement. The diploma really wouldn't matter because the youngster is going on to college anyway. Around high school graduation day, though, you might want to consider taking a vacation trip with the child. Not being able to go through graduation proudly with friends and classmates really seems to hurt young people who fail their competency tests.

One last, improbable alternative is that competency test requirements for the diploma might possibly have been overturned in the courts by the time of your child's graduation. Florida's requirement has been suspended by order of Federal District Judge George Carr until the 1982–83 school year. He based his decision mainly on the argument that students should have been told of the requirement starting with the time they entered high school (the first ones to whom it applied were sophomores at the time of its introduction).

New York's requirement has been challenged in the courts by the Northport-East Northport School District on Long Island, at this time of writing. In June 1979, the district had awarded diplomas to two un-identified and otherwise undescribed "handicapped" students, a boy and a girl, who had met district requirements but who had not passed the required state tests.

Explaining the district's legal stand, Joseph Beattie, president of its school board, declared: "It has been our policy to award diplomas to students who fulfill specialized requirements which have been estab-lished under the Individual Education Program.

"Those requirements are worked out for each special student by counselors, teachers and special education teachers, and we feel that the competency test regulations violate federal laws which protect the handicapped students and give them the rights to the same educational opportunities and benefits as other students.

"In our view," he added, "a high school diploma is one of those benefits."

Vital Countermeasures against Testing Dangers

Competency tests such as those described above pose possible threats to your child only at the end of high school. But standardized tests of other kinds might endanger your child's future in hidden, insidious ways at any time from kindergarten on. Various ways in which this might happen were outlined at the start of the chapter.

Countermeasures for you to take against such dangers are given here. They can prove vital at decisive points in your child's schooling. We first summarize these countermeasures so that you can have them ready for use all through your child's schooling. Then we explain how and when to use each countermeasure.

Countermeasures to Prevent Harm to Your Child through Testing

1. Find out what your child's test scores are, getting clear explana-tions of all their varying forms.
2. Find out how the school interprets your child's test scores, and what, if any, actions it is taking on the basis of them.

3. Question the accuracy and validity of any test scores that seem low to you, based on other evidence.
4. Challenge potentially limiting class placements of your child that are based only or largely on test scores.
5. Keep your own spirits high even though your child may have low scores that generally agree with all other evidence.

1. Find Out What Your Child's Test Scores Are

You will want to arm yourself with the facts. This means knowing at the outset what your child's test scores are.

Finding out may be simple or involved, depending on practices in your schools. It would be simplest if teachers go over them with you in regular conferences about your child's progress.

If your school is among the few that do this, take enough time to understand clearly each evaluation of your child, including the teacher's own marks and comments on the child's report card, as well as any and all test scores themselves. Take notes if you wish on each mark for schoolwork, score on a test, comment, and any suggestions the teacher may have.

Test scores in particular are given in a bewildering variety of forms. Ask the teacher not only to show or tell you each score but to explain the meaning of the form in which it is given. Regardless of the form, remember this: Any test score should enable you to see how your child's performance on the test stands in relation to the test performance of some specific group (or groups) of children.

For example, a score of your child "at the forty-fifth percentile" means that your child's mark on the test ranks ahead of the scores of 45 percent of the children in a specific group. Ideally, that group is a representative one, comparable in essential respects to your child—such as a representative group of children nationwide in the same grade as your child.

Quite a few teachers know little about the very important background needed for correctly interpreting the test scores earned by their pupils. Uninformed teachers tend to make snap judgments on the basis of scores and to apply them with inflexible rules dictated by school administrators or specialists.

If this is true of the teachers you confer with, they may not be able to explain the meaning of your child's scores clearly. In that case, you should set a meeting with someone like the school psychologist or guidance counselor who does have the background for making the scores clear to you.

It is likely that your schools don't make it a practice to discuss test scores in regular teacher-parent conferences. If so, make an appointment through the school office with someone who can tell you all about your child's test scores (this would probably be an officer like the school psychologist or an assistant principal). You can give interest as your reason for wanting the conference.

Such a request from you could not be legally refused in almost any part of the country. Your child's official school record must be shown and explained to you at your request under the present laws or regulations of most states today. And test scores are very likely to be part of that record.

How often should you check up on your child's test scores like this? It's a good idea to do it as much as once a year if your school is among the numerous ones that give standardized tests in every grade. Otherwise, find out when the school administers tests and ask about your child's scores each time the youngster is tested.

2. Find Out How the School Interprets Your Child's Test Scores

When you learn what your child's test scores are, you should ask two more questions:

How do the teachers and administrators interpret the scores? That is, what do the scores mean about how your child is developing, and how the child might best be taught?

Are any actions concerning the child being taken on the basis of the test scores?

The answers to these questions will bring out in the open any possible "halo" effects from tests that may be beneficial, or any possibly unwarranted downgrading effects.

Asking these questions can also alert you in advance to a planned placement of your child in school, whether good or bad. And knowing ahead of time about an approaching bad placement (like the ones covered in Chapter 5) can put you in a good position to work on having a better placement arranged.

3. Question Any Test Scores that Seem Low to You, Based on Other Evidence

As you saw at the start of the chapter, any one test score earned by your child can fall far below the score that would truly indicate your child's ability.

Keep this clearly in mind whenever you learn about your child's test scores from the teacher or other school official. Be very alert for any scores—in reading comprehension, arithmetic computation, or "mental abilities" generally—that are lower than what you would expect from other things you know about your child. These other things might be your own direct acquaintance with those abilities in daily life or in helping with homework. Or they might be the teacher's own marks and comments on assignments and report cards.

Question any low scores that you notice, especially in talking with teachers. You'll recall how test scores can act powerfully as self-fulfilling prophecies in the minds of teachers. This is a major reason for not letting possibly erroneous low scores remain unquestioned with your child's teacher.

You have two grounds on which to question low scores of your child. One is accuracy. As you saw before, there is some chance that any score earned by your child can be a great deal lower than the child's true score. A score may be inaccurate by a small to large amount; a score that other evidence indicates to be low may reflect a large inaccuracy.

Validity is the other ground on which to base your questions about dubiously low test scores. The key point is that any test score gotten by your child on a test that is not appropriate for that child is invalid—a meaningless, misleading, worthless score.

As an extreme example, your child's score on an IQ or "mental abilities" test that was written in Chinese would be invalid. That's obvious. What isn't so obvious is that any test depending on English language skills (and just about all tests given in schools do depend on English skills) would be invalid if your child had not had typical opportunities to develop skills in standard American English.

Lack of such opportunity would be very notable in the case of a learning disability in language. It would be true if your child happened to be much stronger in Spanish than English—which is the case for millions of children in American public schools. It would be true if your child, like millions more, were far more proficient in Black English than in standard English.

A dialect spoken in many of the country's black communities, Black English has been increasingly recognized in recent years as a highly developed, completely sophisticated language in its own right. A landmark step in its recognition came with the 1979 decision of Federal District Court Judge Charles W. Joiner concerning a school district in Ann Arbor, Michigan. His precedent-setting decision ordered the district to have its teachers trained in ways of identifying pupils who speak Black English and effectively teaching them standard English.

You might be amazed to see how dramatically this matter of standard versus Black English background affects the validity of test scores if you were to take the "Dove Counterbalanced Intelligence Test." For a change, the "Dove" intelligence test puts the shoe on the other foot. It was written in Black English by Adrian Dove, a social worker in the predominantly black community of Watts in Los Angeles, California. He wrote it to measure intelligence as commonly understood in lower-class black America.

Giving it to a small sample of residents of a black neighborhood in New Haven, Connecticut, a Yale University faculty member found that their average score was 97 percent correct answers. Dove test scores for persons unfamiliar with Black English typically run from 15 to 0 percent.

From this, you can get an idea of how important it is to question any low scores your child may receive on tests that are not valid for that child. You might keep in mind also two other common factors that make test results invalid: Test comparison covering material your child hasn't been taught; and comparison of your child's score to the scores of a reference group (or "norming" group) of children to whom your child is not really comparable.

4. Challenge Class Placements Based Largely on Test Scores

Schools often assign children to classes or groups within classes that are intended to do them the most good. On the other hand, class placements of "slow" or "remedial" repeated over a few years can permanently limit a child's development. Schoolmates, teachers, and even the child in time come to see the person so assigned as a permanently limited individual.

Be wary, then, whenever you learn that your child is to be put in some program or group for slower progress or special help. Make sure this assignment is one your child really needs before you agree to it.

Ask searchingly about the basis for such an assignment if you're in any doubt about the need. In a borderline case, the reasons may not be at all strong; on occasion, you may find the teacher or other official justifying the proposed placement mainly on the basis of one or a few test scores.

Should that happen, challenge the potentially limiting placement. Test scores can be grossly inaccurate, as you've seen. Emphasize instead your child's record in schoolwork. The record in schoolwork would probably be strong enough to support your stand if the placement were being urged mainly because of test scores. You should be able to succeed in heading off an action that could cramp and stifle your child's growth.

5. *Keep Your Spirits High Even Though Your Child May Have Low Scores*

One last countermeasure applies to you, and could prove the most important one of all. Keep your own enthusiasm and hopes and affection for your child at the highest pitch, whatever you find out about his or her test scores over the years. Feeling fundamentally that your child is great can be especially important if you see that the test scores are consistently low and consistently agree with everything else you know about the child's abilities.

After all, the most important elements in the worth of an individual stand outside the narrow range of school abilities and tests designed to provide means of assessing them. Value your child for wonderful personal qualities and a unique, individual style and range of accomplishments like those of no one else on earth. Winning means having the spirit of a champion about achievements that are within one's powers. Your confidence and backing represent essential ingredients for developing a dauntless champ.

IO

High School Strategies that Lead to Top Colleges and Careers

High school years can prove especially important for your child's future. They are the years in which the youngster can score a big winning, as most American parents would see it—admission to one of the country's top colleges, with fine prospects for going on to a high-income, high-status career.

Your child can easily realize this kind of winning in high school if the boy or girl really wants to and has one of the right combinations of capabilities and background for it—and if he or she takes the right steps. But without the right steps, the same child can just as easily lose out on success.

For other kinds of children, trying to push them to win in this way can frequently lead to a very painful failure. Different children deserve to and need to win in their own ways in high school. The high school years are just as important for their kinds of winning.

This chapter tells how your child can become well qualified for top colleges and careers, if the child is really cut out for it. It also explains how your child can best succeed in other ways that are truly fulfilling if a top college wouldn't fit.

Getting Off to a Good Start

Heading into high school provides an especially good time for stock-taking and a look ahead by you and your child. Those next few years will see your child grown up physically, and becoming socially ready to leave home for college, work, or adventure. The child should be excited by the prospect of high school, reached at last after seemingly endless years of having been just a little kid. You can capitalize on the excitement felt by the whole family to plan on making the most of these pivotal years.

You should do all you can to make starting high school count for your child in each of three major directions. All three are vital, whether your child proves in time to be a strong top college prospect or far happier pursuing some other future. Here are the three directions and what you can do in each.

1. Learning in School

Regular courses and learning in school continue to be even more important as your child's main work in life. Study workloads generally increase in high school; young people in some high school programs study harder than many college students.

You should accordingly give or arrange for any special help your child may need for comfortable, optimum learning progress. Such help might include sessions to build reading speed (perhaps at a reading skills development center in your school system), or tutoring to clear up areas of math that remain fuzzy. Try to start such special help even before the child enters high school.

Then, in advance talks with advisers and with your child to plan the first high school program of courses, you should work to have your child placed in courses that will be as challenging as possible. Why and how to do this are discussed in the next main section of the chapter.

2. Career

It's not too early to take imminent high school entrance as a timely occasion for you and your child to start seriously considering a career. This means a start on consistent, serious exploration of working and possible jobs for the person. It doesn't mean making anything like a definite choice of future career at this time.

Exploring work and careers at this point is a very good idea, even though most middle-class families postpone all but the dreamiest, blue-sky notions about careers until or even after college years. Exploring careers now can help make clear to your child why some hard courses in high school and college are important. Such discussion can begin providing a comfortable transition for your child from being dependent on you to being self-supporting. Most important of all, it can head off the very real danger of having your child suffer one of the worst kinds of shocks in the lives of young Americans today: finishing their education with high hopes and then not being able to find a job.

Chronic oversupplies of college graduates will move out into the job market every year in the 1980s. Not even graduation from a top college guarantees a good starting job today unless the student has prepared for some field with fair to high employment demand. But you can take vital steps to help your child avoid going jobless, as we explain later.

One of the best ways to help your child explore careers early in high school is by starting to talk often about the various possibilities. Also, try to have the youngster repeatedly visit places where very familiar people work—you, your wife/husband, other relatives, and close family friends.

You can do still other valuable things. Help the child get part-time work outside the home to develop experience. Encourage talks with older young people who are preparing for careers or who have recently started work. Steer the conversation toward careers and what's happening in your own work and field. Libraries and bookstores have many interesting books on careers and working for teenagers. Some of these should be around the house.

3. Activities and Interests

Extracurricular activities can prove essential for admission to a top college. Still more important, such activities are not only fine recreation but can further your child's development significantly in social and personal areas, and even in academic and career directions.

Try hard, then, to interest your child in participating in one or two activities when entering high school—either extracurricular activities in school, or organized activities in the community. These could further an already established interest, as in music, art, or sports, or open a new interest in activities such as newswriting, debate, dramatics, photography, or community service.

In addition, you might also resolve to give your maturing child more encouragement to pursue hobbies and personal reading interests, and more cultural experiences in going to plays, art galleries, museums, zoos, historic sites, and concerts. It can be helpful as well to aid the youngster in learning and talking about current events. Steps like these can broaden a child's educational and social horizons very advantageously.

But be careful not to overdo the cultivation of activities and interests for your child. As we said before, it pressures and strains any child to schedule activities for every waking moment. Kids need intervals of free time to play, think, or just loaf. Moreover, top colleges today generally do not prefer the applicant who is involved in three or more activities; to them, such a youngster tends to look scattered and superficial. They prefer the applicant who has persisted in one activity or interest long enough to accomplish something of genuine significance.

Spotting Educational "Straitjackets" in High School— And Beating Them

You should arm yourself thoroughly in the year before your child enters high school for the conference on the levels and kinds of courses scheduled for your child. This conference and later actions of yours can shape your child's future. Be sure, as well, to talk to your child about these high school courses.

The courses will come up when either you or your child, or both, meet with a school official (probably the assistant principal or guidance counselor) to work out or go over the program planned for the youngster. The meeting should come some weeks before your child graduates from junior high or middle school.

Why is a seemingly routine conference like this so important? Because these high school programs amount to tracks that lead children to dramatically different futures. The highest tracks can prove to be express highways to top colleges and fine careers; the lowest tracks typically carry students only into the lowest-paid clerical or manual jobs, if that.

Moreover, in the typical "comprehensive" high school of today, there's seldom any word of "tracks" or "tracking" for students. Students are supposed to be able to move freely, as their accomplishment warrants, between tracks. But the fact is that the tracks tend to become self-perpetuating. The actual but hidden lower tracks all too often turn into straitjackets on future lives.

For instance, Dolores Spivano headed into the "general" secretarial program in high school on the very plausible basis of final grades of C−, D, and one F she'd gotten in her last junior high year. She'd been home sick a lot that year, and only late in the year did a doctor diagnose the cause as an "unusually severe" case of mononucleosis, which finally cleared up.

Dolores and her family didn't have too much reason to object to her planned secretarial program. They didn't see it as low tracked, nor did they see Dolores herself as particularly bright. They'd thought that the fair number of As she'd gotten in earlier years had come only because she was a hardworking, obedient child.

Her three older brothers were really the bright ones in the family, she believed. Two were already in college, and the financial load on the family was very heavy. Their dad didn't make much money as an insurance clerk. Dolores rather liked the notion that her secretarial program would lead to fairly well paid work right out of high school. She could help out all the sooner with the very tight finances at home.

Through her tenth-grade year, Dolores made exceptional progress in typing and shorthand. She easily got As in all her other courses, even though she also had babysitting jobs three or four nights a week. Her friendships and social life revolved around classmates in the general programs, from whom college-bound kids shied away.

Dolores got a full-time typing job at a local real estate firm for the summer after tenth grade. She was dazzled to bring home $120 a week. And she could still make about $60 a week by continuing to work afternoons and Saturdays after starting back to school with a heavy secretarial courseload that fall.

That same fall, not long after starting her junior year in high school, the high school gave all students the first test for National Merit scholarships ("PSAT-NMSQT," it was called). Dolores thought nothing of it. She and her family had long since dismissed any idea of her going to college.

She had just got a raise to $75 in her part-time job when a printed slip of paper was handed out in school saying that her scores on the test put her ahead of more than some 98 percent of the students nationwide who had taken it. That made her feel good, but she thought it was just some kind of accident, and threw the slip away. She later got a certificate saying something like "semi-finalist," along with directions for taking a further test. She threw those away, too. By now, she saw clearly where she was going and didn't want to be distracted.

However, Dolores could have headed toward quite another future. All the A grades she earned and those scores very strongly suggest that Dolores would have been able to go instead to a very fine college on full financial aid—if she hadn't gotten straitjacketed on a low track in high school.

Jim McGregor, by contrast, didn't need to earn money by working and had very busy and preoccupied parents. A big, bumbling kind of boy, his passion was sports. He played all kinds of sports in much of his spare time. He was good at sports, but not great; enthused but somewhat uncoordinated. He seemed very boyish and immature, despite his size.

In junior high, he hung around with the boys really good in sports and picked up the scorn for studies that some of them affected. His grades slid down to mostly Ds as he wound up junior high.

It's no surprise, then, that he was scheduled to start in courses on the "general academic" track in high school, except for a regular college-prep English course as an experiment. But his real interest at high school was sports. He paid as little attention to studies as possible in his first year. He soured on his English class after an unfortunate early run-in with the teacher; his grade for the year accordingly was D—, while his other grades were Cs and C—s. Naturally, he continued on in the general academic track the following year.

One day in a practice scrimmage Jim dove at an awkward angle for a fumble. After the pile-up of six other players climbed off him, he found he had a broken ankle. That made him something of a hero as he hobbled around school on crutches. It also opened up long stretches of idle time. He somehow started to fill it more and more by reading, just for fun, first in sports and then in almost everything.

By the time Jim got the cast off and the strength in his leg back, he was reading four or five hours a day. He had grown more sure of himself, more independent, more thoughtful. He went out for tennis but held his practice time down. The spring before his senior year, he talked with his counselor and argued hard for a senior year program that included college-prep biology and a combined literature-history course in American studies. Doing his coursework turned out to be really fascinating in the last year, and he astonished himself by winding up with an A— average.

Jim realized then that he might have been doing that kind of work all along. And he knew that he was about three years behind his friends who were going off to college.

"I'd really be going somewhere today," he said, "if only I hadn't been started wrong in high school."

To get your own child started right in high school, your basic rule of thumb should always be to try for the higher track. This is the rule to follow if you want your child prepared as well as possible for college, and unless you see really compelling reasons for your child to start in a lower track.

No one will tell you that your boy or girl is being routed on a lower or higher track. School advisers will talk instead of kinds and levels of courses. But you can see from the chart of "Key Clues to Higher and Lower Tracks in High School" given below which courses mean a lower or a higher track.

You child's marks on report cards through junior high or middle school will have much to do with setting the track for high school. But

Key Clues to Lower and Higher Tracks in High School

	Clues by Course Subjects	*Clues by Course Levels or Kinds*	*Other Clues*
Lowest Tracks	"Business" English (noncollege-prep)	noncollege-prep	leads to "general" diploma
	"Business" or "applied" math (noncollege-prep)		
	Shop subjects		
	Secretarial or business subjects		
	Art, Music, Health & Family Life, Home Economics		
Middle Tracks	English (college-prep) Math (") Social studies (& History) (") Science (") Foreign languages (")	"standard" (average ability) college-prep level; or "enriched" (above average ability) college-prep level	leads to "academic" diploma
Higher Tracks	English (college-prep) Math (") Social studies (& History) (") Science (") Foreign languages (")	"honors" or "accelerated" or (in junior or senior years) "Advanced Placement"	leads to "academic" diploma

NOTE: Terms given in quotations are typical, illustrative ones; the actual terms used by your school may differ but should be recognizably similar.

so will your own and the child's plans. You should be able to get the youngster scheduled for at least some college-prep courses if you insist strongly enough—unless the child seems very clearly not qualified for them. Do insist, if you want to keep college opportunity open for the child.

Be ready to insist on a course-by-course basis, for high schools often track subject by subject rather than for a student's whole study program. College-prep courses are given in five subject areas, widely called solids. (As indicated in the "Key Clues" chart, these subject areas are: English, math, social studies including history, science, and foreign languages.)

The question for a child is usually whether he or she can "carry" the heavy work of some number of "solids." It is hence common for students of about C— to B average ability to schedule three or four solids when starting high school, and for those with higher ability to schedule five solids. For a student to be scheduled for a solid on an accelerated or honors level, quite good marks or keen interest in the subject is normally required.

You would want to get your child started in high school with three or four solids for a good beginning in college-prep work. You should cite signs of high ability or interest in arguing for placement on the honors or accelerated level in one or more subjects.

Getting into one or more courses on that highest, accelerated level when starting high school should be carefully considered by you and your child. You have strong reasons to try for it if the youngster has the interest and ability to handle it, perhaps with much effort. If not, the experience could backfire badly on the child's confidence as a winner. At stake, should the child really have what it takes, is the possibility of getting a whole year's college work done while still in high school— with savings to you of up to $8,000 or more—plus a potent advantage for admission to top colleges. This is explained in the later section on "Advanced Placement" courses.

On the other hand, if you, the child, and the advisers all agree on a compelling need for a lower track, make the best of that track. You'll want to come to that conclusion if a higher track would prove only a punishing experience for your child. Perhaps try for one course on a higher track, and see how it goes. Children who turn out to be badly overloaded can usually be transferred to less demanding (and lower-track) courses during the school year.

By the same token, you might try for transfer to a higher track in a subject in which your child is doing unusually well. However, such up-track transfers are usually made only at the start of a new year or semester (because a child transferring up would otherwise have missed out on much course content already covered by the class).

Finally, for a child with a learning disability, the program of courses in each high school year should be planned for the child's individual needs. Tracks and levels as such should be largely disregarded. Most important, the child's entire instruction should be planned with the help of knowledgeable specialists in learning disabilities.

College-prep studies can certainly be worked into the program of a learning-disabled child, perhaps extensively. But college-prep work should not be more than the youngster can handle. Even young people with severe lags in learning due to disabilities often find it practical to go on to college. You could explore this possibility by making special inquiries at individual colleges that interest the child and yourself. (You may also find it helpful to obtain the list of "Colleges/Universities that Accept Students with Learning Disabilities," from the Association for Children with Learning Disabilities, 4156 Library Rd., Pittsburgh, Pa. 15234.)

Basic Career Skills Courses Can Be Helpful to Your Child

A few other high school courses that your child might choose are particularly important—courses that provide career skills with high employability. It wouldn't be a good idea to emphasize these in the first high school year at the possible expense of solid, college-prep coursework. But the youngster and you might remember to pick up one or two of them later on when scheduling permits. Don't overlook them because of pressure from two other kinds of courses—attractive but noncollege-prep courses in areas like art, music, and shop (woodworking, electricity, etc.), and courses required for the diploma like phys ed, health or hygiene, and citizenship or an equivalent.

Career skills courses can bring a double advantage. Most directly, they can develop at least the rudiments of job skills that are widely employable today; these skills are also highly useful adjuncts in many kinds of professional and managerial careers. Secondarily, taking such courses can help in your child's career development, since they are courses taken specifically to prepare for work.

Typing is one such course; touch typing can be self-taught at home, but mastering it in the enforced routine of a course helps develop proficiency up to the level of at least 40 or 50 words per minute— the level at which a boy or girl can actually get part-time or full-time work almost anywhere in the country. In addition, being able to type student papers helps considerably in getting better grades in high school as well as college.

Bookkeeping or basic accounting represents another useful career skills course, especially with a later course or two in accounting. This is also true of the introductory courses in computer operating and programming that are offered by fairly large numbers of high schools today.

Drafting is another widely employable skill taught in courses given by a number of high schools. One or two courses in drafting would be particularly appropriate for a youngster with a bent for mechanics or building. For a person who might go into any kind of sales or office work, speech courses, if available, could develop a generally advantageous career skill.

You might talk over an interesting point with your child about all these courses. Almost all the courses the youngster takes in high school represent learning a person would need for a career. Which courses connect with which careers—and with *whose* careers, among people the child knows? Which courses give you all that you need for work right now, in areas that seem to have lots of job openings (as judged by glancing over "Help Wanted" ads)?

Improving Study Skills in Your Child

Good study skills can help your child feel like a winner, in high school especially. That's when the academic load can build heavily. Study skills give the youngster the confidence of familiar, organized, proven ways of tackling any assignment, however tough it may first appear.

For youngsters who generally find schoolwork interesting and not too hard, good skills can mean the difference between Bs and As. For borderline boys or girls, they can similarly raise Fs to passing or better.

It's not unlikely that you'll find yourself teaching some study skills to your child. Schools rarely give specific work in them except for pupils who fall seriously behind. Teachers in lower grades often think they'll be covered in higher years; teachers in upper grades assume they've already been taken care of somewhere in earlier years. What actually happens is that kids who succeed have developed their skills on a largely improvised and intuitive basis, but not without gaps.

So, don't be surprised to find yourself sitting down often with the youngster to do a little informal teaching. On one occasion, you may be demonstrating how to get all the meat out of any hard chapter; at other times you could be showing how to take clear notes in outline form on a reading assignment, or helping outline and plan research for a term paper, or explaining ways to cut through the knots in tough word problems in math.

Not only your aid but your comfort can very substantially help your child develop effective study skills and habits. The quality of the background setting you provide for your child's high school study at home counts even more heavily than the specific skills you explain. Your child will best develop skills and pick up pointers from you in a framework of interest, confidence, quiet, and good sense. Rules for you to follow in supplying this foundation for good study skills are given below.

If only for ideas, you and your child should learn of the many detailed techniques for good study explained in one or two of the various books available in libraries and bookstores. One book you might find especially informative is:

Helping Your Teen-Age Student: What Parents Can Do to Improve Reading and Study Skills, by Marvin Cohen (Dutton, 1979).

Others that could be used by your child and yourself include:

How to Study Better and Get Higher Marks, by Eugene Ehrlich (Harper & Row; Apollo Editions, paperback, 1976);

How to Study, by Clifford T. Morgan and James Deese (McGraw-Hill, paperback, 1979);

Effective Study, by Francis P. Robinson (Harper & Row, paperback, 1970);

Thirty Ways to Improve Your Grades, by Harry Shaw (McGraw-Hill, paperback, 1975);

How to Study in College, by Walter Pauk (Houghton Mifflin, 1979).

A two-volume work published in 1979 was written under impressive auspices by educators at Harvard University and Milton Academy (hence the "HM"). It forms a workbook for your youngster and a teacher's guide for your use in working along with the child:

HM Study Skills Program (National Association of Secondary School Principals; grades 8–10 edition, workbook $3.50, teacher's guide $2.50; available from the NASSP at 1904 Association Drive, Reston, Va. 22091. Editions for grades 5–7 and first-year college are scheduled for 1980 publication.)

Rules for You—the Parent—to Help Build Good Study Skills and Habits in Your Child

1. *A Place to Study.* Provide a regular place for homework—reasonably undisturbed and attractive if possible.
2. *A Study Schedule.* Try to have the child study at generally regular times through every week of school.
3. *Managing Study Time.* Help the boy or girl manage study time well—planning ahead, allocating, and putting in proper time for

each subject; and breaking any long assignments into a scheduled series of workable tasks.

4. *Sharing Study Interests.* Share the child's interests, annoyances, and confusions with studies by talking them over, sympathetically and in private; show that you're interested and understanding, but don't intrude.

5. *Your Help with Study—When and How.* Offer help whenever the child asks or seems stymied; something like, "Let's see if we can figure it out together," can strike a good opening note. (It's especially fine when, as you both go along, the child can teach you something.)

6. *Teaching Study Skills.* Be as ready as you can (perhaps with some advance reading or brush-up on the side yourself) to teach skills for good study—like writing down and learning the meaning of each new term in a subject when the term is first met; close analysis, memorization, and practice of new material in math textbooks; reviewing for tests, etc.

7. *Never Be Negative.* Don't ever be negative—that is, criticizing, condescending, sarcastic, or threatening—about your child's abilities or performance in study. Such negative behavior will only tend to make the child hate learning and feel less able.

Helping Your Child Get a Good College-Prep Record

During that spring of his senior year in high school, Joseph Caglione and his folks never knew how close he had come to admission with a large scholarship at that Ivy League college in New England. It was his first choice college. A few days after mid-April, he received only the polished letter expressing regret and commenting generally on the very high qualifications of the whole group of applicants that year.

But in fact, the file folder with his application, school transcript, test score reports, school recommendations, and other papers had been held active for weeks by the admissions committee. Committee members had been much impressed by his A— average, his rank of fourteenth in a class of 800, his entrance test scores at mid-90s percentiles, the counselor's recommendation of him as a very bright, widely liked, and responsible person, his clear and vigorous writing, and especially his long leadership of community youth drives against alcohol abuse that had sharply reduced teenage car accidents.

What really had given them pause was the program of courses he had taken. Not that it didn't meet their college-prep requirements. They didn't set specific requirements, but instead suggested strong college preparation in the college bulletin or viewbook for applicants. This policy was designed mainly to keep the door open for the very rare near-genius with unavoidably erratic preparation, and for very promising youngsters with disadvantaged backgrounds or other handicaps that ruled out their completion of strong college-prep programs.

Joseph didn't fit either of these categories, however. He'd had the opportunity and the ability to do outstanding college-prep work. His family situation, while certainly not affluent, was stable and untroubled. His suburban high school, which they knew through earlier applicants, offered a full range of academic studies with many honors and "Advanced Placement" courses.

Joseph hadn't gotten into any of these higher track courses. He'd instead pursued work on the regular college-prep track. In college-prep courses, his transcript showed four years of English, two years of math, a year each of social studies and U.S. history, two years of science, two years of French, and one year of Spanish. To the admissions committee, this looked surprisingly weak in quantity as well as in level for someone of Joseph's caliber (for reasons explained shortly). The rest of his courses were largely in art, music, phys ed, health, and shop areas.

Much as they liked Joseph's other qualities, committee members had seen again and again that he just didn't compare well against other applicants who had similarly appealing qualities outside their course-work but stronger preparatory studies. On a final show of hands, he had lost out in the committee by only two votes.

Joseph never knew this, of course. In time he got over his disappointment and went instead to his state university (which, incidentally, cost him and his family as much as the Ivy League college would have—for reasons given in Chapter 13).

But it could have been different. Joseph had earlier shied away from chances to get into honors courses. Reflecting attitudes in his circle of friends, he had typically said, "Oh, no thanks. I'm doing OK where I am. That kind of stuff is for weirdos and girls."

Students who take lighter college-prep loads than they can carry comfortably often short-change themselves in many other ways, besides ones like Joe's near-miss on a rare opportunity in life. For college-bound youngsters, the quality and amount of education generally increase with the strength of college-prep studies taken in high school.

But many of the benefits from stronger college-prep work don't appear until later years. They can include:

1. Actual savings of as much as $8,000 in college costs (explained in the following section on Advanced Placement courses);

2. Broader and deeper preparation for college studies, which tends to result in higher marks or grades in college;
3. More extensive development of the student's learning and thinking abilities, which can prove a valuable asset all through a professional or executive career; and
4. Stronger capabilities and qualifications for most scholarship competitions.

Advantages such as these may give you background helpful in persuading your teenager starting in high school to do the right thing by college-prep labors. This can take some urging. Chances are the boy or girl has lots of exciting things besides studying in mind, not to mention friends who scorn high marks and bookworms.

But you and the youngster also need to know what college-prep work of various degrees of difficulty amounts to. The following table gives you a summary. It covers the years from ninth through twelfth grades (with ninth possibly spent in junior high school), and gives the number of years of high school study in each "solid" (academic subject of college-prep caliber) that go into college-prep programs of varying strengths.

College-Prep Programs in High School, Grades 9–12

Subject	Strongest Possible (a rarity)	Strong (enough to get into most colleges)	Fairly Light (but enough to get into many colleges)
English	4 years	4 years	3–4 years
Math	3–4	2–3	1–2
Social studies	3–4	2–3	2
Sciences	3–4	2	1
Foreign languages	3–4	3	0–2
Total no. of "solids" (1-year courses)	16–20	13–15	8–11

Five vital points that you should understand about these college-prep programs follow.

1. *Any* college-prep program is strengthened further by courses taken on the honors (or accelerated) and Advanced Placement levels.

Suppose that Sue Jones took a college-prep program about like the "strong" one in the table, but her college-prep courses were all on the regular level. Bill Evers, on the other hand, racked up about the same numbers of years as Sue in each college-prep subject area but instead got into courses on the honors and Advanced Placement levels in English and math. Bill's program would be a stronger college-prep one than Sue's, even though they'd studied the same number of years in each subject.

Don't push too hard, however, to have your child put in honors or accelerated-level courses in all five of the college-prep subject areas in any or every year unless the child seems to be fantastically able academically and eager for it. The most intensely bright young people in high school usually do honors Advanced Placement work in only three of the subjects, or sometimes four—and at that, they may put in about fifty-five hours a week on studies alone, in addition to their time in activities, home life, work, sports, social life, recreational reading and culture, and (importantly) relaxing.

Again, workload can build incredibly for a high school youngster. Don't, *don't* overdo it.

2. High school students very commonly show higher abilities and interests in some areas rather than others through ninth and tenth grades. Certain students flourish most in the math-science areas; perhaps more take best to the English–social studies–foreign languages areas. The completed college-prep programs of high school seniors accordingly tend to show a concentration in one or the other of these broad areas. A pattern of even length and strength across all subjects— as indicated in the "Strongest Possible" program category in the table— is quite rare.

3. College-prep programs can serve important career preparatory purposes for students going on to four-year colleges. Concentrating courses in certain subject areas can tend either to open up new career fields for a student or to provide preparation for a career already selected.

For instance, students who might later enter medicine or other health care careers acquire essential basic knowledge in general science, biology, chemistry, physics, and in Advanced Placement courses in those sciences. Future engineers and architects similarly need extensive math and sciences, especially physics and possibly also chemistry. Skill in English is one of the pivotal capabilities for future executives and lawyers, who will also often find extensive knowledge in math, sciences, and social studies quite helpful.

In view of this, the subjects in which your child concentrates his or her college-prep studies can directly contribute to and shape the youngster's future career.

Note also that subjects like art, music, phys ed, or home economics can be important for college-prep and career-prep purposes. This can be true for a student who has a very strong present interest in one of them that seems likely to grow still stronger in future years—perhaps as a college major and eventual career field. However, these are not subjects required for college admission except in specialized college programs.

4. It's important for you to understand: in *social studies,* diploma requirements as well as college admissions requirements commonly include one year of American history (typically an eleventh-grade course); in *sciences,* admissions requirements commonly are two years, including one year in a laboratory course (a course typically having two lab sessions a week in addition to classroom sessions); in *foreign languages,* colleges prefer three or more years in one language to develop substantial proficiency, rather than only two years in one language and one or more in a second foreign language.

5. Finally, you should realize that your child could get admitted to any one of many hundreds of respected private colleges today with no prior foreign language study, one or even no years of math study, no lab science, and, in general, very light college-preparatory work. These colleges need students and have greatly relaxed their college-prep requirements in recent decades. Your child would need strong to strongest college-prep work only for one or more of three reasons:

First, in trying for admission to one of the fifty or so most sought-after private colleges in the country.

Second, in trying for admission to one of the more sought-after state universities, which tend to impose college-prep subject requirements more rigidly than the most sought-after private colleges.

Third, in trying to get the most value out of his or her high school studies for advantages in future college study and career, and perhaps for saving thousands of dollars.

Go for Advanced Placement Courses if Appropriate for Your Child

Gregory Hauser recently went right out of Irondequoit High School in Rochester, New York, and on into Michigan State University with credit for more than a year's college study completed—forty-one credits at Michigan State, to be precise. He saved more than $3,500 in college costs. More than $700 in tuition alone at Pennsylvania State University was similarly saved by Sue Weltman, of Watchung Hills, New Jersey.

But perhaps the largest savings of all are realized regularly by more than 250 students entering Harvard University in each current year.

Although they graduated from high school only the spring before, these students enter Harvard as sophomores. They have a full freshman year's credits at Harvard that they earned through courses and exams taken while still in high school. Costs for a dorm student for a year at Harvard total $8,300 as of 1979–80. All 250 students hence save a total of more than $2 million in college costs at Harvard. And, as frosting on the cake, the qualifications that realized these savings also served to give them a leg-up in competition for Harvard admission.

More important, these able young people gained important educational benefits in high school and college. They avoided wasted time and boredom in high school by going on into challenging courses; they avoided having to repeat college courses with content they already knew.

Advanced Placement courses could bring advantages like these to your child. It's not unlikely that your high school gives "AP" courses—more than 4,300 high schools in all parts of the country do. If the local high school doesn't, join with others in the community—especially interested high school teachers—in pushing for their introduction as your child starts high school. Some AP courses could be available by the time your child is ready in another year or two. You can obtain an informative introductory booklet, *A Guide to the Advanced Placement Program,* on request to the program (College Board, 888 Seventh Ave., New York, N.Y. 10019).

What would make AP study appropriate for your son or daughter? The main factors would be above average interest and marks in one or more subjects. Indications of interest and ability might include placement of the child in honors or accelerated-level courses in those subjects in early high school years. Or they might include high B+ or better marks with lots of output (turning in extra assignments, good class participation, tackling special projects or problems) in regular-level college-prep courses. Teachers' recommendations based on such considerations normally get students into AP courses.

It doesn't take exceptional ability for a student to do well in AP courses, a number of high schools have found. If your child's high school is among them, the youngster may be allowed to enter an AP course simply by expressing interest in doing so and getting your approval. That's the policy, for instance, at the two high schools of Pittsfield, Massachusetts, which together offer sixteen AP courses.

In Pittsfield, a student who obviously would not be able to do the work of an AP course is advised against going ahead. But most who say they're interested and have their parents' consent are allowed in. More than seven out of every ten students going into AP courses there achieve at levels of college-caliber quality.

Your child would be ready for any AP course after having finished the prior high school-content courses in the subject at any time before graduating. You see, AP courses are college-level ones given in high school. Most students doing AP work take the college-level courses in their eleventh-or twelfth-grade year. But AP biology, for instance, is sometimes taken in the tenth-grade year, usually in the case of students who've had the regular one-year high school biology lab course in ninth grade.

Here are the subjects in which your child might take AP courses, grouped by the five college-prep subject areas about which we've been talking:

**Advanced Placement Courses—Subjects
in Which They Can Be Offered**

English
   "Advanced Placement English" (one course, covering typical college freshman-year English)
Math
   "Advanced Placement Mathematics" (or "Calculus")
Social Studies
   American History
   European History
Sciences
   Biology
   Chemistry
   Physics
Foreign Languages
   "Classics"—Latin (third year)
   French
   German
Other
   Art (a history of art course, or a studio art course)
   Music (a listening and literature course, or a theory course)

These are the dozen subjects in which Advanced Placement Examinations corresponding to the AP courses are offered in 1980. (Additions and refinements are regularly made in courses and exams.) Participating high schools give the exams in one week of May every year, usually the third week. Outlines for the courses and the corresponding exams are provided, along with much other coordination, explanation, development, and research, by the Advanced Placement Program of the College Entrance Examination Board.

Few, if any, high schools give AP courses in all twelve subjects. Offerings in a half dozen or so are more typical.

What would a typical AP agenda for your child look like? It would start with above average performance in at least one subject early in high school. The subject or subjects would be ones in which the school does (or will) offer an AP course or two.

Your child finishes all courses in the subject leading up to the AP course(s), with continued above average performance. The youngster gets recommended for and enrolled in the AP course(s).

In May, the child takes the AP exam for that course in the school. Taking the exam isn't required, but it is necessary in order to get AP work considered for credit by colleges.

AP exam marks earned by your child could range from a high of 5 to a low of 1. Each college sets its own policy on which exams and which marks will be good for credit (and how much credit) toward the college's degree.

An AP exam mark of at least 3 or "qualified" earned by your child would be good for credit at any one of many hundreds of colleges (though some colleges might set the minimum at 2, or at 4, or not recognize the exam for credit at all).

Your child's exam marks would be reported to the colleges where the boy or girl is (or will be) applying for admission. The college your child finally attends would notify him/her of its AP credit decisions before registration at the college.

Benefits could be considerable. More than 1,000 colleges grant credit for AP. Some 200 others besides Harvard grant a full year's credit for qaulifying scores on three or four AP exams—including Stanford, Yale, Vassar, Notre Dame, California State University at Fresno, and the Universities of Hawaii, Denver, Maryland, Wisconsin, and Minnesota.

As you see, if your child has a chance and a hankering for AP studies, there's good reason to give them a try. If workable, they represent one very beneficial way to win in high school.

Make the Most of It if Your Child Heads for Work Instead of College

Depending on how you look at it, high school can prove especially welcome for other quite different kinds of youngsters—the many boys and girls who just don't enjoy inactive, abstract, bookish studies. For them, high school can mark the beginning of being able to learn and work for much of their time at other things they really like. It's possible for them to flourish as never before.

You'd be foolish to feel disappointed if your child proves to be a youngster like this through the first term or so of high school. And it would be worse to try to force the child through a heavy college-prep program and on into four years of college.

Plenty of fine career opportunities stand open for young people who don't get four years of college. The widely held notion to the contrary simply doesn't square with the facts. In nationwide projections, there are three times as many job openings a year for persons without four-year degrees as there are for persons with them. A number of careers open to persons without four-year degrees can lead to incomes easily as high as those of many four-year college graduates.

Harry Feldsman, for instance, had the good luck to become interested in a career as a restaurant cook and chef. Schoolwork was hard for him because of a learning disability. He regretted the fact that his school didn't offer vocational courses in "food service," as a number of high schools do. But he started learning a lot anyway by working as a part-time helper in restaurant kitchens, and went on to take the food service program at a local community college.

Now, some six years after high school, Harry makes $19,000 a year as the capable chief cook for a large, fashionable restaurant. He recently talked about running into an old high school buddy, Ben Perkins, and comparing notes on how they'd done. Ben had gone on not only to four years of college but to graduate study and college teaching. Harry felt sad to hear how Ben had to hustle to line up work every year, teaching only a course or two at each of three or four different colleges, and even at that wound up making only about $7,500 a year.

Stella Brit was interested in clothes and social life in high school, and terribly bored by all her academic subjects except, to her surprise, math. She was an extremely active young lady, bursting with energy. What she really liked was the afterschool job she got at a downtown clothing boutique. She took art and dressmaking courses in high school, as well as courses in merchandising to help with her job. For the same reason she took speech, too. She also got into dramatics and did a lot of costume design and some acting.

After graduation, Stella went right to work as a salesperson for a big department store in a nationwide chain. Four years later, as many of her old high school friends were finishing college, she was promoted to the job of assistant buyer of women's clothes for the store at an annual salary of $21,000.

Some of the largest and most satisfying income possibilities open to young people who go from high school into such fields are as owners of their own businesses. People with skills and experience like Harry's often find it possible to open their own restaurants—and restaurant chains. Merchandisers like Stella have obvious capabilities for establishing stores. Auto mechanics can advance into well-paid jobs as chief mechanics and service managers, and on to running their own garages. Young people skilled and experienced in carpentry can start very profitable small businesses in home repairs and remodeling.

Even while still in high school, some young people who don't like academic work can show an impressive head for business. At the age of sixteen, Mike Glickman was asked by a realtor and family friend to deliver listings of houses for sale to other real estate offices in suburbs outside Los Angeles. Not long after, young Mike founded his own business, Brokers Specialized Services, to deliver such listings for realtors in and around Los Angeles.

By the time Mike was nineteen, his firm had thirty employees; he had also become the youngest person ever licensed as a broker with his local realty board, and made sales of more than $1 million before the end of his first year's brokering. He puts his current income at $100,000 or more a year. And he notes, "Every day, I wake up with a new idea for business."

Mike's family had wanted him to go to college and law school, but he never went. He says, "That kind of stuff never appealed to me."

In Middletown, Ohio, Roger Connors got interested in business when he visited a flower shop at the age of thirteen as part of a career-day program. Two years later, he began selling flowers from the basement of his home, and at seventeen he bought a flower shop for $12,000. He now runs two "Flowers by Roger" shops that together have annual gross sales of $100,000. Roger Connors and realtor Mike Glickman are only two of the diverse young entrepreneurs profiled in a striking, recent article by Jessica Holland entitled "Teen-Age Tycoons," that appeared in *The New York Times Magazine* (Aug. 18, 1979).

Make the most of it, then, if your child seems to be heading toward work rather than college while in high school. These examples suggest how much can be made of the many opportunities outside the college route. If opportunities like these seem best for your child, here's what to do.

1. Watch Early for Overload in College-Prep Courses. Starting no later than the ninth grade, watch carefully to see how your child does in college-prep courses. These courses can overload young people who have stronger bents in directions other than academics. Such youngsters will often show far more than usual annoyance with college-prep work.

If poor marks and resentment over one or more of these courses consistently signal overload for your child, set an early meeting with your child's guidance counselor in high school. In addition, go out of your way to let your child know that you think he/she is still just great, and that you feel sympathy rather than blame over the poor marks and difficulties with the courses. To offset further having your child's edge as a winner dulled by academic frustrations, encourage the youngster to do more in those activities or hobbies that especially bolster the teenager's confidence and high spirits.

Talk to your child about possibly shifting to some other courses that are more interesting, and ask for his/her ideas along those lines. Through the current term, help the child to put in reasonable time on the disagreeable courses and to avoid getting discouraged about them.

2. Confer with the Counselor on Better Courses and Possible Career Guidance. You and your child should next meet with the guidance counselor. Talk over the child's marks and reactions in college-prep work so far, and find out about all the other possible courses that might be better suited to the youngster's interests and talents. See which ones might be planned for the coming term. Perhaps it would be possible and constructive to shift into one of them while the current term is still under way. Such discussion should result in a better program of courses for the next term—a program more interesting and satisfying to your child, and one in which he or she can work confidently and successfully.

Ask, too, about the possibility of getting guidance for your youngster on good career possibilities to explore. Say that you think career guidance would be helpful to your child for educational planning, in view of the fact that some better course possibilities are in occupational areas rather than college-prep ones.

Starting to set career goals now can be important for your child. It's possible the youngster will be beginning work or specialized career training after high school graduation, just a few years away. In that event, your child would find it very helpful to have developed a clear idea of where he or she is going.

3. Help Your Child Develop and Get Enthused about Career Goals that Don't Involve Four Years of College. Over the coming months or longer, help your child to work out career goals that don't involve getting a four-year college degree. Career guidance from a professional may well help in this endeavor—guidance either from a school counselor (along the lines of your inquiry), or through a private counseling bureau suggested by the school counselor (or by the school psychologist serving your high school).

Professional career guidance provides no magic answers. Rather, it should help your child think carefully about possible future careers, and get extensive information and perspective—on the person's own interests and capabilities, and on all key facets of promising careers. You can help considerably in the process by talking with the youngster about all the ideas and questions that arise from the counseling.

Decisions about career goals will be left to your child, and won't be reached by the counselor. Professionals in the field only provide information, point out alternative possibilities, and outline the likely consequences of one or another choice. Making the choice itself is entirely up to the individual being counseled.

In time, your child should settle on career goals that look both appealing and practical. You can increase his or her natural satisfaction and enthusiasm for those goals by your own interest and support. Perhaps you could help your child meet and talk with people already pursuing the career, and share further discoveries in reading and hearing more about the career. You might also help your child find part-time work that would be good experience in the career field.

4. Join in Planning Your Child's Program through High School, and Possibly Short Training After. In settling on a career goal, your child will already have worked out a general plan of sound education and training for it. With each new term or year of high school, though, there will be specific details of courses, hours, and optional choices that you could join your youngster in planning. Also, quite a few careers entered without four-year college degrees today are best prepared for both in high school and in short training after graduation—at a community college for two years or less, or in a private occupational school. It would be helpful for you to join with your child in planning for such studies after high school.

Many more of these attractive careers that your child could enter without first having four years of college are described in Chapter 13, Better Ways than College to Careers for Many Teenagers. That chapter also gives a fuller explanation of the preparation after high school needed for such careers.

Winning Attitudes for Your Child Down the High School Homestretch

As your child advances on through junior and senior years of high school, he or she should have good reason to feel satisfied with schoolwork, activities, and especially goals for the immediate future. You and the school will have worked to assure this by actions like the ones outlined in this chapter.

On the one hand, your child may be heading for a good or top college with the best preparation. On the other, he or she may be progressing through present and possibly future education for early entrance into an interesting, rewarding career.

Either way, the child will be developing through pivotal high school years near or at the peak of his or her unique potential. The youngster will also be graduating with self-confidence, a sense of real accomplishment, and enthusiasm for what lies ahead. Qualities like these are all the hallmarks of a winner.

11

Winning Admission to America's Top Colleges

"Oh, Susan's going to Stanford."

"Yale? Why yes, Don will be starting there next fall."

Casual remarks like these speak volumes. So do the decal stickers you see on the rear windows of cars proclaiming, *Duke University,* or *University of Notre Dame,* or *Princeton.*

Going to one of America's most sought-after colleges represents a very conspicuous way for a teenager to be a winner today. Winning like this can of course bring your child special advantages. In general, among the advantages are an education and classmates of a quality that many of America's "best families" strive to assure for their own children. This chapter tells how your child actually could win admission to a top college—if workable and wanted by your child.

Besides those that impress almost everyone, there are many other top colleges about which you may not even know. These colleges can be excellent choices for young people of wide ranges of ability and background. They are attended by some students just as able as any who go to the most sought-after colleges—and even by numbers of young people from very influential families. This chapter tells you about these colleges, too—which might well be better for your child than the familiar top colleges.

Admissions tests like the "SAT" loom large as hurdles at the gates of top colleges. These tests can count heavily for acceptance and scholarships. We explain here what it really takes to get high scores on the tests —and also the circumstances in which you should understand that high scores are not important at all.

The chapter goes on to tell how your child can succeed through every other step of admission to whatever college would prove best for genuine winning.

Sure-Fire Timing for Admission—To a Good College

You and your child will have to take many steps to do an effective job of planning and gaining admission to college. Sure-fire timing of those steps can help your child to realize the best possible chances for fine college education and scholarship aid. Good timing is especially important for getting into a top college, and it's most helpful for getting into any good college.

What's called for from you both can be seen most readily in the chart below. Then let's quickly go through the opening steps of the schedule, ones that will get you and the child off to a good start.

Your Schedule for Sure-Fire Timing of College Admissions Steps

When	*Your Steps* Eleventh-grade year	*Your Child's Steps*
Fall–Winter	See seriously how much your family can afford for college—and check on range of college costs (see Chapter 12). Possibly increase savings or family earnings.	Aim for high accomplishment in studies and activities. Take the PSAT-NMSQT test (October). Closely examine full information on a range of at least three possible colleges.
Spring	Start visiting most likely or attractive colleges (continue in summer or possibly early fall).	Start guidance counselor conferences, talks with college representatives, college visits. Perhaps take "SAT" and "Achievement Tests" as may be required by colleges you're applying to.

When	*Your Steps* Eleventh-grade year	*Your Child's Steps*
		Search out information on all scholarships and other financial aid for which possibly eligible. Make near-final college choices.

When	*Your Steps* Twelfth-grade year	*Your Child's Steps*
Fall	Last college visits. Make specific financing plans for all main college alternatives.	Make college choices final and send applications for admission with financial aid. (The dates on which applications for admission and financial aid are due vary from Jan. 1 through June 1 or later.) Possibly try "Early Decision." Send other applications for scholarships and financial aid (except Basic Grants). Possibly retake SAT or take "ACT" test.
December		Possibly be told of admission under "Early Decision."
December on		Get decisions from colleges with "rolling admissions" policies.
January	Fill out and send in "FAF" or "FFS" confidential statement form on family finances and apply for Basic Grant.	

When	*Your Steps* Twelfth-grade year	*Your Child's Steps*
Mid-April		Get admissions decisions from top colleges (mailed about April 15).
May 1		Deadline for reply to top college admissions offers.
May–June	Set actual college financing plans.	Possibly apply for 7 percent guaranteed loan.

Fall/Winter of Eleventh-Grade Year—Vital Early Steps for You. On your part, you should start thinking seriously about financing college costs some two years before your child enters. This would first brace you for the shock—four years' study at top colleges can cost as much as $35,000 to $40,000 today, while four years as a dorm student even at a well-known state university commonly involves out-of-pocket costs totaling $12,000 to $16,000 or more.

Most important, starting this early will give you time to increase your family income or savings for heavy college costs. In families with college-bound children, income is often increased by having the mother resume or start work. Planning on such a step two years early provides time for the mother's training for higher-paid work than might be possible without planning ahead. Of course, the college-bound teenager can also build up savings through work—during the school year as advisable for best performance in studies and activities, and during summer vacations, generally as much as possible.

Savings of your own for just the first college expenses might total, if possible, from $2,000 to $5,000, for you may have to pay such amounts for the youngster's first term in the August before he/she enters. You would probably be able to borrow the money then, but doing so could involve additional costs for interest.

On any substantial savings for imminent college costs—even those earned by your child—hold them in your name, rather than in the name of your child (if, as is likely, your family is determined to have financial need for college in the special, complex system for determining need explained in Chapter 12). Savings held in the child's name would reduce the amount in scholarships or other financial aid for college he/she would get (for any amounts of such aid adjusted according to need—

and much aid is so adjusted today). You and your son or daughter might find it helpful to put savings into a separate savings account in your name but to be used only toward college education.

Fall/Winter of Eleventh-Grade Year—Vital Early Steps for Your Child. Your college-bound youngster should similarly take three important steps early in the eleventh-grade year. The first, broad one works best when undertaken in a natural, relaxed way by the teenager. And it will develop in this way if the child has built the confidence, zest, and sense of responsibility of a winner. This step is to aim with growing maturity for as high an accomplishment as is reasonably practical in all studies and activities already under way. Such an aim can be pursued as much with pride in attainment now as with ambition for the best possible future chances with colleges.

A second step might come up routinely in your child's school, but it's still helpful to anticipate in case it's not routine. This is for the youngster to take a two-hour test very widely given in schools every October for high school juniors. The impossibly long name of the test is "Preliminary Scholastic Aptitude Test—National Merit Scholarship Qualifying Test." It's understandably known most often by its inscrutable initials, PSAT-NMSQT, and is usually administered in the school on the last Saturday of October.

From the test, your child will get an advance idea of how he or she is likely to score later on the regular SAT or Scholastic Aptitude Test of the College Entrance Examination Board. Taking the Preliminary SAT should also give your child helpful practice (while in addition starting the child in competition for a National Merit Scholarship worth $1,000 and much prestige). The country's most sought-after colleges generally require the SAT for admissions applicants, as do more than 1,000 other colleges.

A third helpful step in the fall or winter of eleventh grade is for the teenager to pick and become familiar with a range of three colleges that might be possible choices. Which three is not too important at this stage, but they should be picked to represent colleges of quite different kinds in costs and admissions difficulty. For example, they might include a high-cost private college, a moderate-cost private college, and a low-cost state college or university. They could be located in different parts of the country in which the teenager might be interested for college-going years.

Your child can get the names, addresses, and summary information for choosing three such colleges from college directories or guides in the school or public library. The youngster should then write to each college selected to request information and application forms. He/she should then look over this literature closely, to become familiar in some detail with such features as admissions requirements, scholarship offerings, study programs, student life, and campus facilities. Doing this should give your child a concrete idea of many of the things to be taken into consideration about a college.

Getting Down to Cases in Spring of Eleventh-Grade Year. Your child and you should start making actual choices of colleges to which to apply through the spring semester of the child's high school junior year. In that semester college guidance conferences with the child and yourself will probably begin. Much can be learned and accomplished in these sessions with your child's guidance counselor, especially if you come to them with a background of initial information, several specific ideas for colleges, and questions thought out in advance.

Spring of the junior year is also a time when your child will probably have opportunities to talk with representatives of various colleges who are visiting the school or the area. Such meetings are obviously informative and useful for giving your child answers about his/her specific chances for admission and scholarship aid at each specific college.

Talking with friends, teachers, and other young people, plus poring over college guides and catalogues, will help your child gradually to focus on several colleges as the most attractive or practical possibilities. The youngster might well start making inspection and interview visits of these colleges in March or April of the junior year (writing or phoning admissions offices in advance to make appointments).

One or both parents will probably go along on at least some of these college visits. That's fine if agreeable with the teenager, but be sure to excuse yourself and step out if you happen to be standing by at the start of formal admissions interviews. Colleges want to interview the applicant, not the parents.

Three more important steps should probably be taken by your child in this busy spring of the junior year. The youngster is likely to take the regular, three-hour SAT one Saturday morning in mid-spring. On the afternoon of that Saturday (or other Saturdays that are scheduled College Board test dates), the child would take one-hour College Board "Achievement Tests" if required by some colleges he/she has in mind (these are tests of knowledge in specific subjects, such as chemistry, American history, or English composition).

Then, too, your child should spend some time in the school's guidance office and library searching out leads to all possible sources of scholarships and other financial aid for which to apply.

Finally, the youngster should sort out all the information and impressions and make near-final choices of colleges to which to apply.

You will, of course, want to talk over these possibilities, especially in connection with money.

That same idea of a "spread" of colleges suggested earlier can be helpful in making near-final choices (unless the youngster is completely satisfied with one or two colleges virtually certain both for admission and financial workability). A set of near-final choices might accordingly include at least some appealing colleges that are long shots for admission and sufficient financial aid; some reasonably sure for admission and sufficient aid; and some very sure for admission and affordability even without any special aid. The spread of choices can be particularly important if your child is trying for a top college.

For the twelfth grade or high school senior year, your child and you face an even more intensive round of steps. If your child were trying for one or more top colleges, this is the year in which admission to such a college could actually be won. We accordingly explain your actions in the senior year in the story of admission to widely known top colleges that is recounted next.

How Your Child Could Win Admission to a Widely Known Top College

Suppose that your child's senior year in high school has just begun and the youngster has become interested in one of the country's widely known top colleges.

If in the Northeast, it might be one of the eight Ivy League colleges— Brown, Columbia, Cornell, Dartmouth, Harvard, Penn (University of Pennsylvania), Princeton, or Yale. Or it could be one of the many others there closely associated with the Ivy League, like the "little three" (Amherst, Wesleyan, and Williams), the "Seven Sisters" (Barnard, Bryn Mawr, Mt. Holyoke, Radcliffe, Smith, Vassar, and Wellesley), or still others, including Bowdoin, Middlebury, Colgate, MIT (Massachusetts Institute of Technology), Rutgers, Swarthmore, Haverford, or Johns Hopkins.

In the South or Midwest it might be a college like Duke, University of Virginia, Oberlin, University of Chicago, or Notre Dame. In the West it could be Stanford, Caltech (California Institute of Technology), one of the Claremont Colleges (Pomona, Scripps, Claremont Men's, Harvey Mudd, and Pitzer), or the University of California at Berkeley.

By and large, these colleges admit only one out of every three or more of their applicants (among out-of-state applicants, for the state universities). In this sense, they are among the most sought-after colleges in the land.

Wide esteem and sterling reputation may have stirred the interest of your child in a well-known top college like one of these. If it's early in the teenager's high school senior year, he/she should decide now whether or not to apply. Application deadlines for these colleges may come as early as January 1 of the student's senior year. Would the chances of admission (with scholarship aid if needed) be sufficient to justify applying?

Here's a full explanation of how to tell. Let's begin with the example of Dorothy Swane. She well illustrates one type of student who almost always wins admission to such eminent colleges.

At seventeen, Dorothy had distinguished herself mainly by rare brilliance in high school studies in Oak Park, Illinois, a Chicago suburb. Almost all her courses there were on the honors and Advanced Placement levels. She completed no less than four of the AP courses with about an A− average and AP exam marks of 4s and 5s (the two highest possible).

Mathematics is Dorothy's very special strength beyond all-around excellence in studies. She took two math courses at a nearby college while still in high school. The teacher heading the school's math department wrote a recommendation confirming her extensive recreational learning in the subject and praising her as "one of the most promising young mathematicians I've ever been privileged to teach."

Dorothy also served as vice president of the school's math club and played on the girl's field hockey team. On her college application, she wrote a warm, sincere, deft essay about her excitement with seeing similar forms in math, music, literature, and sports.

On all academic indicators of ability, she stood very high. She ranked as the number three student in her graduating class, with an overall average in college-prep subjects of 3.94 out of a possible 4.00. Her SAT scores were 721 for "verbal" abilities and 800 for "mathematical" abilities (the latter is the highest possible on the 200-to-800-score scale used for the SAT; small numbers of students every year earn such perfect math scores on the SAT). Her Math and Physics Achievement Test scores were in the high 700s.

Princeton was happy to admit someone like Dorothy. She typified the extremely bright, impressively accomplished, and personally well-balanced applicant top colleges almost always accept.

As director of admissions at Harvard College, John P. Reardon Jr., designated students like Dorothy as being in "our real scholar category," who regularly win acceptance. Commenting further on such students, he said: "Of course, as far as possible, we take the very best of those from all over the country who will be heading into scholarly research and teaching."

The qualifications of such a "real scholar" as Dorothy, who has very high top college admissions chances, have been summarized conveniently for your reference. Moreover, there are three more categories of students with unusually high admissions chances whose winning characteristics for top colleges similarly can be summarized for you. So can the qualities of still another category of students who represent the largest group admitted by top colleges—but for whom, unfortunately, admissions chances are only about fifty-fifty.

These categories of students are summed up in the table below. If a well-known top college interests your child, the table can be used to check his/her possible fit.

The qualifications of students typifying these categories have long been familiar to persons with inside knowledge of the workings of admissions at top colleges. But they are portrayed with special insight by Richard Moll, director of admissions at Vassar College, in his book *Playing the Private College Admissions Game*.[1] He perceptively points out that applicants to such colleges "compete against each other within categories, not against all other candidates judged by a single admissions standard." And he illustrates his point graphically: "The Merit Scholar, the extraordinarily talented violinist, the Stanford alumnus' son, the nifty all-round kid and the black are not going to nudge one another out of the running. They're competing against others of like interest and talent for that particular group's fair share of the class."

What It Takes to Win Admission at Top Colleges: Does Your Child Fit One of These Categories?
(The admissions criteria for each category of student
are arranged in descending order of importance)

Real Scholar Category
99% Sure Admission

Special quality	very special brilliance demonstrated in one or two subjects
College-prep program	heavy honors and AP courses with about an A— average
Recommendations	strongly favorable overall and confirming special brilliance
SATs (and Achievement Tests, if any)	high 700s (or about 675s and up outside specialties)
Class rank—public school	top 5 percent
Class rank—private school	top 15 percent
Activities	some evidence of participation desirable

Top Athlete Category
99% Sure Admission

Special quality	all-state or other top high school record held in a major intercollegiate sport
SATs (and Achievement Tests, if any)	about 450 or higher
College-prep program	"fairly light" or stronger with at least a C— average
Recommendations	very strong from high school coach(es); others generally favorable
Other	not very important

Alumni Child Category
99% Sure Admission

Special quality	child or other close relative of an alumnus/alumna
College-prep program	"strong" helpful, with B or better average
Class rank	above top 25 percent (top 50%, private school)
SATs (or Achievement Tests, if any)	about 550s or higher
Activities	genuine accomplishment in one activity or hobby helpful
Recommendations	strong recommendations helpful

Minority-Group Category
75% Admissions Chances

Special quality	impressive evidence of drive and strong motivation (plus high potential ability) to overcome handicaps in getting an education
Class rank	top 5 percent (if from a depressed-area high school)
College-prep program	as strong as circumstances permitted, with at least some grades of B and A
SATs (and Achievement Tests, if any)	about 400s and up

Activities	impressive effort demonstrated in work and/or activity or hobby
Recommendations	very strong motivation and potential academic abilities

Large, Typical-Applicant Category
50% Admissions Chances

Special quality	some striking distinction in actual accomplishments (music, writing, art, community service, 4-H club, school activity, hobby, etc.)
Good writing ability	evidence in application essays
College-prep program	"strong" with some honors and AP courses, and at least a B+ to A− average
Class rank	about top 15 percent (top 25%, private school)
SATs (and Achievement Tests, if any)	about high 500s and up
Recommendations	strongly favorable on academic work and very strong on applicant's special quality of distinction.

Accordingly, you or your child should gauge the youngster's chances of admission to a well-known top college by the benchmarks for his/her category shown in the table. (Those benchmarks, by the way, originated with the authors of this book, based on their experience and judgment.) It's likely your child will represent someone in the "Large, Typical-Applicant Category." You may have difficulty in telling what is meant by the first characteristic needed by such applicants: "some striking distinction in actual accomplishments."

Here it may help to know that J. Fred Jewett, dean of admissions and financial aid at Harvard, told one of the co-authors: "We want students who, while very able academically, also can do one or two things really well—things in which they've displayed spontaneous action and unusual accomplishment." And a former admissions director at Princeton commented: "In nonacademic areas, the quality of what the applicant has accomplished is far more important than merely the nature and number of activities." He added: "It's not just that this boy or girl has held offices. We ask how good a newspaper editor this person has been, or how effective he or she was as a student council president."

Yale's dean of undergraduate admissions, Worth David, has remarked, "We're looking first for people who are academically qualified, but among those, we're looking for young people who demonstrate unusual motivation.

"This can be in an academic area, or it can be nonacademic," he continued. "It can be in an extracurricular activity, community service, sports, arts, politics, or almost anything. The opportunities are endless. Insofar as the area of a student's special drive and interest is concerned, what we're looking for is demonstrated evidence of what the boy or girl has done—not just general superlatives but evidence of actual accomplishments."

Judging your child's chances of admission to a top college can also be very substantially aided by talking them over with the child's guidance counselor, or even with admissions staff members of the college itself.

Carrying Out All the Steps of Winning Admission

Suppose that you've judged those top college admissions chances for your child early in the high school senior year, and that they look possible to promising. From that point on, you and the child would proceed as follows to win admission in reality—to that well-known top college, as well as to other good colleges for the youngster.

No applicant should count on certain admission to a well-known top college in advance, however stupendously qualified. Decisions are made only in the actual workings of the college's admissions process, and the accidents of who else may be applying and of the judgments made in the process can result in decisions against any one applicant.

For this reason, your child should certainly apply to at least one or two other colleges where admission is virtually certain (as we suggested earlier). And you and your child should be very careful to avoid any sense that it will be a crushing disappointment not to get into the chosen top college.

Particularly good counsel on this hazard has been given by Dean David of Yale. He said: "What parents have to be very careful about is that they don't lead the youngster to believe that he or she will let them down if he or she doesn't get into Yale and, in letting them down, prove that they're failures as parents. Doing this could be deeply unfair. Whether Yale accepts or rejects is simply a reflection of Yale's admissions."

So, in the early fall of the senior year, your child should make final decisions on several other colleges as well as the first choice. This may involve a last-minute visit or two to colleges not yet seen. The youngster will then go through all the work of filling out applications—most probably applying not just for admission but for admission with financial aid. Applying for admission with aid rarely prejudices one's chances. At the same time, the parents could well spend some time making specific financing plans for each college to which the teenager is applying. (In planning for perhaps more expensive colleges, see Chapter 12 on how the gaps between what you can afford and what college will cost might be filled by scholarships and other financial aid.)

Your child will also complete applications to all additional sources of scholarships and financial aid other than colleges, with one major exception—the source for a federal "Basic Grant" (or Basic Educational Opportunity Grant, explained with full detail in Chapter 12).

In the fall of the senior year, your child may also want to take the SAT again to try for a higher score than in the junior year; or he/she may instead take the similar ACT entrance examination if required (many hundreds of colleges require this test of the American College Testing Program instead of the SAT).

Should your child choose to apply to a college under an "Early Decision" plan (an option offered by many colleges), word of acceptance could arrive as early as December or January of the senior year—giving the youngster and you relief from long suspense.

Other colleges that operate "rolling admissions" plans could inform your child of acceptance or rejection at any time from about December on through winter and spring. Under a rolling admissions system, applicants are notified of admissions decisions within a few weeks after receipt by the college of all the required credentials (application form, high school transcript, school recommendations, test score reports, etc.).

After January 1 of the senior year—and specifically, after you have finished your federal income tax return for the preceding calendar year —you as the parent will probably tackle the task of giving detailed information about the family's financial situation on one of two forms widely required from the parents of applicants for college financial aid. Data on the forms are held in complete confidence. Your data would be given on either the "FAF" (Financial Aid Form of the College Scholarship Service) or the "FFS" (Family Financial Statement of the ACT Program).

You can apply for one of the very advantageous Basic Grants simply by checking a box on either of these forms. If you do, you will want to comply with a Basic Grants application requirement to base the family financial information you provide on your income tax return for the preceding calendar year.

Suspense will mount as you near April 15 of the senior year, if your child has applied to one or more well-known top colleges. That's the approximate date on which many colleges mail letters to applicants on their admissions and scholarship aid decisions.

Your child may prove fortunate enough to have admissions and aid offers from two or more very attractive colleges. If so, deciding which one to accept could prove hard. Decisions should nevertheless be promptly made and reported back in letters. Top colleges usually require replies to their offers by about May 1.

As all the suspense and excitement of the preceding weeks subsides, you will want to work out details for financing studies at the new college. Those could well include having your child apply for one of the "Guaranteed Student Loans" available for college, which are offered on uniquely advantageous, subsidized terms regardless of financial need (as explained in Chapter 12). Millions of families a year use these guaranteed loans to close their college-financing gaps.

How to Boost Your Child's Scores on the SAT and Other College Entrance Tests

How high your child scores on college entrance tests—in particular, the SAT—might have a substantial effect on the child's chances for admission to a well-known top college, as you have just seen. You may well wonder: What could the youngster and you do, if anything, to increase his/her scores on the SAT?

Questions on exactly this point became a burning public issue in mid-1979. Since the 1950s, the organizations that jointly provide the SAT (the College Entrance Examination Board and Educational Testing Service or ETS) had maintained on the basis of research that intensive coaching or cramming for just a few weeks or months could realize only negligible increases in SAT scores. Nevertheless, many public and private secondary schools have long given SAT-prep sessions for interested juniors and seniors. Numerous commercial coaching programs claiming to raise SAT scores have increasingly sprung up and flourished; various thick books with SAT drill questions and test-taking tips have appeared and sell strongly in bookstores.

Commercial coaching programs particularly concerned the College Board in its anti-coaching stand, though board officers also wanted to counter the distraction from regular studies represented by SAT-prep sessions in schools. The commercial programs typically cost $100 or more. Were they truly effective, the SAT would be unfair to young people who could not afford such fees. Moreover, the SAT would be educationally invalid as a measure of basic "aptitudes" for college study fostered through long years of effort in school and personal intellectual growth.

Note carefully that this question of coachability bears on only the SAT among college entrance tests. Achievement Tests of the College Board examine students on learning in specific college-prep courses. The board has never claimed that cramming or coaching in the relevant course content for Achievement Tests would not improve test scores in much the same way as for a regular classroom final exam. But Achievement Tests do not play as conspicuous a role in top college admission as the SAT.

Also, though the ACT exam is required by many colleges instead of the SAT and is taken by about a million college-bound students a year, it too is basically an achievement test examining students on course content. Its several parts broadly cover learning in such subject areas as English, math, social studies, and sciences. Cramming in these subjects might improve scores on the test. However, little if any interest in coaching for the ACT has developed because it rarely figures in top college admissions. It is most notably required by large, renowned state universities outside the Northeast.

Public interest in SAT coaching flared in mid-1979 with the final release of a highly controversial, long-rumored report of an investigation by the Federal Trade Commission (FTC). The report was withheld from the public for some months. Its main findings as finally issued were that the SAT coaching programs of one of the largest commercial coaching enterprises, Stanley H. Kaplan Educational Centers, Inc., resulted in average gains in each of the two SAT scores, verbal and mathematical, of 25 points for students described as "underachievers."

Some confusion surrounds the study on which the findings are based. It was initiated by a staff attorney in the Boston office of the FTC, Arthur E. Levine, and ran for three years. Mr. Levine had admirably noted the discrepancy between the College Board/ETS position on the ineffectiveness of coaching and the advertised claims of the Kaplan Centers that students finishing their SAT coaching could realize score gains of as much as 100 points.

But the FTC's Consumer Protection Bureau in Washington termed the original study "seriously flawed," and based its public report on a reanalysis of the statistics on the original study. Average gains of 50 points found in the original study were scaled down to 25 points in the reanalysis. The final report also found that, of two coaching schools studied, only Kaplan's had proven effective. And in the report, the underachievers realizing the gains were said to be persons who score lower on standardized tests than would be expected from such indications as their course grades.

In reply, the College Board reaffirmed its position that, on the basis of its own research studies and analyses, coaching defined as intensive

drill or cramming on sample test questions does not substantially increase SAT scores. But Robert J. Kingston, then board president,
pointed out that "this kind of intense cramming should be differentiated
from instruction in test-taking skills, and instruction in mathematical
and verbal reasoning abilities." He also stated: "It may be that some
individuals, perhaps underachievers, can be helped by certain kinds of
training." The board pledged to its hundreds of member colleges and
secondary schools that it would continue to investigate and report on
the matter.

In the face of all this uproar, what should you and your child do?
Should your son or daughter be sure to take Kaplan's SAT course if
vying for a well-known top college? It's given, by the way, at more than
eighty Kaplan centers coast to coast and costs some $275 for ten
weekly sessions.

There's no great harm in trying, if you want—and if it's no hardship. Or, as alternatives, the youngster could take coaching sessions in
his/her school or the coaching course of another commercial sponsor,
or else practice independently with one of the commercially published
SAT drill books available from a library or bookstore.

As still another possibility, your child could use the free, official drill
book issued by the College Board since 1978 to students taking the
SAT. Called *Taking the SAT,* it includes a complete, three-hour sample
test with brief explanations, timing instructions, and practice answer
sheet. In the board's official view, this is all your child really needs for
any special preparation. It represents the latest version of a series of
board publications designed to help students get ready for the SAT that
were introduced when one of the co-authors of this book was the editor
on the College Board staff in the 1950s.

Students using any form of independent practice or organized coaching to prepare for the SAT should make sure to review or learn the
mathematics it involves. Working the test's math section calls for a
basic knowledge of arithmetic, first-year high school algebra, and plane
geometry, plus considerable reasoning skill in applying that knowledge.
For example, the forty-eight-page book on *Taking the SAT* includes
about three and a half pages of mathematical definitions, formulas, operations, and concepts needed in answering the math questions on the
test. And the College Board has long stated that students enrolled in a
math course when they take the SAT tend to earn math scores averaging
about 10 points higher than comparable students not currently studying
math.

News media reported widely on other government actions concerning the SAT in 1979, but these developments will have little or no effect
on how your youngster might prepare for the SAT. New York Governor

Hugh Carey pushed through a state law requiring public release of an SAT edition and correct answers for it within thirty days of receipt of their scores by students who had taken it. (The same requirements apply to other admissions tests for college and graduate school.) Actual SAT editions had previously been kept secret. However, being able to see authentic old SATs should make little difference to your child because masses of sample questions and answers have already been widely available. The one apparent change will be that your child will have to pay higher fees for the SAT (than the $8.25 in 1979), at least in New York State. These higher costs cover the need to develop, try out, and analyze large numbers of additional SAT questions.

Naturally, you are likely to be interested in having your child boost his/her SAT scores if the first scores earned seemed lower than expected or hoped (such as scores on the PSAT in the fall of the high school junior year, or on the regular SAT in the spring of that year). Should your child's first scores seem disappointingly low, he/she might consider taking the SAT an extra time after some brush-up (perhaps using the free book on *Taking the SAT*) before trying extensive coaching.

By chance alone, students who earned low initial SAT scores tend to get higher scores on a second testing. College Board statistics show that one in every twenty such students will see score increases of 100 or more points—just by chance, without any coaching or other special preparation.

If your child should be a lucky one in twenty who automatically gains 100 or more points, he/she would probably not need to consider any extra coaching effort or further SAT-taking. And if the child is not lucky, the extra practice on the test should prove some advantage.

These chance effects should remind you of the warning we made about all standardized testing in Chapter 9. As with IQ and other tests, scores on the SAT for any individual child—including your own—are scientifically inaccurate indications of actual abilities. The College Board regularly warns users about this, and a good many college admissions officers accordingly give greater weight to other indicators of ability, such as high school academic record and recommendations. As the admissions director of an Ivy League college once told a co-author, "The SAT is a measure of ability, but I have seen boys with test scores in the 700s flunk out, and I have seen boys with test scores in the 300s graduate."

Basically, three factors can boost a child's SAT scores. The first and by far the most effective for most young people is real excellence in school studies, including mathematics. Most of the students who get high SAT scores are those who, year after year, have gotten excellent marks in high school and who go on to get excellent marks in college.

But there are exceptions who somehow don't test well, but still get excellent marks in high school and college.

The second factor for boosting SAT scores is being test-wise, having highly developed skills at taking and scoring well on tests. It is this faculty that independent practice or organized coaching is most likely to develop. But students who have consistently received excellent school marks have usually developed these skills over years of taking other standardized tests in school.

The third factor, as you've just seen above, is chance. It's too bad that at least some element of chance enters into admissions decisions at well-known top colleges. However, it does—and it would do so even if the SAT were not used.

But you can still counter even this factor of chance in raising your child to be a winner. You could do this, not by trying to boost SAT scores in some esoteric way, but by helping your child make the most of college with whatever scores have been earned. In the next section we explain how to do this through one of the many fine alternatives open to your child beyond the few well-known top colleges.

Finding Lesser-Known Top Colleges for Your Child

You and your college-bound youngster have every reason to keep your minds—and especially your enthusiasms—open about other colleges besides well-known top ones. Fixation only on a Dartmouth or a Stanford would be foolish. Trying for these colleges is all right; but don't count at all heavily on it. As you saw, no one student, however qualified, can be certain of getting into such a college.

There is a tremendous range of other fine choices open to you and your child. Among them are literally hundreds of lesser-known top colleges that are just as superb for all practical purposes as the most celebrated ones. Making some of these your first choices could be wise. For almost all of them, your child will not need qualifications up in the stratosphere for admission. About B average work in moderately strong college-prep studies will often suffice for acceptance to most of them; a great many admit students with about C averages. Moreover, in numerous instances, their costs can be much lower than those of well-known top colleges. Here are just a few samples of these lesser-known top colleges:

Washington University in St. Louis, Missouri, has ten Nobel Prize winners on its faculty; writers on the faculty who regularly teach undergraduate courses have won such honors as the National Book Award, the Bollingen Prize, and the Roethke Award. (It also has about the eighteenth largest endowment of any U.S. university, more than $134 million; University of Texas, incidentally, has the second largest, more than a half billion dollars.)

Brandeis University in Waltham, Massachusetts, ranks ahead of Amherst and Harvard in the number of male bachelor's degree graduates who go on to earn the Ph.D.

Carleton College in Northfield, Minnesota, occupies a 1,000-acre campus and has long attracted hundreds of students a year from other states coast to coast. "Carls" (as its students dub themselves) may opt to live in residence halls grouped by such fields of interest as French or Ecology. They may also carry out part of their study in any of fourteen overseas programs in Asia, Europe, and Latin America.

Lawrence University in Appleton, Wisconsin, has had administrators who went on to become presidents of more than ten other colleges— including Brown, Duke, and Harvard.

Knox College in Galesburg, Illinois, counts among its historic alumni the country's first black U.S. senator, Hiram Revels, and the poet Carl Sandburg. Its distinguished faculty stresses teaching, and it places more than 80 percent of its pre-med graduates in U.S. medical schools. It is also the college immortalized as the "Dear Old Siwash" for which football heroes would "do or die" in the widely popular novels of George Fitch, Class of 1897.

Kenyon College in Gambier, Ohio, was founded by settlers from New England in 1824 and is the oldest college in continuous operation west of the Alleghenies. Affiliated with the Episcopal Church, it sees more than half its graduates continue on into advanced professional or academic studies. It was a major originator of the Advanced Placement Program (described in Chapter 10), which was called in its early stages "the Kenyon Plan."

Washington and Lee University in Lexington, Virginia, is the nation's sixth oldest college (founded 1749). Washington himself endowed it in 1798. No less than General Robert E. Lee revived it after the Civil War, served as its president, and is buried in its chapel. About half of its alumni have become physicians or lawyers.

University of the South in Sewanee, Tennessee, has a spectacular 10,000-acre campus on a plateau 1,000 feet above the surrounding valley. The nationally respected literary magazine *Sewanee Review* is published there, and its studies in literature are understandably strong and popular. Recreations enjoyed nearby include hiking, spelunking, mountaineering, skiing, and white-water canoeing.

Franklin and Marshall College in Lancaster, Pennsylvania, regularly has one of the highest percentages of pre-medical graduates accepted by medical schools among all colleges in the country.

State University College at Purchase, New York, is a rather new college (established in 1971), with a luxurious rural campus and extraordinarily fine facilities and faculty members for college programs in theater and the arts. It's the fitting central campus for such studies of the vast system of the State University of New York, and also offers a wide range of other liberal arts studies. New York City's extraordinary cultural resources are only a forty-five-minute drive away.

A great many institutions of another whole group also rank as top colleges in many respects, such as ability and social background represented in the student body, faculty prowess, research reputation, and size and quality of academic resources and facilities. These are the oldest or leading state universities of each state throughout the central, Southern, and Western regions of the country.

You should surely consider a good state university for your child if a chief interest of yours is collegiate eminence. Among them, for instance, are such strong and respected institutions as the University of North Carolina at Chapel Hill, University of Michigan at Ann Arbor, University of Minnesota-Minneapolis-St. Paul, Indiana University (which has some of the strongest music programs offered anywhere), University of Wisconsin at Madison, University of Colorado at Boulder, and University of Washington in Seattle. But this mere sampling of lesser-known top colleges cannot really serve your specific interests and situation. It is given only to suggest possibilities for consideration.

For suggestions of colleges that would fit your particular plans, you or your child should ask the guidance counselor or well-informed teachers. You might also search in general college directories. A book that could prove unusually helpful for this purpose is by a co-author of this one; it's the *Hawes Comprehensive Guide to Colleges*,[2] and it uses findings based on research to rate colleges on features that include their social prestige and their relative output of distinguished graduates. Well-known top colleges come out very high on these ratings—but so do hundreds of other lesser-known top colleges.

You would be well advised to look thoroughly into appropriate colleges like these in addition to, or instead of, well-known top colleges. Such a distinguished choice could actually prove near-ideal for your child in terms of admission, cost, scholarship aid, study programs, academic pressures, location, and general character.

What Really Counts—Not So Much the Reputation of the College as What Your Child Does There

Especially harrowing memories of a certain kind haunt a friend of the authors, who once worked in the dean's office at Yale. He recalls very vividly the failing students called into the office who were asked to leave shortly after the spring semester mid-term exams of their freshman year. These were students who had been put on academic probation after first-semester grades, and who had failed on most or all of their following mid-terms.

"It would be just awful to see them," he said. "They were very badly shaken. They looked hollow-eyed, haggard, thin, white as a sheet, utterly exhausted. They would have been straining night and day for months to keep up and catch up, but the academic load had proven just too crushing for them. Of course, they represented mistakes made over in the admissions office. They could otherwise have managed quite well at any one of hundreds of other colleges. At Yale, though, they'd gotten absolutely beat. You couldn't help realizing that the experience would leave a bad scar for the rest of their lives."

While extreme, these recollections show dramatically that the experience and sense of accomplishment your child has in college counts far more than its renown. At one of the best colleges, these students had suffered the worst possible disaster to their self-confidence and growth.

For your child, then, college should be a challenging, but strongly positive experience. Make sure that the college chosen is one where your child will enjoy the reinforcement of continued success. Such reinforcement heavily outweighs whatever lack of prestige the college may have. Assuring a productive experience in college is the prime consideration.

A close second consideration is the record and reputation your child develops through college. It's clearly desirable to have the youngster finish college with a reputation as a good to outstanding student. That's worth more, not only personally but in the job market, than graduating with a weak record from a college even of towering reputation.

In consequence, don't worry about having your child go to a college of only modest reputation. It makes no difference if the college is one where the boy or girl can develop well and is the best that can be managed under the circumstances. The reputation your child builds there by solid accomplishment counts more in the world than the reputation of the college itself. And the experience of real accomplishment within the powers of the child's unique potential will surely develop further strength as a winner.

CHAPTER

I2

◆

Getting Thousands of Dollars in College Scholarships

By the time Julie R. graduated from Harvard-Radcliffe College one recent June, she had spent more than $19,000 in tuition over her four years of studies, and another $10,000 in room and board. There had also been hundreds of dollars a year for books, laundry, recreation, and airfare home to visit her family during vacations. All told, going to college had cost Julie more than $35,000.

When you look at those figures, you might feel like turning to the next chapter and trying to persuade your child that college isn't such a good idea after all. But what if your youngster really wants to go to college and has the ability and interest to be a winner there? Yes, it can be discouragingly expensive; but there are dozens of places where you can get financial aid to help you and your child make it through.

First, let's dispel a few myths. Contrary to what you may think, your child doesn't have to be a straight A student, artistic genius, or star athlete in order to qualify for financial help; nor do you have to be living below the poverty line. More than $12 billion will be available in the 1980–81 school year, and the chances are that you can get some of that money.

Of course your child's education may not cost as much as Julie's did. While prices are going up an average of 8 percent a year, most schools are not as expensive as Harvard. If your child is planning to attend a public university or college, for instance, you can probably cut at least three-fourths off the price of Julie's tuition.

This chapter will give you an idea of what you can expect to pay at various types of colleges. Then it will show you the kinds of aid programs that are available to help you with those costs. Finally, you'll find advice on how, when, and where to apply for that aid, including some tips to improve your chances.

The Bad News

A typical student at Bennington College in Vermont in 1979 paid $6,590 just in tuition and fees, according to a survey of 1,842 colleges conducted by the College Board. Meanwhile, a student at the University of Hawaii at Hilo paid $110. Within those two extremes, the cost of tuition can range widely, depending on the type of school.

The schools referred to in this chapter are four-year undergraduate institutions. Tuition can be as low as $50 at a two-year community college, or as high as $7,000–10,000 at medical school. In addition, there are some special types of colleges that offer low tuition through unusual programs—external degree colleges where pupils study at home; military service academies that will pay all your child's school expenses; co-op work-study programs in which students alternate classwork with paid jobs. Because those programs are so limited and specialized, however, they will not be included in this general discussion of costs and colleges. You can find more information about them in a book called *How to Get the Money to Pay for College.*[1]

In general, the College Board found tuition and fees averaged $2,923 at a private four-year college or university in the 1979–80 school year, and $680 at public schools. However, if you are not a resident of the state where a public school is located, you may be saddled with an extra charge—$450 per year at the State University of New York, for example, and as high as $2,400 at the University of California at Berkeley.

To those fees you must add the expense of books and supplies, personal items, room and board, and transportation. Books and supplies in the College Board survey cost about the same, roughly $230 a year, at both public and private schools; so did personal expenses, from $490 to $558. You can save on housing if your child lives at home with you, of course, but even then you must consider what you spend on food, laundry, and other items. The College Board found an average of $850 to $963 just for room and board for pupils living with their families. By comparison, the average cost of a dormitory at a public school was

$1,550, and at a private school, $1,629. For students living in private houses or apartments at college, housing and food averaged $1,791 at public schools and $1,754 at private schools.

Students who commute to school from their family home can also expect to spend money for daily transportation. On the other hand, those who go away to college will probably travel home for vacations about three times a year. The College Board found that students living with their families spent an average of $367 for transportation if they attended a private school and $440 at a public school. Those who lived at their schools spent from $246 to $318, on the average, for transportation.

To summarize all those figures, here is what a typical student in each category in the survey spent for all expenses in 1979–80: living with family and commuting to public school, $2,735; living with family and commuting to private school, $4,977; living in a dormitory at a public school, $3,258; living in a dormitory at a private school, $5,526; living in private housing at a public school, $3,576; living in private housing at a private school, $5,733.

That's still not the end of your calculations. Now you have to multiply those totals by the four years your child will probably spend at college. And don't forget that costs are going up. Tuition and fees increased by an average of 6.4 percent from 1978–79 to 1979–80 at public schools, 9.4 percent at private schools. Housing, food, transportation, and other items are also getting more expensive.

There are a couple of additional factors you should consider, too. While public schools generally cost less than private ones, that isn't always the case. Prestige also affects the price. Thus, for an out-of-state student at a high-prestige public school like the University of North Carolina at Chapel Hill or the University of Wisconsin at Madison, tuition and fees ($2,239 in 1979–80 at Chapel Hill, $3,155 at Madison) are actually higher than for a student at a non-Ivy League private college such as Baylor University in Texas ($2,000). Of course, the high-status private schools like Bennington are still the most expensive of all.

Finally, consider geography. College costs in the South and the West are usually lower, especially for the lesser-known private schools, than they are in the Middle Atlantic and New England states. The cost of living in the South and West also tends to be less expensive.

The Good News

Even if your child commutes from home to a public school in the South, that's still some $11,000 at least that you're going to have to pay over four years. But it doesn't all have to come out of your bank account.

Although the whole subject of financial aid can be a confusing tangle of bureaucracies, in essence it boils down to three general sources and about four basic varieties. The sources are federal and state governments, the colleges themselves, and private organizations. The varieties include grants based mainly on financial need, scholarships based on special abilities or personal qualifications, loans, and work-study programs. As for the amount you can get—it can range from $100 to the full cost of tuition, room and board, and books.

It's true that most programs are open only to students who can demonstrate financial need. However, there are programs through which you can get aid for college regardless of your income. Even the definition of need may be broader than you think. For instance, your child could qualify for the federal Basic Educational Opportunity Grant program (BEOG), a major source of student aid, even if your family income is as high as $25,000 or, in some cases, $40,000. That's because the program takes into consideration the cost of the college you choose plus certain financial obligations that cut into your income.

Usually, the amount of aid you can get will be adjusted according to your need. In 1980–81, the average Basic Grant will probably be $1,050, up to a maximum of $1,800. Your child must be a U.S. citizen or permanent resident who intends to become a citizen, must not have earned a bachelor's degree already, and must be admitted for or enrolled in college.

Later in this chapter we help you determine whether you meet the criteria for financial need. Meanwhile, the next few pages list some more of the programs based on need, and then the programs that don't require proof of need.

Programs Based on Need

Undergraduates with "exceptional financial need" who would not be able to continue their education without aid can get from $200 to $1,500 a year through the federal Supplemental Educational Opportunity Grant program (SEOG), with at least a matching amount added to that by their state or college. The grant may be renewed each year up to a total of $4,000 for a four-year undergraduate program, $5,000 for a five-year program.

Each state also has aid programs, usually limited to colleges within the state. The money may be granted on a competitive basis in addition to the basis of need. In 1976–77 (the last year for which figures are available), the amount of aid averaged $440 to students at public schools and $833 to those at private schools.

Many colleges, particularly the private ones, offer their own scholarships to students with financial need. At Harvard, all freshmen who fit that category can receive some kind of aid to cover their total need. Stanford University in California gives full aid to 44 percent of freshmen with financial need.

If one of your child's parents or grandparents is a Native American or Native Alaskan belonging to a tribe recognized by the U.S. Bureau of Indian Affairs, your son or daughter may be eligible for a special grant from the Bureau. The amount can run from $100 to $2,300, depending on need.

Among private organizations, a whole range of scholarships and grants is available. Because they are generally offered by groups with a particular geographic, religious, ethnic, or occupational interest, most of these grants are based on a student's talents, interests, community involvement, religion, ethnic background, or geographical location, as well as need. In some cases, clubs or unions will limit their grants to children of employees or members.

The awards usually aren't large, and they are often competitive. They may require that applicants write an essay, perform in a contest, or show a certain level of academic achievement. Some of the types of groups that offer this aid are chambers of commerce, private corporations, fraternal organizations, churches, newspapers, 4-H clubs, veterans groups, and PTAs.

No-Need Programs

Even if you don't qualify under the category of need, there are several other sources of financial help open to you. But be prepared to find these programs more competitive. Instead of income, it will be ability, achievement, or a special personal qualification that is usually the determining factor.

Your best bet is probably with the private sector rather than the government. Increasing numbers of colleges are offering so-called no-need scholarships for students with high academic standing or athletic skill, regardless of income. Fordham University in New York is a typical example. There are 116 grants for athletes and 15 scholarships, each worth full tuition and room and board, for honor students. Butler University in Indiana gives twenty-nine scholarships based on debate, music or dance auditions, plus seven athletic grants. These scholarships will generally be found at non-Ivy League schools.

Scholarships for sports stars—widely known as "athletic grants-in-aid" and covering tuition, room, board, and laundry—are offered by many hundreds of colleges. Women athletes who have become outstanding in sports during their high school years now have as fair a chance of winning such athletic scholarships as male athletes. This resulted from federal action culminating in an order issued by the U.S. Department of Health, Education and Welfare in late 1979 requiring colleges to provide "proportionately equal" scholarships for men's and women's sports programs.

One of the leaders in the effort to secure equal rights for women student athletes is Ewald B. Nyquist, former New York State Commissioner of Education and now vice president for academic affairs at Pace University. Mr. Nyquist also served as chairperson of the influential Commission on Collegiate Athletics of the American Council on Education.

Mr. Nyquist hailed the new opportunities for women athletes by saying in an interview with one of the co-authors, "Congress and the courts have finally learned that Adam gave up a rib for a better cause. The law now mandates equal treatment of women in intercollegiate athletics. The result is a spectacular increase in the number of athletic scholarships available for women. For instance, from 1974 to 1977, the number of colleges offering athletic scholarships to women increased from 60 to more than 500 colleges."

He added: "Colleges must now give financial aid to men and women athletes in proportion to their participation in sports, even if it means robbing Peter to pay Paula.

"What this means is that a woman student athlete with superior ability in any of several popular intercollegiate sports and with at least average academic ability now has an equal chance with men athletes of winning an athletic scholarship.

"It is a new day—women have the right to participate, to compete, to achieve, to excel," he emphasized. "In short, cheerleading is not enough."

In order to get a scholarship from private organizations, you won't necessarily have to demonstrate that you have financial need. Pamela Bates, a California high school senior, won a $1,000 National Merit Scholarship even though her parents' income was close to $35,000. The scholarship was based on Pamela's score on the Scholastic Aptitude Test (SAT) given by the College Board, as well as her grades and extracurricular activities in school. And that $1,000 wasn't the end of Pamela's good fortune. Because many private companies, foundations, and colleges use the Merit awards as a framework for their own aid programs, Pamela was flooded with letters from private colleges offering her scholarship money.

Another major private program that doesn't require financial need is the Betty Crocker Search for Leadership in Family Living. About 100 students a year, particularly young women interested in homemaking, are awarded from $500 to $5,000 through this contest.

There are a few federal and state government programs also based on special factors rather than need. Probably the most widespread is the Social Security benefits program. No matter what your family income is, your child may get monthly Social Security payments averaging $70 if one parent is disabled, $80 if one is retired, or $127 if one is deceased. The parent must have contributed to Social Security while working, and your child must be a full-time unmarried student between the ages of eighteen and twenty-two. (The only way that income matters in this program is if your child earns more than $3,000 a year, independent of the family income. Then the payments will be reduced.)

Other special federal grants are available, regardless of need, to students who agree to work in law enforcement after they graduate, and to students who sign up for the Reserve Officer Training Corps (ROTC). If your son or daughter joins the armed forces in active duty after 1977, he/she can get government aid through a special two-for-one savings plan: for every $1 that your child contributes out of his/her military pay while in service (minimum $50 a month, maximum $75), the government will contribute $2.

What if you can't get any outright grants or scholarships? You can still obtain help through various loan and work-study programs. Of course these programs will mean an extra burden for your child, either a debt to repay or else a part-time job during the school year. Still, the interest rates and payment schedules on the loans are generally lighter than those for commercial loans. The work-study programs will save your child the effort of job hunting independently.

For students who can't prove financial need, the major source of loans is the Graduated Student Loan Program (GSLP) of federal and state governments. Your child can borrow $2,500 per year of undergraduate work, to a maximum of $7,500 through the entire course of undergraduate study. The basic interest rate in most states is 7 percent, plus a fee of one-half of 1 percent. Usually your child won't have to begin repaying the money until nine to twelve months after leaving college, and usually no interest is charged while the student is in school. Up to ten years is allowed for repayment.

National Direct Student Loans (NDSL) are available at a limited number of colleges for students who do have financial need. The amount here is smaller—a maximum of $5,000 for the entire undergraduate program—but the interest rate is a low 3 percent. The payment schedule is similar to that for the GSLP.

Other federal loans are open to students in law enforcement and nursing. Some colleges and private lenders, too, will lower their interest rates on special student loans.

Through the College Work-Study Program, the federal government gives some $400 million a year to schools to provide part-time jobs for students with financial need. The jobs may be on or off campus, at public or private agencies.

As we said earlier, altogether, more than $12 billion in aid should be available in the 1980–81 school year. Since a single program often will not provide enough money to cover the full cost of college, you might find yourself patching together several different grants, scholarships, and loans to meet your need. Your child's college can help you to devise this package.

How Do You Determine Financial Need?

Now that you know all this aid money is waiting for you, what's the best way to win your share of it? Because financial need is the basis for so many grants—and because you may have to fill out a financial aid form even if you don't have need—the place to start is with your economic situation.

Calculating your need is a lot like filling out a tax return. In fact, you may want to get your tax accountant's help. First you have to figure out your income, the value of any property you own, the amount your child may contribute, and the deductions that reduce your income.

Then you should assess how much you can realistically afford to contribute toward your child's education. Don't forget to include those nonliquid types of assets such as bonds, government securities, stocks, insurance, valuable collections, and real estate. Selling off your trove of rare coins or mortgaging your house to pay for college is a drastic step, but it may be one you will have to consider. How much are your assets worth now compared to their potential value in the future? Perhaps you can borrow against them. Consider, too, the tax aspects of your holdings.

Finally, look at the costs of the various colleges your child is considering. Your need, and therefore your eligibility for aid, will vary depending on how expensive a particular college is.

One way to increase your child's chances of getting aid is to prove that he/she is self-supporting. But there are some strict rules on this. Eligibility covers a period of three years—the year you apply, the preceding year, and the year for which you want aid. During that time, you can't claim your child as a tax deduction; your child can't have lived with you for more than two consecutive weeks; and you can't give your child more than $600 in cash or equivalents.

Because different programs have different standards for determining need, there's no single figure this book can give you to let you know whether you'll qualify for aid. If you want more detailed assistance in calculating your need, a pamphlet called *Meeting College Costs,* published by the College Board, is available from most high school counselors.

You May Be Surprised at the Places You Can Find Aid

There's one basic piece of advice you should follow in looking for financial aid: Don't dismiss any possible source until you check it out. Money may be waiting in the places where you least expect it.

Start in your own community. Your child's high school guidance office should have a list of sources of funds. Find out if your chamber of commerce, PTA, or large local corporations have any aid programs for youngsters who live in your area. Your company, union, church, veterans group, civic organization, fraternal club, or any other group you belong to may offer scholarships for the children of members. Keep an eye out for stories in your newspaper about pupils who win grants.

If your child has a job, the company he/she works for might help out. Similarly, the Evans Scholarship Foundation in Golf, Illinois, gives grants to college-bound pupils who have been golf caddies for two or more years. Many companies and foundations have scholarship funds for students who want to enter particular occupations, so check with professional groups and teachers.

Your child's talents in a particular field could open more doors to money. Especially if your son or daughter is an outstanding athlete, talk to the school coach about college scholarships. Students interested in science may compete for some forty grants, ranging from $250 to $10,000, offered through the Science Talent Search of the Westinghouse Educational Foundation (1719 N St., N.W., Washington, D.C. 20036). Members of 4-H farm youth clubs in about a dozen Western and Midwestern counties may be eligible for the scholarship program of the Union Pacific Railroad (headquartered at 1416 Dodge St., Omaha, Neb. 68102).

Of course your child should also apply for the government aid mentioned earlier; in particular, try the Basic Educational Opportunity Grant. Information and applications for the various programs are usually available through the colleges your child is applying to, your state's department of higher education, or the particular government agency (Social Security, Bureau of Indian Affairs) that oversees the program.

There are a few national organizations that will help you in your search. They include: The Citizens Scholarship Foundation of America (1 South St., Concord, N.H. 03301), with 200 local chapters that each award scholarships to students in their communities; the National Association of Secondary School Principals (1904 Association Drive, Reston, Va. 22091), which has a list of contests that offer scholarships; and computer services like the College Scholarship Information Bank (College Entrance Examination Board, 888 Seventh Ave., New York, N.Y. 10019), and Scholarship Search (1775 Broadway, New York, N.Y. 10019). Or, if you're willing to spend a lot of time, you can hunt through directories of aid programs, such as the *Student Aid Annual* (issued by Chronicle Guidance Publications, Inc.), and the annual catalogue of *Financial Aids for Higher Education* (published by William Brown Co.).

Probably your child's best bet for general help is to take the SAT of the College Board and use the Board's Student Search Service. The service, for no extra charge, will route your child's application to colleges that are interested in such students.

Finally, for more information on the types of aid available and advice on applying, you might want to turn again to *How to Get the Money to Pay for College.*[2]

Choose a College that Will Offer You Money

The school that your son or daughter applies to can also improve his/her chances of getting financial aid. Keep in mind two important factors: How much aid does the school offer? And how desirable is your child to that school?

The second factor may surprise you, if you've tended to think more in terms of how much you desire a certain college. But remember that you're raising your youngster to be a winner, and winners are what most colleges are looking for. Colleges use scholarships to attract the students they want.

The students they're most interested in are those with outstanding athletic skills, academic ability, or extracurricular activities (for instance, school presidents, winners of major art awards). Remember all the scholarships that were offered to Pamela, the National Merit Scholar? Private schools in particular are trying to increase the number of minority pupils enrolled. Another prime consideration is variety: few, if any, schools want a student body all from the same geographical area or with the same academic interests.

Of course, the most prestigious schools have little trouble attracting the applicants they want, with or without scholarship aid. But the great majority of colleges are not that lucky, and they have to reach out and compete for students. Thus, an academic record that wouldn't even get your child into Harvard could win him/her a scholarship to another school.

That was the case with Joseph Dixon. Although he had a good B+ grade average, in the top 15 percent of his class, and he'd scored in the seventy-eighth percentile on the SAT, Joseph knew that he'd need better grades to be accepted by an Ivy League college. So he concentrated his efforts on the next range of schools, the lesser-known private and public universities.

Because he lives in Pennsylvania, Joseph started by looking at institutions in that state. But from his high school counselor, Joseph learned that he might actually have a better chance to get a scholarship at a school in another part of the country. Colleges are always seeking to broaden the geographic variety of their student bodies and they will offer financial aid to attract applicants from far away. Joseph's counselor particularly recommended private schools in the West and Midwest, because those schools are in direct competition with large, less-expensive state university systems.

When you consider a school's financial aid package, you should look at the number of scholarships and grants available, the requirements, the percentage of students who receive aid, how much of the total expense that aid covers, and whether aid extends beyond the freshman year. One good source of this information is the *Hawes Comprehensive Guide to Colleges,* mentioned earlier. Another source is *The College Handbook,* published by the College Entrance Examination Board. You'll probably find that schools with higher tuition offer more aid—but that still may not make them less expensive than low-tuition schools.

Joseph ended up with scholarship offers from three moderately prestigious private colleges in the Midwest. He decided on Carleton College, a small school near St. Paul, Minnesota. Although the tuition was a steep $4,037, Carleton offered Joseph a $2,000 scholarship plus a campus job to help with the rest of the cost.

The Paperwork

Every aid program has its price: forms to fill out and fees to pay. Generally it will cost you $4 or $5 for your financial statement, plus $1.50 to $3 for each college that statement is sent to. Competitive contests can require that your child write an essay or take an achievement test. Other programs may want personal interviews, transcripts of your child's grades, or recommendations from high school. All in all, applying for money can cost some $100 in fees and hours in paperwork.

The work is somewhat simplified because most programs use one of two standard forms, the Financial Aid Form (FAF) of the College Scholarship Service or the Family Financial Statement (FFS) of the American College Testing Program. In fact, that's all you need in order to apply for the Basic Grant. Another time-saver, mentioned earlier, is to sign up for the Student Search Service of the College Board when your child takes the SAT. Similarly, you should apply for financial aid from an individual college at the same time that you apply for admission.

And start planning early. Deadlines for most aid programs can be as early as October of your child's senior year, generally no later than December. In fact, the test for the National Merit Scholarship must be taken in October of the *junior* year. On the other hand, the Financial Aid Form must not be sent out until after January 1.

Fortunately, federal loan programs such as the GSLP have later deadlines than the aid programs. Try for outright grants and scholarships before settling for a loan or work study.

Yes, for all your work and expense, your child may still end up with nothing more than a loan or a token $100 grant. And you may wonder if it's even worth bothering.

Look at it this way: you can't get anything at all unless you apply. You may just get $100, or you may get $1,000. But however much it is, it's money that you don't have to pay out of your own pocket. If a loan or a job or a small grant makes the difference as to whether your child can go to the college that will help him or her become a winner—then isn't it worth it?

13

Better Ways than College
to Careers for Many Teenagers

You've probably heard at least one story about someone who dropped out of school in eighth grade, went to work on a factory assembly line, and ended up twenty years later as the multi-million-dollar president of a major company. It probably sounded like a fantasy to you, the kind of thing that could only happy 100 years ago.

Well, it's still happening today. Consider Fred L. Turner, who started out frying hamburgers at a McDonald's restaurant, dropped out of college, and eventually became chief executive of the McDonald Corporation. Of course, such extreme success doesn't happen often, but the moral of the story is this: Your child can be a winner without going to college.

A four-year college education isn't the right route for all young people, and those who don't want to go to college shouldn't feel that they have to. There are plenty of other paths to a satisfying, well-paying career. A study by the U.S. Department of Health, Education and Welfare in 1972 found that a majority of men earning $15,000 or more in 1970 never graduated from college. More than three-quarters of the job openings forecast for the mid-1980s will be in career areas that do not require a bachelor's degree.

The areas range from medicine, computers, and banking, to cooking, commercial art, and forestry. People without college degrees work as police officers and nurses, technicians and paraprofessionals. Some run their own businesses. Generally, the jobs require one or two years of education beyond high school—usually at a far lower cost than a four-year bachelor's degree—and many provide training on the job.

In fact, opportunities are so good that even some college graduates are abandoning their diplomas and going back for training in non-college careers. That was the case with Charles Ridgeway, for example. After searching unsuccessfully for two years, the only job Charles could find, even with a four-year degree in biology, was a position as a mail clerk. So he switched careers and enrolled in a two-year training program to become a medical lab technician. Similarly, Vicky Logan found that her bachelor's degree in music education was useless once she realized that teaching was the wrong career for her. Her main ambition is still singing, but to earn a living right now she took a four-month training course in electrolysis (a branch of the beauty field) and works for a major Manhattan beauty salon.

Almost any area your youngster is interested in probably has good career opportunities that don't require four years of college. This chapter will show you some of the fastest-growing of those careers and tell you what kind of training your child will need to prepare for them. For a start, let's look at one of the most prestigious fields of all, medicine.

Your Child Doesn't Have to Be a Doctor to Work in Medicine

Ella D. always wanted a career in the area of health care, but she didn't want to go through the years of college required to become a physician. So, with just two years at a Massachusetts community college, Ella fulfilled her ambition by becoming a medical assistant. Working first for a dermatologist and now for an allergist/internist, Ella takes patients' blood pressure, gives tests for anemia, and screens laboratory slides. She also does some bookkeeping and clerical work. "I love it," Ella says. "It's helping people."

The health care industry now employs approximately 6 percent of all workers in the United States, and the number is growing rapidly. As medicine becomes more complex and specialized, a range of support jobs as aides, assistants, and technicians has developed for each medical specialty, none of them requiring a four-year college degree. Here are some of the specific career fields that the U.S. Bureau of Labor Statistics (BLS) predicts will have a particularly high rate of job openings in the 1980s:

Medical assistant: These assistants work under a physician's direction in helping provide medical care to patients. They often work in physicians' offices. Employment prospects for them are excellent. They are also called physician's assistant or associate.

Dental hygienist: The BLS foresees an astounding increase of nearly 157 percent in job opportunities as dental care continues to improve. Hygienists work in dentists' offices, cleaning teeth, taking X-rays, and preparing tests.

Respiratory therapist or technician: Using respirators and positive-pressure breathing machines, therapists and technicians provide treatment for patients with breathing difficulty and teach the patients how to use the equipment themselves. The growth rate in this field is also expected to be extraordinarily high, 110 percent.

Occupational therapy (OT) assistant: OT assistants work with patients who are mentally or physically disabled. The work can range from teaching the patients how to dress themselves to helping them learn a new craft. Job openings are expected to increase by a healthy 81 percent.

Physical therapist (PT) assistant or aide: Like OT assistants, PT assistants and aides work with people who are physically handicapped. Their work concentrates on the physical aspect of rehabilitation, including exercise, massage, and teaching patients to use artificial limbs. A 71 percent growth rate is expected in employment.

Lab technician: Technicians specialize in a specific medical field, helping to carry out tests or making medical equipment. Job opportunities depend on the field: there will be a strong demand for dental and ophthalmic (eyeglass) lab technicians, a lower demand for medical lab technicians.

Emergency medical technician (EMT): This is one of the newest and fastest-growing fields in health care. As the first medical personnel at the scene of an emergency, EMTs administer immediate treatment to victims of such crises as shock, accidents, and heart attacks. Although some EMTs now work as volunteers, the trend is toward full-time, paid professionals.

Nurse: Jobs in nursing cover almost the whole range of the medical field. Licensed practical nurses (LPNs) and registered nurses (RNs) work in physicians' offices, private homes, schools, businesses, and in every ward of a hospital. They may specialize in surgery, psychiatry, maternity care, or intensive care, to name just a few fields. Their work includes giving medication, assisting in examinations, and comforting patients. Demand for LPNs is expected to shoot up by 95 percent, while the need for the more highly trained RNs will increase by 50 percent.

Available Jobs in a Wide Range of Fields

Those eight job categories are only some of the possibilities available in the field of medicine—and medicine is only one field. It would be impossible here to list all the careers with good employment opportunities that your child could choose among without needing a four-year bachelor's degree. The next few pages will give you a few examples of the range of fields and the specific jobs in those fields that should have the most potential in the years ahead.

The computer industry is a particularly good example. Twenty years ago it hardly existed, yet today it is one of the areas with the biggest projected growth rate for jobs. As computers find their way into more and more aspects of daily life, there will be a large demand for *computer service technicians* to maintain the intricate machinery. A smaller number of *programmers* (the ones who plan and write the programs that are fed into computers) will also be needed. The one place where growth is expected to be slow is in the area of *console and keypunch operators,* an area which involves entering and retrieving data into and from a computer.

Law is another field where jobs are booming. *Legal assistants* (also known as paralegal specialists) help lawyers in their research. *Court reporters* (also known as certified shorthand reporters) record everything that is said in a legal proceeding, using special stenographic machines.

For a different aspect of law, your child might consider *police work.* It is, of course, an exceptionally demanding job: a typical day can involve anything from a high-speed chase after a murder suspect to testifying in court about a suspect's arrest. But the kind of work a police officer does depends a good deal on where he or she works. In a small town, most days may be spent directing traffic, breaking up a domestic argument, even delivering a baby in an emergency. Larger police departments tend to assign their officers to specialized areas such as radio communications, riot control, or detective work. Opportunities should be most numerous with state police departments, where the work mainly involves patrolling the highways.

Americans are eating out more and more these days, and that means a growing need for professional *cooks.* The variety of jobs is as wide as the variety of food we eat, everything from fast-food hamburgers to gourmet foreign meals. Larger restaurants often hire several cooks and chefs, each concentrating on a certain type of food, such as salads, sauces, desserts.

As we keep filling our lives with more complex machinery, specialized technicians will be needed to repair and maintain those machines. Surprisingly, one of the biggest growth rates is in the field of *motorcycle mechanics,* with job openings expected to expand at a rate of 98 percent. Other high-growth careers are *business machine servicing technician* (50 percent) and *industrial machine repairer* (66 percent). Opportunities for general *appliance servicing technicians* (those who service such everyday items as refrigerators, toasters, and washing machines), *TV-stereo-radio service technicians,* and *aircraft mechanics* are expected to grow at a slower rate.

The need for *secretaries* should increase at a healthy 47 percent—and your child's chances will be improved if he/she is qualified in the full range of secretarial skills, including typing, filing, simple bookkeeping, and stenography. There will be fewer opportunities for *typists* and *receptionists* with only selected secretarial skills. Another advantage of secretarial work is that part-time and temporary jobs are often available.

Registered land surveyors will be in great demand as the United States continues to develop new streets, housing, shopping centers, and recreation areas. Working in the field, surveyors measure precise boundaries, help set land valuation, and gather data used for making maps.

Another career that sometimes overlaps with surveying is that of a *forestry technician.* With the growing national interest in the environment, technicians will be needed to battle fires and floods, inspect trees for disease, work on replanting forests, and help surveyors build roads.

As *offset printing* replaces the old method of letterpresses, there will be openings for several different types of jobs in that field. Camera operators photograph the copy that is to be printed; lithographic artists sharpen and reshape the images on the negative of the photograph; strippers put together all the negatives into the positions they are to appear on a page; platemakers transfer those negatives to a printing plate; and offset press operators run the printing press. For the industry overall, job openings are expected to grow at a rate of 30 percent.

Banks will also be needing various types of employees. *Tellers* handle such customer transactions as cashing checks or withdrawing and depositing funds, and in larger banks, they may specialize in a particular type of transaction (loans, payroll, foreign exchange, etc.). Bank *clerks* do the behind-the-scenes work of bookkeeping, accounting, and record-keeping.

If your child is interested in part-time work, *cosmetology* might be a good career. Cosmetologists (also known as hairdressers and beauticians) cut and style hair, give manicures and facials, and provide advice on makeup. They can work both full and part time.

For many women, becoming an *airline flight attendant,* or stewardess, has always seemed like a glamorous career. Now the field is open to men as well. Since attendants are responsible for the safety and comfort of passengers on an airplane, their duties can range from serving meals to caring for a child who is traveling alone. This is a particularly good career for people who like to visit new places and don't want a regular nine-to-five schedule. An extra fringe benefit is the discount most airlines allow attendants when they fly on personal trips.

Finally, there's the option of *running one's own business.* The possibilities here are as varied as the types of businesses you can find in the Yellow Pages, from a crafts boutique to a telephone-answering service, from a restaurant to a computer software firm.

You and your youngster may want to look into a book on such high-demand career fields for which college isn't needed. Written by one of the co-authors, it is *Careers Today: Leading Growth Fields Entered by Short Training,* by Gene R. Hawes, Mark Hawes, and Christine Fleming.[1]

Why College May Not Be the Best Route for Your Child

With so many different fields to choose among, your child doesn't have to go to college in order to pursue a satisfying career. So think of college as just one of the many alternatives. The first thing to determine is whether college is the best alternative for your son or daughter.

The decision is a complex one that involves almost every aspect of your youngster's life—experience in school so far, interests, hobbies, personality, long-range goals. When their son, Stephen, was in tenth grade, Phyllis and Jim Davis sat down with him to talk about that decision.

They started by looking at Stephen's educational background during the past nine years. Although his grades were better than average, Stephen had never really liked going to school. At the slightest sign of a cold or stomachache, he always asked if he could stay home. Jim and Phyllis constantly had to remind him to do his homework. Stephen rarely read books just for pleasure.

The Davises went to Stephen's school to talk to his teachers and guidance counselor, who said that Stephen didn't seem to have the interest in academics that he would need if he were to do well in college. According to his scores on various standardized tests, Stephen had the potential to earn good grades, but only if he worked hard.

Stephen himself wasn't sure if he wanted to go to college. After spending almost his entire life in school, it might be good to do something else and earn some money once he finished high school, instead of devoting another four years to studying. Maybe after he'd been working at a job for a while, Stephen suggested, he could decide then to go on to college.

But what kind of job did Stephen have in mind? Because some careers do require a bachelor's degree, that question could determine whether or not Stephen went to college. So, Stephen and his parents started looking at his classes and hobbies to see which general fields interested him most.

Any career such as bookkeeping, banking, or land surveying was eliminated immediately: Stephen hated math. Since he liked working with people, a public service job as an airline flight attendant, cook, or police officer might be a good idea. Another advantage to police work was that Stephen enjoyed being out of doors. Because he was also very good at making things with his hands, perhaps he might want to work in offset printing, in a medical lab, or as a mechanic.

Although that analysis still left Stephen with a list of about a dozen different fields to consider, he had moved an important step closer to a decision on college. All of the career fields that interested him offered job possibilities that wouldn't require a four-year bachelor's degree.

You and your child should go through the same sort of process that the Davises did. Once you have a general idea of the career field or fields that sound good, you can find out more details about particular jobs in those fields. Talk to people working in those areas, and visit their places of work. Look at the salary levels, the possibilities for advancement, the working conditions. Even in one career, there can be a variety of alternatives, such as working in an office, at a research lab, in the field, or with the public. Would your child rather work a steady nine-to-five schedule or odd hours? How long does your child want to spend in training before getting out to work? Does he or she like to travel? Another important aspect to consider is whether jobs are available in the geographic area where your child wants to live.

There are certain character traits that are particularly important if your son or daughter is thinking about running his or her own business. An independent business owner must be a self-starter, the kind of person who can work on his or her own and stick to the job even when there's no boss to report to. The business owner must also be good at managing other people.

Winning a Job in a Winning Career

Finally, your child settles on a career that sounds fulfilling and satisfying—a career that could be a winner. The next step is to find out what preparation your child needs in order to get a job in that career.

In most cases, he/she can start in high school by taking classes that will give some background in the field. For instance, while most appliance technicians are trained on the job, applicants who've taken high school courses in electricity, chemistry, and shop math will have an advantage. Secretaries can cut down on the amount of time they will need for training if they've learned shorthand or typing in high school. Some schools actually offer full vocational training programs in such areas as auto mechanics. Even if no specific classes are available in a career area, it's important to finish high school. While a high school diploma isn't always officially required, in every career it's an advantage.

Some extracurricular activities during high school may also help. A part-time job as a sales clerk will give your youngster important experience in working with the public. Volunteering in a hospital can provide a background in medicine. These extra activities may prove to be a crucial advantage when your child applies for a job.

Most career fields require some formal training after high school. Usually, there are three basic sources: high school adult education vocational programs; community colleges; and private trade or technical schools. The first two are generally the least expensive, while private school courses may take less time to complete. But the length of time depends more on the career than on the school. Training for work as an emergency medical technician can be accomplished in just eighty-one hours; but registered nurses may go to school for as long as four years.

At the end of a two-year community college course, students often earn an associate's degree, and those class credits can usually be transferred later to a four-year college.

If your child attends a private trade or technical school, be sure to check that school's credentials carefully. Find out what employers think of the program, and check its status with the Better Business Bureau. Be especially wary of a school's claims regarding the number of graduates who've found employment. Unfortunately, many private schools are more interested in making a profit than in training students for careers, and they may advertise inflated success rates.

Two other good sources of training are the armed forces and apprenticeship programs. However, the types of careers where such training is available are limited, and competition for apprenticeships is keen.

In some fields, special examinations or certain personal qualifications are required, even after training is completed. Nurses and cosmetologists, for instance, must pass a licensing exam. Police officers must meet specific physical requirements, pass a competitive written exam, and undergo a check of their backgrounds.

Of course, there are also careers where the real training is on the job and no particular schooling is needed before hand. But your child's previous educational, volunteer, and working experience is still important. Louise Regalla's history is a good example.

Louise decided to become an airline flight attendant because she likes to travel and she wanted the freedom that an airline career would allow her in scheduling her time. (Attendants can often put in all their required hours of flight time at the start of the month, leaving the last two weeks free.) Getting a job wouldn't be easy, Louise knew. In fact, after her first interview, she was sure she hadn't made it; the five other women interviewed with her all seemed much prettier and more knowledgeable.

Because there aren't really any formal qualifications for the job beyond certain age, height, weight, and health requirements, there wasn't much Louise could do to improve her chances. A nursing background would have helped, but she didn't have that. Since she wasn't applying to any international airlines, it didn't matter whether she was fluent in a foreign language. There was no school she could go to for extra training.

However, Louise did have some crucial advantages. After four years as a sales clerk in Boston, she had experience working with the public. She'd almost completed her two-year associate's degree in business administration at a community college, and airlines prefer attendants with some college study. Louise got the job.

What Kind of Training Will Your Child Need?

To get an idea of the different kinds of education or experience that may be needed, consider this list of the requirements for each of the careers mentioned earlier in this chapter:

Medical assistant: A one- or two-year medical assisting program at a community college or private occupational school is the most common way of getting into the field. Passing the certification exam offered by the American Association of Medical Assistants is not necessary, but it helps.

Dental hygienist: Hygienists must have graduated from an accredited dental hygienist school, usually a two-year program at a community college or technical institute. Then they must pass written and clinical exams to earn a hygienist's license.

Respiratory therapist or technician: Post-high school education in respiratory therapy at a school at (or affiliated with) a large hospital can last from eighteen months to four years.

Occupational therapy assistant: OT training programs are offered at community colleges (usually two years), private vocational schools (usually one year), or through the armed forces.

Physical therapist assistant or aide: For aides, on-the-job training is available. Assistants should have a two-year associate's degree from a community college.

Lab technician: The requirements depend on the exact field. Generally, training lasts from nine months to two years after high school and is available at community colleges, vocational schools, and hospitals.

Emergency medical technician: An eighty-one-hour training program is usually offered by police, fire, and health departments. EMTs must be at least eighteen years old and have a high school diploma and valid driver's license. Chances will be improved if an applicant passes the practical and written exams offered by the National Registry of Emergency Medical Technicians.

Nurse: LPNs need a one-year, state-approved training program through a hospital, community college, public school, or health agency. RNs may go to college for two to four years to earn an associate's degree, nursing diploma, or bachelor's degree. LPNs and RNs must also pass state licensing exams.

Computer service technician: Technicians should complete a one- or two-year training program in basic electronics or computer technology at a technical school or community college. (High school math and physics courses also help.)

Computer programmer: Two years of college or vocational school training in computer science or programming are a definite advantage.

Computer console or keypunch operator: Although only a high school diploma is required, one or two years of training in computer operations after high school will give your youngster an edge. Applicants may also be asked to take aptitude tests for speed, accuracy, and logic.

Legal assistant: Paralegal programs at colleges and law schools last from a few months to four years, generally two years. Some schools even require a college degree or a certain score on the Scholastic Aptitude Test of the College Board in order to get into a paralegal training program.

Court reporter: Most reporters complete a two-year program, usually at a private school that is approved by the National Shorthand Reporters Association. They typically can take dictation at a rate of at least 225 words per minute.

Police officer: After passing stringent physical exams and competitive written exams, officers receive their training on the job. Usually a high school diploma is required, and state police must be U.S. citizens at least twenty-one years old. A two-year community college degree in law enforcement will help an applicant get a job.

Cook: Many cooks learn their trade by starting as kitchen helpers. Those who want to start at higher levels take programs offered at community colleges, private institutes, and high schools.

Motorcycle mechanic: There are no formal requirements, but a high school diploma and courses in mechanics, science, and math are an advantage.

Business machine servicing technician: Employers prefer to hire people with at least a year of post-high school training in electronics. Job applicants may be tested for mechanical aptitude, manual dexterity, general intelligence, and knowledge of electronics.

Industrial machine repairer: Most repairers work their way up by starting as helpers, or else they enter four-year apprenticeship programs. They may also study mechanical technology at a community college or private technical institute.

Appliance servicing technician: Usually training is provided on the job. High school students may want to take classes in electricity, electronics, chemistry, shop math, and blueprint reading, and some community colleges and private trade schools also offer courses in appliance repair.

TV-stereo-radio service technician: People who want to be technicians can enter an apprenticeship program, learn skills in the armed forces, or take a two-year program in electronics technology at a community college.

Aircraft mechanic: There are two basic ways to learn the trade: through a three- or four-year apprenticeship program, or in a two-year course at a private trade school certified by the Federal Aviation Administration. Many mechanics also learn the trade in the armed forces.

Secretary: Secretaries should have graduated from high school and completed at least one year of college. Training programs, lasting from a few months to two years, are available in high schools, community colleges, and private occupational schools.

Typist: Employers will probably expect a minimal speed of 40 to 50 words per minute, plus a high school diploma. Almost all high schools offer typing classes, as do adult education programs, public colleges, and private occupational schools.

Receptionist: A high school diploma, with courses in bookkeeping, typing, English, and business, will be an advantage.

Registered land surveyor: Surveying programs last from one to four years at community colleges and private vocational schools. A good high school background includes algebra, trigonometry, geometry, drafting, and mechanical drawing.

Forestry technician: While technicians can learn on the job or through government-sponsored training programs, the best method is probably a one- or two-year program at a community college, technical institute, or university. If the program is not recognized by the Society of American Foresters, investigate it carefully.

Offset printing employee: High school graduates may enter the field through apprenticeship programs (four or five years) or two-year programs at community colleges and technical institutes. While in high school, students can get a good background by taking classes in printing, photography, art, math, chemistry, and physics.

Bank teller: A high school diploma and some clerical experience will provide an edge in getting hired. Most training is on the job.

Bank clerk: Any high school or post-high school courses in related fields will help: bookkeeping, business arithmetic, typing, office machine operation. The American Institute of Banking offers part-time courses.

Cosmetologist: All cosmetologists must pass a state licensing exam. To prepare for it, they usually take courses in public or private schools lasting at least six months.

Airline flight attendant: Two years of college are preferred, but not required.

Business owner: The type of business that a person owns will determine the kind of background needed. For general advice, the U.S. Small Business Administration is a good source.

Today's Decision Is Not Forever

As Stephen Davis pointed out to his parents, deciding not to go to college now doesn't close off the possibility of enrolling later. If, in a few years, your youngster wants to change careers or advance to a position where a bachelor's degree is a prerequisite, there will still be a chance to go back to school. In fact, there are some definite advantages to postponing college until after a person has been at a job for a few years. Often colleges want students who've had some experience in the working world. And more and more companies are offering tuition programs as a fringe benefit, where they pay for part of their employees' school tuition.

In some of the careers described in this chapter—particularly those in medicine, forestry, surveying, and computers—a four-year college degree will be necessary for your youngster to move up the career ladder. However, all that's needed in most fields is experience, ability, and perhaps a type of advanced certification. Taking further training courses will always help, of course, but that doesn't have to mean a full four years of college.

How high can your child go without that college diploma? Remember Fred Turner of McDonald's at the beginning of the chapter. The important point is that a lot of factors are involved in making your child a winner—and college should be only one of them.

I4

Essential Steps to Full
Independence for Your Child

By your child's late teens, if all has gone well, the young man or woman will have taken one of two broad directions: either a four-year college degree program, or shorter education to prepare for a good career field. Things will be very different from ten or twelve years before. Your son or daughter will often be telling you how to run your life, instead of the reverse, and will be away independently most of the time, busy with his or her own learning, work, interests, friends, and fun.

Clearly, the child can soon be completely independent of you through the workings of a powerful drive for self-direction that you yourself helped generate over the years. That complete freedom will be realized with minimal help from you, or even none at all. Still, in your long endeavor of raising a winner, certain steps remain. They can be essential in helping the youngster avoid possibly painful floundering, hardship, or wasted effort in getting off to a winning start in adult life. Here are those important followthrough steps.

Helping Your Child Set Important Directions

Setting a good career direction will probably continue to be one of the main areas in which you can most productively help your child on into early adult years. On the one hand, your son or daughter may have decided to head into a career right after high school, or after a year or two of career study beyond high school. In that case, career choices will necessarily have been made in high school (as described in Chapter 10), and your child will probably have started training for one of the growth careers entered by short training (such as those highlighted in Chapter 13). In addition, though, the youngster may well have many detailed questions about career directions to settle, such as where and with what type of organization to start work. Your interest and thoughts on such questions as these can prove quite helpful.

On the other hand, your boy or girl may have entered a four-year college program for the bachelor's degree. In this case, it's especially important for the youngster to set good career directions, and you can help in this endeavor. Setting good career directions while getting a college education is important because many young people finish college today unprepared for any careers in which jobs are available.

Such unprepared graduates must often settle for jobs they could have gotten right out of high school—as taxi drivers, waiters or waitresses, mail clerks or shipping clerks, or gas station attendants. We've seen this happen in recent years to a number of college graduates we know. You may have seen it among families you know. It can be a very bitter experience—a real blow to a young graduate's confidence and enthusiasm.

However, the experience of going jobless after college can be avoided entirely. To be sure of starting successfully in a career after college, the student should be certain to do one or both of two things: get a good preparation to enter a leading growth field for college graduates; and develop job skills that are in high demand.

By a leading growth field, we mean any career area normally entered by college graduates that has unusually abundant job opportunities or growth possibilities. Among such careers at present are those of architects, engineers, accountants, marketing specialists, hospital administrators, physical therapists, computer systems analysts, and geologists. These are only a few of many possible examples. Guidance counselors in high schools or career placement officers in colleges can identify such areas and can help you find other information about them. They are also treated in various books on careers, including one by a co-author of this book, *Careers Tomorrow; Leading Growth Fields for College Graduates,* by Gene R. Hawes, New American Library/Plume, 1979.

The second precaution a student should take to assure getting a job after college is to develop job skills in high demand. Among skills of this kind are computer programming, basic accounting, drafting, selling, and even expert typewriting. You may recall that we also urged students to acquire one or two of these marketable skills while still in high school. Acquiring and getting some work experience with them either in high school or college can substantially increase the chances for getting a career entry job after college.

Again, specialists in the placement office at the college should be able to advise the student on which kinds of skills might be most advantageous, and how they might be developed at the college in courses, and perhaps also in part-time jobs or student activities.

Placement offices at colleges can aid students with career questions in a number of additional ways. They can help students improve such job-getting skills as resumé writing and interviewing. They can also help the graduating senior with planning and carrying out an effective job campaign.

Your New Roles: Boss No More, but Morale-Booster, Balance-Wheel, Banker, Special Friend

Your influence on the young man or woman by this time—concerning career direction or almost anything else—is very likely to be indirect and by suggestion. The vital reason for this, of course, is that you want a person of around age twenty to be able to make his or her own decisions wisely. In fact, as part of your efforts to raise a winner, you have been trying for quite a few years to bring the youngster up to such a point of independent judgment.

For all the new independence, though, you have some very important continuing roles to play. You will need to go on being a morale-booster, first of all. The young man or woman will run into reverses and disappointments. You can be important at times like these for comfort and reassurance. Serving as something of a balance-wheel is a related function you'll continue to perform. You'll need to go on taking some of the ache out of transient sorrows and adding touches of practicality to wild-eyed schemes.

Being the banker for your grown son or daughter represents one of the most delicate and essential roles for you to play. Obviously your help in financing an expensive education for a professional career can make an enormous difference. Your money can help the youngster through business or personal reverses that may come in getting started in work or family life. Both you and your adult child will have reservations about special funds; the child will want to avoid feeling obligated, while you will want to avoid compromising his/her independence. But maturity and tact on both your parts can make it possible to resolve such concerns.

Most important of all, you will have become special friends to each other. You will certainly go on enjoying one another's company. That son or daughter whom you've raised to be a winner will surely go on turning to you, not only for advice but for fun and for your special quality of understanding.

References

Note that additional references also appear under the following section on Further Resources for each chapter.

CHAPTER 1

1. L. Rainwater and R. Coleman, *Social Standing in America*. New York: Basic Books, 1979.

CHAPTER 2

1. Sylvia Richardson, Milton Brutten, and Charles Mangel, *Something Is Wrong with My Child*. New York: Harcourt Brace Jovanovich, 1973.
2. Thomas Gordon, *Parent Effectiveness Training*. New York: Peter H. Wyden, 1970.
3. Jessie Bernard, *The Future of Motherhood*. New York: Dial Press, 1975.
4. Lee Salk, *What Every Child Would Like His Parents to Know about Divorce*. New York: Harper & Row, 1978.
5. Nancy Friday, *My Mother My Self: The Daughter's Search for Identity*. New York: Delacorte, 1977.

CHAPTER 3

1. Jerome Brunner, *Toward a Theory of Instruction,* Cambridge, Mass.: Belknap Press, 1973.
2. Leo Buscaglea, *Love*. Thorofare, N.J.: Charles B. Slack, Inc., 1972.
3. Terrell H. Bell, *Active Parent Concern*. Englewood Cliffs, N.J.: Prentice-Hall, 1976.
4. Christopher J. Jencks, *Who Gets Ahead in America: The Determinants of Economic Success in America*. New York: Basic Books, 1979.
5. Helen G. and Martin S. Weiss, *Home Is a Learning Place*. Boston: Little, Brown, 1976.

CHAPTER 4

1. Joseph Heller, *Something Happened.* New York: Alfred A. Knopf, 1974.
2. Harold B. Levy, M.D., *Square Pegs Round Holes.* Boston: Little, Brown, 1973.
3. Alfred North Whitehead, *The Aims of Education.* New York: Macmillan, 1929.
4. Marcia Chambers, "Teaching Licensing Considered," *New York Times,* July 3, 1979.
5. Charlotte Des Jardines, "How to Organize an Effective Parent Group to Move Bureaucracies," Massachusetts *ACLD Gazette.* June 1979.
6. Ronald and Beatrice Gross, *The Children's Rights Movement, Overcoming the Oppression of Young People.* New York: Doubleday, 1977.
7. Paul Graubard, "Little Brother Is Watching You," *Psychology Today,* New York: March 1974.

CHAPTER 5

1. Paula Bernstein, "How to Talk to Your Child's Teacher," *Redbook,* November 1978.
2. Victor and Mildred G. Goertzel, *Cradles of Eminence.* Boston: Little, Brown, 1950.
3. "America's Teachers, Are They to Blame?" *U.S. News and World Report,* Sept. 11, 1978.
4. *Ibid.*
5. Helen G. and Martin S. Weiss, *Basic Language Kit.* Great Barrington, Mass.: Treehouse Associates, 1979.
6. Lena Williams, " 'Star Wars' Battles School Reading Slump," *New York Times,* Nov. 23, 1978.
7. Weiss, *op. cit.*
8. Robert Reinhold, "California High School Panel to Urge Drastic Changes in Traditional Studies," *New York Times,* March 2, 1978.
9. Fred Hechinger, "Many Schools Rely on the Hickory Stick," *New York Times,* July 24, 1979.
10. Irwin Hyman and James Wise, *Corporal Punishment in American Education.* Philadelphia: Temple University Press, 1979.
11. Fred M. Hechinger, "Smaller Classes Found to Produce Subtle Changes," *New York Times,* April 10, 1979.

CHAPTER 6

1. Eve Block, Jenny Covill-Servo, and Margery Fischer Rosen, *Failing Students—Failing Schools,* Statewide Youth Advocacy Project of the New York Civil Liberties Union, Rochester, New York, 1979.

CHAPTER 7

1. Howard P. Rome, M.D., "The Myriad Problems of Dyslexics," *Psychiatric Annals* 7, No. 9 (September 1977).

2. NINDS, Monograph 9, "Disorders of Central Processing in Children," Department of Health, Education and Welfare, Washington, D.C.

3. Public Law 91-230, April 1970.

4. Slogan of the Massachusetts ACLD, 11 River Street, Wellesley, Mass.

5. National ACLD, 4166 Library Road, Pittsburgh, Pa. 15234; National Orton Society, 8415 Bellona Lane, Towson, Md. 21204. The second is an organization of educators, psychiatrists, psychologists, and other professionals researching and working with children with learning disabilities.

6. CACLD (Connecticut Association for Children with Learning Disabilities), 20 North Main Street, South Norwalk, Conn. 06854; New York Orton Society, 80 Fifth Ave., New York, N.Y. 10011.

7. See for example the Massachusetts ACLD *Gazette,* 11 River Street, Wellesley, Mass. and CANHC Library Center, 645 Odin Drive, Pleasant Hills, Calif. 94523.

8. Diana McGuiness, "How Schools Discriminate Against Boys," *Human Nature Magazine,* February 1979.

CHAPTER 8

1. S. P. Marland, *Education of the Gifted and Talented.* Washington, D.C.: U.S. Printing Office, 1971.

2. Jessica Holland, "Teen Tycoons," *New York Times Sunday Magazine,* Aug. 19, 1979.

3. Interview with Marjorie Zerin, M.A., Mf.C.C., and Edward Zerin, Ph.D. Mf.C.C., Westlake, California, Center for Marital and Family Counseling.

4. N. R. Tempest, *Teaching Clever Children.* London: Routledge and Kegan Paul, 1974.

5. Marsha M. Correll, *Teaching the Gifted and Talented.* Bloomington, Indiana: Phi Delta Kappa, Inc., 1978.

6. Milton Rockmire, "Creating Creativity," *American Way,* March 1979.

7. Bruce O. Boston, ed., *The Gifted and the Talented: Developing Elementary and Secondary School Programs,* Council for Exceptional Children, Reston, Virginia, 1975.

8. Kenneth Brower, *The Starship and the Canoe.* New York: Holt, Rinehart and Winston, 1978.

CHAPTER 9

1. R. Rosenthal and L. Jacobson, *Pygmalion in the Classroom.* New York: Holt, Rinehart and Winston, 1968.

2. Nancy Larrick, *Parent's Guide to Children's Reading.* New York: Doubleday, 1975.

CHAPTER 11

1. Richard Moll, *Playing the Private College Admissions Game.* New York: Times Books, 1979.

2. Gene R. Hawes, *Hawes Comprehensive Guide to Colleges.* New York: NAL/Plume, 1978.

CHAPTER 12

1. Gene R. Hawes and David M. Brownstone, *How to Get the Money to Pay for College.* New York: David McKay, 1978.
2. *Ibid.*

CHAPTER 13

1. Gene R. Hawes, Mark Hawes, and Christine Fleming, *Careers Today: Leading Growth Fields Entered by Short Training.* New York: NAL/Plume, 1977.

Further Resources

———◆———

In raising your child to be a winner, you may find it helpful to consult additional books and organizations given in this section. They are arranged by chapter, and by topic within each chapter in the order in which the topics are covered. In a number of cases, these resources are also briefly identified and discussed in the chapters.

CHAPTER 2
How You Talk and React to Your Child Sets the Foundations

On how parents relate to their children:

Richardson, Sylvia, M.D., Milton Brutten, Ph.D., and Charles Mangel, *Something Is Wrong with My Child.* New York: Harcourt Brace Jovanovich, 1973.

Ginott, Haim, Ph.D., Psychologist, *Between Parent and Child.* New York: Macmillan, 1972; *Between Parent and Teenager,* New York: Macmillan, 1969.

Gordon, Thomas, Ph.D., Psychologist, *Parent Effectiveness Training.* New York: Peter H. Wyden, 1970.

Despert, J. Louise, M.D., Psychoanalyst specializing in working with emotional problems of childhood. *Children of Divorce.* New York: Doubleday, 1953.

Bernard, Jessie, *The Future of Motherhood.* New York: Dial Press, 1975.

Szasz, Thomas, M.D., Psychiatrist, Professor of Psychiatry at SUNY Medical Center, Syracuse, N.Y., *The Second Sin.* New York: Anchor-Doubleday, 1974.

Friday, Nancy, *My Mother My Self: The Daughter's Search for Identity.* New York: Delacorte, 1977.

Elkind, David, Ph.D., Psychologist, *The Child and Society.* New York: Oxford University Press, 1979.

Additional Resources for Chapter 2

Siegel, Ernest, Ph.D., Rita Siegel, and Paul Siegel, *Help for the Lonely Child*. New York: E. P. Dutton, 1979. Dr. Ernest Siegel is Professor of Special Education at Adelphi University.

CHAPTER 3
Building Essential Readiness from Earliest Years

On understanding how your child gets ready to learn:

Chess, Stella, M.D., Psychoanalyst, *How to Help Your Child Get the Most Out of School*. New York: Doubleday, 1973.

Hunt, J. McVicker, Ph.D., Psychologist, "Psychological Development: Early Experience," *Annual Review of Psychology,* No. 30, 1970, pp. 103–43.

Hunt, J. McVicker, *Intelligence and Experience*. New York: Ronal Press, 1961.

Pines, Maya, Writer, *Revolution in Learning, The Years Birth to Six*. New York: Harper & Row, 1967.

Piaget, Jean, Ph.D., Former Professor of Developmental Psychology at the Sorbonne, Paris, France. *The Origins of Intelligence in Children*. New York: International Universal Press, 1952. See also *The Child's Conception of Numbers*. London: Routledge & Kegan Paul, 1952.

Jencks, Christopher, Ph.D., Professor of Sociology at Harvard University, *Who Gets Ahead in America: The Determinants of Economic Success in Amercia*. New York: Basic Books, 1979.

Badger, Earladeen, Teacher, *Teaching Guide, Infant Learning Program*. Paoli, Pa.: The Instructo Corp., 1971.

Weiss, Helen Ginandes and Martin S., *Home Is a Learning Place*. Boston: Little, Brown, 1976.

Ellkind David, Ph.D., Psychologist, "Growing Up Faster," *Psychology Today,* February 1979.

Other Resources on School Readiness

Brearley, Molly, *The Teaching of Young Children*. New York: Schocken Books, 1970.

De Hirsch, Katrina and Jeanette J. Jansky, Ph.D., with William S. Langford, *Predicting School Failure*. New York: Harper & Row, 1966.

Gesell, Arnold, M.D., and Frances L. Ilg, M.D., *The Child from Five to Ten*. New York: Harper & Row, 1946.

Ilg, Frances L., M.D., and Louise Bates Ames, Ph.D., *School Readiness*. New York: Harper & Row, 1964.

On communicating with your child:

Ackerman, Paul and Kappelman, Murray, *Signals: What Your Child Is Really Telling You*. New York: The Dial Press/James Wade, 1978.

CHAPTER 4
School Putdowns and Halos: How Kids, Teachers, and Parents Interact

On parents' and children's rights:

Levy, Harold B., M.D., *Square Pegs, Round Holes.* Boston: Little, Brown, 1973.

Gross, Beatrice and Ronald, *The Children's Rights Movement.* New York: Doubleday, 1977.

Des Jardines, Charlotte, "How to Organize an Effective Parent Group," Mass. ACLD *Gazette,* June 1979.

"You Have New Rights—Use Them!" *Closer Look,* Fall 1977, National Information Center for the Handicapped, P.O. Box 1492, Washington, D.C. 20013.

National Committee for Citizens in Education, *Network—Newsletter for Parents,* Suite 410, Wilde Lake Village Green, Columbia, Md., 21044.

On parents interacting with kids:

Ginott, Haim G., Ph.D., Psychologist, *Between Parent and Teenager.* New York: Macmillan, 1969.

On parents interacting with teachers:

Bernstein, Paula, Writer, "How to Talk Back to Your Child's Teacher," *Redbook,* November 1978.

On historical biographies of famous winners and their experiences in education:

Goertzel, Victor and Mildred G., *Cradles for Eminence.* Boston: Little, Brown, 1950.

On teenagers with problems:

Weiss, Helen Ginandes and Martin S., *Basic Language Kit.* Great Barrington, Mass.: Treehouse Associates, 1979.

CHAPTER 7
Learning Disability: The Hidden Handicap You Can Overcome

On what a learning disability really is:

Rome, Howard P., M.D., Psychiatrist, "The Myriad Problems of Dyslexics," *Psychiatric Annals,* No. 9, September 1977.

NINDS (National Institute of Neurologic Diseases), Monograph 9, *Disorders of the Central Processing of Children,* Dept. of Health, Education and Welfare, Washington, D.C., August 1969.

Public Law 91-230, April 1970, *Definition of Specific Learning Disabilities* (for a review of research), U.S. Government Printing Office, Washington, D.C. 20402.

On parent perception:

Reik, Theodore, Ph.D., Psychologist, *Listening with the Third Ear.* New York: Pyramid, 1964.

On personal perception of a learning-disabled adult:

Simpson, Eileen, *Reversals, A Personal Account of Victory Over Dyslexia.* Boston: Houghton Mifflin, 1979.

Further Resources on Learning Disabilities

On home activities that teach:

Weiss, Helen Ginandes and Martin S., *Home Is a Learning Place.* Boston: Little, Brown, 1976.

On developing social skills:

Siegel, Ernest, Ph.D., Rita and Paul Siegel, *Help for the Lonely Child.* New York: E. P. Dutton, 1979.

On adolescent learning problems:

Weiss, Helen Ginandes and Martin S., *Survival Manual.* Great Barrington, Mass: Treehouse Associates, 1974.

Weiss, Helen Ginandes and Martin S., *Basic Language Kit, A Teaching-Tutoring Aid for Adolescents and Young Adults.* Great Barrington, Mass.: Treehouse Associates, 1979.

CHAPTER 8
Your "Burden of Great Potential"—The Gifted Child

On education of the gifted child:

Marland, S. P., *Education of the Gifted and Talented.* Washington, D.C.: U.S. Government Printing Office, 1971.

Rockmire, Milton, "Creating Creativity," *American Way* magazine, March 1979.

On the self-fulfilling prophecy with children:

Rosenthal, Robert, Ph.D., and Lenore Jacobson, *Pygmalion in the Classroom.* New York: Holt, Rinehart & Winston, 1968.

Additional Resources on Gifted Children

Office of the Gifted and Talented (Federal Government), Dept. of Education, Washington, D.C.

Cushenberg, David C., Ph.D., and Helen Howell, Ph.D., *Reading and the Gifted Child*. Springfield, Ill.: Charles C. Thomas, 1974.

Martinson, Ruth A., *The Identification of the Gifted and Talented*. Office of the Superintendent of Schools, Ventura, Calif., 1974.

Gowan, John Curtis and E. Paul Torrance, *Educating the Ablest*. Itasca, Ill.: F. E. Peacock, 1971.

Torrance, E. Paul, Ph.D., *Talent and Education*. Minneapolis: University of Minnesota Press, 1960.

CHAPTER 9
The Myth of Testing—And Vital Countermeasures

On how teachers' expectations can boost test scores:

Rosenthal, Robert and Lenore Jacobson, *Pygmalion in the Classroom*. New York: Holt, Rinehart & Winston, 1968.

On how to build reading ability:

Larrick, Nancy, *Parent's Guide to Children's Reading*. New York: Doubleday, 1975.

On puzzles for imaginative thinking:

Leeming, Joseph, *Fun with Pencil and Paper*. Philadelphia: Lippincott, 1955.

Beard, Isabel R., *Puzzles and Riddles*. Chicago: Follett, 1969.

On colleges for students with learning disabilities:

An up-to-date list of colleges that accept students with learning disabilities is available on request from Association for Children with Learning Disabilities, 4156 Library Rd., Pittsburgh, Pa. 15234.

CHAPTER 10
High School Strategies that Lead to Top Colleges and Careers

On key factors in study skills for your child:

Cohen, Marvin, *Helping Your Teen-Age Student: What Parents Can Do to Improve Reading and Study Skills*. New York: Dutton, 1979.

Ehrlich, Eugene, *How to Study Better and Get Higher Marks*. New York: Harper & Row, 1976.

Morgan, Clifford T. and James Deese, *How to Study*. New York: McGraw-Hill, 1979.
Robinson, Francis P., *Effective Study*. New York: Harper & Row, 1970.
Pauk, Walter, *How to Study in College*. Boston: Houghton Mifflin, 1979.

CHAPTER 11
Winning Admission to America's Top Colleges

On gaining college admission:

Moll, Richard, *Playing the Private College Admissions Game*. New York: Times Books, 1979.
Hawes, Gene R., *Hawes Comprehensive Guide to Colleges*. New York: New American Library/Plume, 1978.

CHAPTER 12
Getting Thousands of Dollars in College Scholarships

Directories of aid programs:

Student Aid Annual. Monrovia, N.Y.: Chronicle Guidance Publications.
Financial Aids for Higher Education (annual). Dubuque, Iowa: William Brown Co.

On obtaining aid:

Hawes, Gene R. and David M. Brownstone, *How to Get the Money to Pay for College*. New York: McKay, 1977.

CHAPTER 13
Better Ways than College to Careers for Many Teenagers

On high-employment career fields:

Hawes, Gene R., Mark Hawes, and Christine Fleming, *Careers Today; Leading Growth Fields Entered by Short Training*. New York: New American Library/Plume, 1977.

CHAPTER 14
Essential Steps to Full Independence for Your Child

On growth career fields for college graduates:

Hawes, Gene R., *Careers Tomorrow; Leading Growth Fields for College Graduates*. New York: New American Library/Plume, 1979.

Appendix 1:
Private Schools

———◆———

This appendix amplifies the explanations and information on private schools that appear in Chapter 6.

Further Varieties of Private Schools—Including One for Home Instruction

You might find it particularly helpful for your child to go to a school with one of the special philosophies or programs you can find among private schools, especially boarding schools.

Many young people who have floundered badly in the high-pressure academic setting of public high schools in suburbs, for instance, can develop well in the low-pressure, noncompetitive, individualized settings provided by certain private schools. The Stowe School in Vermont, for example, is run by a joint student-faculty council and offers a combined program of college-prep studies without pressure and many sports and outdoor activities, including those of the "Outward Bound" variety. Also in Vermont, the Lyndon Institute offers not only college-prep work but high school majors in vocational areas, including business, homemaking, forestry, auto mechanics, dairying, and building trades. It provides close supervision to develop good study and health habits, and self-discipline. The Blue Ridge School in Dyke, Virginia, offers a noncompetitive program for boys of average academic capacity. The staff seeks to prepare a student to deal effectively with ideas and people by instilling in him confidence and respect for his own abilities: boys are given realistic challenges they can meet, and, inspired by their success, gain an awareness of their individual worth.

Sailing looms large as a focus of activity and development for students at some schools. The Flint School teaches aboard its two large, steel-hulled schooners as they voyage to foreign ports from its base in Sarasota, Florida. Endowed by an old Massachusetts whaling family, The Tabor Academy in Marion has all students sail its seventy-strong fleet of sailboats, operates an oceanography motor cruiser, and offers weekend and three-week Bermuda cruises aboard its ninety-two-foot schooner. The two Admiral Farragut academies, in New Jersey and Florida, offer junior naval training, preparatory study for all U.S. service academies like Annapolis and West Point, and sailing on their own fleet of boats.

You may well want to consider the question of which kind of school or program—either coed or single-sex—is most appropriate for your child. You, the child, and the child's advisers may all have strong preferences on whether the child's private school environment should be all boys, all girls, or boys and girls. You will find schools with different degrees of mixing the sexes. At a few schools, only some classes are coed; at others, the boys' and girls' schools are "coordinated" but are several miles apart.

Among private schools are also a number of military academies for parents interested in traditional discipline and service-academy preparation. Well-known ones include Culver Military Academy in Indiana, New York Military Academy near West Point, and Texas Military Institute.

Under unusual circumstances, you might find it helpful to turn to one of the few private schools where your child does not have to attend daily classes. The Calvert School in Baltimore, a regular coed day school for kindergarten through eighth grade, also provides home instruction courses covering the complete schoolwork in those grades. Any parent can teach the course for each grade to a son or daughter who cannot attend school—if wanted, with the help of an optional advisory teaching service. Each course includes books, paper, pencils, workbooks, pictures, and other materials, with a day-to-day instruction manual for the inexperienced home teacher.

The courses are made available for American children who cannot attend school for any compelling reason, such as residence in a foreign country or an area far from a school, travel with parents, or some serious physical handicap. Tuition fees for a course range from some $90 to $160. Some parents find it helpful to use these courses for enrichment of a child's schooling, particularly the courses for grades 3 to 8. (Information is available from Calvert at Tuscany Road, Baltimore, Md. 21210.) Calvert advises parents living in the United States who plan to use the courses for complete home teaching of their children to secure first the approval of their local school principal or superintendent because of school attendance laws.

If your child happens to have begun a busy professional career before high school graduation—perhaps in acting, dance, music, or modeling—you might be interested in the Professional Children's School. Located near the Lincoln Center for the Performing Arts in New York City, this school conducts regular day school classes. For pupils who have to be on the road or otherwise away from school for their professional work, however, it also provides daily lessons and assignments with which pupils can regularly continue their education.

A most unusual alternative to private high school after the ninth grade for mature, goal-oriented boys and girls is a private institution combining school and college studies—Simon's Rock Early College in Great Barrington, Massachusetts. Simon's Rock operates as a division of Bard College (in Annandale-on-Hudson, N.Y.), and awards fully accredited college degrees in an accelerated program that can shorten the time needed to earn the bachelor's degree by two years. Students can enter Simon's Rock after the ninth grade (usual first year of a four-year high school). For those who do, tenth-grade work represents a transitional year, eleventh- and twelfth-grade studies lead to the associate's college degree, and thirteenth- and fourteenth-year studies lead to the bachelor's. Simon's Rock students can transfer their credits to Bard. Recipients of bachelor's degrees awarded by Simon's Rock have been admitted to graduate study at such institutions as Harvard University, Princeton University, and Massachusetts Institute of Technology (MIT).

"St. Grottlesex" Top Boarding Schools for High Academic and Social Aims

You may well have received the impression that a number of the private boarding schools in America are widely considered to be among the very best, in both academic work and social standing. The reputations of such schools have developed in large part because they educate relatively large numbers of children from American families of long-established wealth and social position. They tend to carry on the aristocratic tradition of British boarding schools, and often used to be whimsically referred to as the "St. Grottlesex" schools, in an amalgam of the names of three (St. Paul's in New Hampshire, Groton, and Middlesex).

Schools of this order may interest you if you have finally decided against public school for your child. But don't be rigid about insisting on one of these. Your child could go to any one of hundreds of other private schools that also have high cultural standards and an excellent social climate. St. Grottlesex schools tend to be highly competitive in admission and high in cost (though they often have substantial scholarship and other financial aid funds). So do check out admissions chances and costs as well as suitability for your child before having the child become a committed applicant at one of these schools.

Now that you're forewarned, here are many examples of private boarding schools considered to be among the best by upper-class families. All are now coed boarding schools that day students can attend also, unless otherwise noted. Many are in the states of the original thirteen colonies, especially those of New England.

Those in Massachusetts include: "Andover," officially Phillips Academy in Andover; Brooks School (boys), North Andover; Concord Academy, Concord (where Middlesex School is also located); Dana Hall (girls), Wellesley; Deerfield Academy (boys), Deerfield; Groton School, Groton; and Northfield-Mount Hermon School, East Northfield.

Among those in Connecticut are: Choate/Rosemary Hall, Wallingford; Kent School, Kent; Miss Porter's School (girls), Farmington; and Taft School, Watertown.

Such prestigious boarding schools in other Northeast states include: in New Hampshire, "Exeter"—Phillips Academy in Exeter, and St. Paul's

School in Concord; in Rhode Island, Portsmouth Abbey School (boys), Portsmouth; in New York State, Emma Willard School (girls), Troy, and The Masters School (girls), Dobbs Ferry; in New Jersey, Lawrenceville School (boys), Lawrenceville; and in Maryland, Oldfields School (girls), Glencoe.

Among those in Virginia are such well-known exclusive girls' schools as Chatham Hall, Chatham; Foxcroft School, Middleburg; and The Madeira School, Greenway.

Some of the "best schools" are located in the West. Among them: in Arizona, Orme School, Mayer, and Verde Valley School, Sedona; Colorado Rocky Mountain School, Carbondale, Colorado and in California, Castilleja School (girls), Palo Alto, and Thacher School, Ojai.

"Best" boarding schools shade off imperceptibly into many other very highly regarded private schools. For example, here are quite a few more boarding schools that informed persons would deem easily as high in prestige and quality as many of those named above:

California—Athenian School (in Danville)

Connecticut—Avon Old Farms, boys (Avon), Cheshire Academy (Cheshire), Ethel Walker School, girls (Simsbury), The Gunnery (Washington), Hotchkiss School (Lakeville), Loomis Chaffee School (Windsor), Pomfret School (Pomfret), Westover School, girls (Middlebury), Wykeham Rise, girls (Washington)

Maryland—St. Timothy's School, girls (Stevenson)

Massachusetts—Berkshire School (Sheffield), Governor Dummer (Byfield), Milton Academy (Milton), Tabor Academy, boys (Marion), mentioned earlier as notable for sailing

New Hampshire—New Hampton School (New Hampton)

New Jersey—Hun School (Princeton), Purnell School, girls (Pottersville)

New York—St. Paul's School, boys (Garden City)

Pennsylvania—Hill School, boys (Pottstown), Westtown School (Westtown)

Rhode Island—St. George's School (Newport)

Vermont—Putney School (Putney).

Still more boarding schools could be added to such a "best" list. Moreover, numbers of private schools for day students rank with these best boarding schools in social standing and academic prowess.

Rest assured you can also locate private schools to satisfy many other kinds of interests you may have in mind. Let us cite only a few examples. You can send your child to American schools in a foreign country or to foreign schools in this country—as with the Lycée Français in New York City, for example. Some parents like the serene, undogmatic atmosphere of private schools sponsored by the religious Society of Friends, or Quakers. Westtown School, mentioned above, is one of the better-known Quaker schools; among others are George School in Newtown, Pennsylvania, and Oakwood School in Poughkeepsie, New York.

Private Schooling Advantages for Admission to Top Colleges

Parents often consider turning to private schools—especially ones like those named above—as an especially good means of getting their children admitted to the more highly regarded and sought-after colleges. But it's not necessarily true that even outstanding private schools can enhance the chances that any very bright boy or girl will be admitted by a renowned college.

For instance, suppose that your son or daughter is reasonably happy in a public high school, is doing superb academic work in strong college-prep studies and even college-level "Advanced Placement" courses, and also finds time for some significant accomplishment in a school activity, hobby, or community endeavor. In a case like this, the public high school would probably prove just as effective in helping your child win admission to a Dartmouth or a Stanford as would any fine private school.

If your child seems to have roughly average talents and motivation for academic studies and is developing happily and confidently in public high school, you also need not bother with considering private school for any notable increase in college admission chances. Further, colleges that have in the past admitted a high proportion of prep school graduates are tending now to look for a more representative cross section of students, more varied economically and geographically. You could undercut the child's growth as a winner by pushing for a college that would be academically overwhelming and hence most unwise. There are hundreds of other excellent colleges for a youngster like this.

Nevertheless, there are some circumstances in which a strong private school can bring advantages for admission to a top college—if your child evidences high potential for studies and activities but actually functions rather far below that potential for instance. Such young people are typically cultivated far more intensively by private schools than by public schools, and the heads of private schools usually urge enrolling a child early enough to make a difference.

"Kids ought to be transferred between the eighth and ninth grades, and preferably between the sixth and seventh," remarks Donald Barr, headmaster of the Hackley School in Tarrytown, New York. "Give the private school a chance to turn out new work habits and get a record ready for college."

You might accordingly look into private school for more effective development of your child, with prospects of entering better colleges, if the child shows clear signs of much more talent than is being used. If your child is an immature twelve-year-old when private school seems advisable, you might have the youngster start as a day student rather than a boarder.

Of course, should your child have some hampering trouble like a learning disability with which your public school cannot help, a private school with just the right program would prove very important in preparing the child for college.

Getting Full Details on Private Schools

A number of ways for finding private schools and getting complete information about them are open to you, once you decide on such a school. Friends of yours who have sent their children to private schools could prove rich sources of initial information; sympathetic teachers or other people in your child's public school might have good suggestions about private schools, even though the school as a whole has failed to meet the needs of your child. In addition, learning consultants, physicians, or other professionals whom you may have been consulting should be able to advise you. Ads or stories about private schools in your local newspapers might be another good source to watch. Your public library should have listings and possibly further information about private schools in your area and beyond. Reputable though often expensive advice is available from private advisers who are members of the Independent Educational Counselors Association (110 Great Rd., Bedford, Mass. 01730; nationwide list of members is sent on request).

One very detailed and informative directory you are likely to find in public libraries is *The Handbook of Private Schools; An Annual Descriptive Survey of Independent Education* (issued by Porter Sargent Publishers, Inc., Boston, Mass.). Nationwide in scope, the *Handbook* is revised annually. It gives entries on some 1,900 private day and boarding schools offering elementary and high school instruction. Extensive information is given in each entry, answering just about all basic questions you might have on type of studies, instructional and activities programs, entrance tests, enrollments, costs, scholarships, endowments, facilities, and history. One illuminating item reports, for secondary schools, the numbers of graduates in a recent class who entered specified colleges.

If your child has any variety of developmental, organic, or emotional handicap, especially a severe one, you may be interested in consulting a similar work also issued by Porter Sargent: *Directory for Exceptional Children*. Revised every few years, it identifies more than 3,000 schools, clinics, organizations, and facilities for children with handicaps, among them the emotionally disturbed, socially maladjusted, cerebral palsied, orthopedically handicapped, mentally retarded, blind or partially sighted, deaf or hard of hearing, and speech handicapped. Added in the 1978 edition is a new section on "academic programs for the learning-disabled."

Once you have learned of possible private schools for your child through individuals, listings, or directories, your main source of information is the schools themselves. Suggestions for drawing on the schools for information are given in Chapter 6.

Facilities for Older Children with Learning Difficulties

———◆———

This appendix provides resource information for parents and professionals about secondary level students, college entrance, and vocational training.

No one recommendation can be made that is appropriate for all secondary level youngsters exhibiting learning difficulties. All of the facilities or programs mentioned below must be evaluated with a specific student's needs and educational skills in mind. Consultation with the directors of each program and a competent psychologist, learning consultant, or guidance counselor is strongly recommended. The school or program should also be visited by parents and students and time spent in classes observing; living on campus overnight can also be extremely helpful.

General Sources of Information

National ACLD
4156 Library Road
Pittsburgh, Pa. 15234
(Send for their Directory of Post-Secondary Programs)

The Orton Society
8415 Bellona Lane
Towson, Md. 21204
(Contact their local chapters for school recommendations)

ATP for Handicapped Students
Educational Testing Service
Box 592
Princeton, N.J. 08540
(For information concerning SATs and PSATs with extended time)

Partners in Publishing (Pip: College Helps Newsletter)
National Director of Four-Year Colleges, Two-Year Colleges, and Post-High School Training Programs for Young People
Box 50347
Tulsa, Okla. 74150
(approx. $7)

Directory of Educational Facilities for the Learning-Disabled, Novato, Calif.: Academic Therapy Publications, 1979.

List of Colleges with Services for Learning-Disabled Students, Greenwich, Conn., Greenwich Association for the Public Schools, 1976.

Special Schools and Colleges

(Schools with supportive college programs that meet the needs of students with learning disabilities so they can progress in college studies regardless of their disabilities)

Missouri Southern College
Joplin, Miss. 64801
(Flexible entrance policies, special math and English programs, tutoring, counseling, and support services)

New England Trade Institute
(Socrates J. Chaloge, President)
359 Franklin Street
Manchester, N.H. 03100

Southern Vermont College
Monument Road
Bennington, Vt. 05201

University of Maine
Augusta, Maine 04330
(By special arrangement)

S. Illinois University
Carbondale, Ill. 62901
(Attn: Barbara Cordone)

Fort Myers Jr. College
Fort Myers, Fla. 33901
(Support and remedial services)

Lindenwood College
St. Charles, Miss. 63301
(Performing arts; special arrangements for individual students)

Otumwah College
Otumwah Hts., Iowa 52501
(Special supplementary services)

E. Texas State University
Commerce, Tex. 75428

Wayne County Community College
4612 Woodward Avenue
Detroit, Mich. 48201

Mercer University
Atlanta, Ga. 30303

Miami-Dade Community College
Miami, Fla. 33167
(2 years)

Westminister College
Fulton, Miss. 62551

Wright State University
Dayton, Ohio 45431

Loras College
Dubuque, Iowa 52001
(Accepts approx. 8 students per year)

Lincoln College
Lincoln, Ill. 62656
(2 years)

Regis College
3539 West 50th Street
Denver, Col. 80221

Xavier University
Dana and Victory Parkway
Cincinnati, Ohio 45207

Springhill College
Springhill, La. 71075

Pennsylvania State University
Waynesburg, Pa. 15370

Ventura College
Ventura, Calif. 93003

Kendall College
Evanston, Ill. 60204

College of DuPage
Lambert Road and 22nd Street
Glen Ellyn, Ill. 60137
(Attn: Van Burke)

Colleges Providing Full Service Programs for Learning-Disabled Students

College of the Ozarks
Clarksville, Ark. 72810

Hardin Simmons University
Abilene, Texas 79601

State University of New York
College at Farmingdale
Long Island, N.Y. 11735
(Developmental program)

Curry College
The Lab School
Milton, Mass. 02186
(Attn: Dr. G. Webb)

Conestoga College of Applied Arts
and Technology
Kitchener
Ontario, Canada
(Attn: E. Shirley Dickson)

Annhurst College
Woodstock, Conn. 06281
(Learning Enrichment for
Academic Progress—LEAP)

Kingsboro Community College
2001 Oriental Avenue
Brooklyn, N.Y. 11235
(Attn: Dr. I. Rosenthal)

New College at Hofstra University
Hofstra University
Hempstead, N.Y. 11550

Life Skills and Vocational Workshops

Para-Educator Center for Young
Adults
New York University School of
Education, Health, Nursing and
Arts Professions
1 Washington Square
New York, N.Y. 10003
(A postgraduate program)

Post-High School Summer Programs

Goddard College
Plainfield, Vt. 05667
(Skills Center)

Eagle Hill School
Hardwicke, Mass. 01037
(Attn: Charles Cavanaugh)

Pine Ridge School
Box 138 G
Williston, Vt. 05495
(Attn: Kay Goranson)

Eagle Hill School
Greenwich, Conn. 06830

Landmark School
Prides Crossing, Mass. 01095
(Attn: Dr. Charles Drake)

Life Skills Training Materials

Technical Tools Today
MIND, 1 Kings Highway North
Westport, Conn. 06880
(An audio-visual program)

Michigan Products Inc.
P.O. Box 24155
1200 Keystone Avenue
Lansing, Mich. 48909

Project Discover
Allison Associates
Box 313
Troy, N.Y. 12180

Frank E. Richards Co.
Box 66
Phoenix, N.Y. 12043
(Meeting basic competency reading math)

PAL Practical Living Series
Xerox
1250 Fairwood Avenue
P.O. Box 444
Columbus, Ohio 43210

Basic Living Skills
Interpretive Education
2406 Winter Drive
Kalamazoo, Mich. 49002

Index

winners (*continued*)
examples of genuine, 13–15; income equated with success, 9–10; from infancy to age two, building a, 43–47; schools that educate, 117–18; self-confidence, 3, 4, 11, 13, 118, 186–87, 194; status by association, 9–10; teacher's stereotypes of, 68, 85, 91, 119, 170–72; what is a winner?, 9–13
Woods, Jerry, 85
Woods, Willy, 85
word skills, games to build, 197–98
workaholics, 14–15

workshops for teachers, 74, 77, 93, 109
work-study programs, 257, 260, 261
Wright brothers, 166
writing: basic competency skills in, 115; gifted children interested in, 185; poor coordination, 121; readiness for, 58–59; symptoms of problems, 139–40, 142–43; tape recorder to aid, 109, 144

Yale University, 130, 227, 239, 244, 252–53
Yarrow, Freddie, 110, 112–13